CU00827994

A

COLLECTION

OF

LEGAL MAXIMS

IN

LAW AND EQUITY,

WITH

ENGLISH TRANSLATIONS.

BY

S. S. PELOUBET.

"Maxime ita dicta quia maxima est ejus dignitas et certissima auctoritas, atque quod maxime omnibus probetur." —*Coke, Litt.* 11. *a.*

NEW-YORK:

GEORGE S. DIOSSY.

1880.

PREFACE.

THE purpose of this work is to collect in a small compass, all the principal Legal Maxims in Law and Equity which are found scattered through the various law-books, and giving under each an approved English translation.

It is intended for the student preparing for the bar, and for the practicing lawyer, who may desire to find a maxim which will apply to, and illustrate, the case before him.

Where a maxim has been found to have been used in various forms, by transposing the words, care has been taken to use only one form, thus avoiding the duplication of similar maxims

Use has been made of the several collections of Legal Maxims heretofore published, but, so far as possible, reference has been made to the authority where the maxim may be found, and the connection in which it was used.

The work contains a full index, which will enable the student to find any maxim upon the subject desired.

NEW YORK, April 10, 1880.   S. S. P.

AUTHORITIES

CONSULTED IN THIS WORK.

Abb. P. R................Abbott's N. Y. Practice Reports.
And....................Anderson's Reports.

Bac. Aph...............Bacon's Aphorisms.
Bac. Max...............Bacon's Maxims.
Bac...................Bacon's Works. 15 vols.
Barb. N. Y.............Barbour's N. Y. Reports.
Bar. & Ald.............Barnewall & Alderson's Reports.
Bell, Dic..............Bell's Dictionary, Law of Scotland.
Best, Ev...... ....Best on Evidence.
Bing...................Bingham's Reports.
Black. Com.............Blackstone's Commentaries.
Bl. (W.)..............W. Blackstone's Reports.
Bon. Tr. Pr............Bonnier, Traité des Preuves.
Bou. Inst..............Bouvier's Institutes.
Bou. ....Bouvier's Law Dictionary.
Bract..................Bracton de Legibus et Consuetudini,
                        bus Angliæ.
Bradf. Surr............Bradford's N. Y. Surrogate Reports.
Branch, Pr.............Branch's Principia Legis et Æquitatis.
Br....................Broom's Legal Maxims.

Brown, Law Dic.........Brown's Law Dict.   Am. Ed.
Buls.. ....Bulstrode's Reports.
Burr....................Burrow's Reports.

Cal. Lex................Calvini Lexicon Juridicum.
Cary....................Cary's Reports.
Chan. C.................Chancery Cases.
Chan. Prec..............Chancery Precedents.
Cicero............. .....
Code.....................Codex Justiniani.
Coke, Litt..............Coke on Littleton.
Coke....................Coke's Reports.
Cowp....................Cowper's Reports.
Cro. Car................Croke's Reports.   (Charles I.)
Cro. Eliz...............Croke's Reports.   (Elizabeth.)
Cro. Jac................Croke's Reports. (James I.)
Curt. C. C ....Curtis' C. C. Reports.
Cush. Mass.............Cushing's Mass. Reports.

Dav.....................Davies' Reports.
Denio, N. Y.............Denio's N. Y. Reports.
Dig.....................Digest, or Pandects of Justinian.
Doct. & Stud...........Doctor & Student.
Dod. Adm................Dodson's Admiralty Reports.
Duer on Ins.............Duer on Insurance.
Dyer....................Dyer's Reports.

East... ....East's Reports.
Eden............. ....Eden's Reports.
Elles. Post.............Ellesmere Postnati.
Ersk. Inst..............Erskine's Institutes, Law of Scotland.
Exch....................Exchequer Reports.

Fer. Rom. Hist..........Ferrier's Roman History.
Finch, Law..............Finch's Law.
Fleta...................Fleta,   seu   Commentarius   Juris
                          Angliæ.

Fortesc..................Fortescue de Laudibus Legum
                   Angliæ.
Foster, Cr. Law.........Foster's Crown Law.
Francis.................Francis' Maxims.
Free....................Freeman's Reports.

Gilb............ ....Gilbert's Reports.
Gilb. Ten...............Gilbert on Tenures.
Godb...................Godbolt's Reports.
Godolph...............ₗ...Godolphin's Orphan's Legacy.
Grat...................Grattan's Va. Reports.
Gr. Ev.................Greenleaf on Evidence.
Grotius................Grotius de Jure Belli ac Pacis and
                   de Æquitate.
Guy. Inst. Feod.........Guyot's Institutes Feodales.

Hale, Hist. C. L.........:.Hale's History of Common Law.
Hale, Pl. Cr.............Hale's Pleas of the Crown.
Halk....................Halkerston's Maxims.
Hard...................Hardre's Reports.
Hein. El. Jur. Civ.......Heineccii Elementæ Juris Civilis.
Hill. Real Prop.........Hilliard's Real Property.
Hill, N. Y.............Hill's N. Y. Reports.
Hob...................Hobart's Reports.
Holt...................Holt's Reports.
Home, L. T............Home's (Ld. Kames) Law Tracts.
How. St. Tr...........Howell's State Trials.

Inst. 1. 2. 3.............Institutes of Justinian.
2. 3. 4. Inst.............Institutes of Lord Coke.

Jenk. Cent..............Jenkins' Centuries or Reports.
Johns. Ch...............Johnson's N. Y. Chancery Reports.
Johns, N. Y............Johnson's N. Y. Reports.
Jur. Civ................Corpus Juris Civilis.

Kames' Eq.............Kames' Principles of Equity.

Keb......................Keble's Reports.
Keil..... ....Keilway's Reports.
Kent, Com..............Kent's Commentaries.

Lane.. ....Lane's Reports.
Lans. N. Y.............Lansing's N. Y. Sup. Court Reports.
Leon....................Leonard's Reports.
Litt.....................Littleton's Tenures.
Lofft.....................Lofft's Reports, Appendix.
Ld. Raym ....Lord Raymond's Reports.

Mack. Civ. Law.........Mackeldey's Civil Law.
Mass ....Massachusetts Reports.
Maule & S..............Maule & Selwyn's Reports.
Merlin, Qu. de Dr.......Merlin, Questions de Droit.
Metc....................Metcalf's Mass. Reports.
Mod....................Modern Reports.
Montes. Es. des Lois.....Montesquieu's Esprit des Lois.
Moore.. ....F. Moore's Reports.

N. Y....................N. Y. Court of Appeals Reports.
Noy....................Noy's Maxims.

Off. Ex.................Wentworth's Office of Executor.

Paige, Ch. N. Y.........Paige's N. Y. Chancery Reports.
P. Will..................Peere Williams' Reports.
Pet. Adm...............Peters' Admiralty Decisions.
P. Syrus...............Publius Syrus', The Mimi.
Phill. Dom..............Phillimore on Domicil.
Phill. Ev................Phillipps on Evidence.
Plowd.... ....Plowden's Reports.
Pothier, Ev.............Pothier on Evidence.
Pothier, Ob.............Pothier on Obligations.

Q. B......... ....Queen's Bench Reports.

Rawle....................Rawle's Penn. Reports.
Reeves.... ....Reeves' History of English Law.
Reg. Brev...............Registrum Brevium.
Riley.. ....Riley's Latin Dictionary.
Rol..... ....Rolle's Reports.

Salk....................Salkeld's Reports.
Sandf. Ch. N. Y.........Sandford's N. Y. Chancery Reports.
Shelford, M. & D.......Shelford on Marriage and Divorce.
Shep. Touch............Sheppard's Touchstone.
Sid...................Siderfin's Reports.
Stark. Ev..............Starkie on Evidence.
Story, Bailm.... ....Story on Bailments.
Story, Cont.............Story on Contracts.
Story, Eq. Jur..........Story's Equity Jurisprudence.
Sum. C. C..............Sumner's Circuit Court Reports.

Taunt...................Taunton's Reports.
Tayler.................Tayler's Law Glossary, 9th Edition.
Tray...................Traynor's Maxims.

Vaugh..................Vaughan's Reports.
Vent...................Ventris' Reports.
Ver....................Vernon's Reports.
Vin. Abr...............Viner's Abridgment.
Vin. Com..............Vinnius' Commentary on Justinian.

Wend. N. Y.............Wendell's N. Y. Reports.
Whart... ....Wharton's Law Lexicon.
Wils...................Wilson's Reports.
Wing ....Wingate's Maxims.
Wright, Ten............Wright on Tenures.

Year B.... ....Year Books.

LEGAL MAXIMS.

A.

1. **A communi observantia non est rece-dendum.** (COKE, LITT. 186. a.)—Common observ-ance is not to be departed from.

2. **A digniori fieri debet denominatio et resolutio.** (WING. 265.)—The title and exposition ought to be made from that which is most worthy.

3. **A facto ad jus non datur consequentia.** A fact does not necessarily constitute a right.

4. **A latere ascendit jus.** (BRACT. 20.)—A right ascends collaterally.

5. **A l'impossible nul n'est tenu.** (2 BOU. 116.)—No one is bound to do what is impossible.

6. **A non posse ad non esse sequitur argumentum necessario negative, licit non affirmative.** (Hob. 336.)—If a thing be not possible, an argument in the negative may be deduced, namely, that it has no existence ; but an argument in the affirmative cannot be deduced, namely, that if a thing is possible it is in existence.

7. **A piratis aut latronibus capti liberi permanent.** (Dig. 49. 15. 19. 2.)—Things do not change their ownership when captured by pirates and robbers.

8. **A principalioribus seu dignioribus est inchoandum.** (Coke, Litt. 18.)—We should begin with the principal and most worthy parts.

9. **A rescriptis valet argumentum.** (Coke, Litt. 11. a.)—An argument drawn from rescripts is sound.

10. **A summo remedio ad inferiorem actionem, non habetur ingressus, neque auxilium.** (Fleta lib. 6. c. 1.)—From the highest remedy to a lower action there is neither ingress nor assistance.

11. **A verbis legis non est recedendum.** (5. Coke, 118.)—From the words of the law there is no receding.

12. **Ab alio expectes, alteri quod feceris.** (P. Syrus, 1.)—Expect from others the same treatment that they receive from you.

13. **Ab assuetis non fit injuria.** (Jenk.

Cent. 8.)—No injury is done by things long acquiesced in.

14. **Abbreviationum ille numerus et sensus accipiendus est, ut concessio non sit inanis.** (9 Coke, 48.)—In abbreviations, that number and sense is to be taken by which the meaning is not rendered void.

15. **Absentem accipere debemus eum qui non est eo loci in quo petitur.** (Dig. 50. 16. 199.)—We must call him absent who is not in that place in which he is sought.

16. **Absentia ejusqui reipublicæ causa abest, neque ei neque alii damnosa esse debet.** (Dig. 50. 17. 140.)—The absence of him who is employed in the service of the State, ought not to be prejudicial to him nor to others.

17. **Absoluta sententia expositione non indiget.** (2 Inst. 533.)—An absolute sentence needs no exposition.

18. **Absolutum dominium in omnibus licitis.**—Absolute power in all things lawful.

19. **Absurdum est affirmare (re judicata) credendum esse, non judici.** (12 Coke, 25.)—It is absurd to affirm that the record of judgment is to be relied upon, and not the judge.

20. **Abundans cautela non nocet.** (11 Coke, 6.)—Abundant caution does no injury.

21. **Accessorium non ducit, sed sequitur suum principale.** (Coke, Litt. 152 a.)—An accessory does not lead, but follows his principal.

22. **Accessorium sequitur naturam rei cui accedit.** (COKE, LITT. 152.)—The incident follows the nature of the thing to which it is accessory.

23. **Accessorius sequitur naturam sui principalis.** (3 INST. 139.)—An accessory follows the nature of its principal.

24. **Accipere quid ut justitiam facias, non est tam accipere quam extorquere.** (LOFFT, 72.)—To accept anything as a reward for doing justice, is not accepting but extorting.

25. **Accusare nemo se debet, nisi coram Deo.** (HARD. 139.)—No one is bound to accuse himself, except before God.

26. **Accusator post rationabile tempus non est audiendus, nisi se bene de cmissione excusaverit.** (MOORE, 817.)—An accuser should not be heard after a reasonable time has expired, unless he can account satisfactorily for the delay.

27. **Acta exteriora indicant interiora secreta.** (8 COKE, 146.)—External actions show the secret intentions.

28. **Actio casus apud nostrates ea est, qua ut inter bonos bene agere opporteat, et sine fraudatione.** (LOFFT, 623.)—In pleading a cause among our countrymen we should act fairly as becomes good men, and not defraud anyone.

29. **Actio contra defunctum coepta continuatus in hæredes.** (HOB. 103.)—An action against a deceased person continues in the heirs.

30. **Actio est jus prosequendi in judicio quod**

alicui debetur. (COKE, LITT. 285. a.)—An action
is the right of prosecuting to judgment that which
is one's due.

31. **Actio non datur non damnificato.** (JENK.
CENT. 69.)—An action is not given to him who is
not injured.

32. **Actio non facit reum, nisi mens sit rea.**
(LOFFT, 37)—An action does not make one guilty,
unless the intention be bad.

33. **Actio pænalis in hæredemnon datur, nisi
forte ex damno locupletior hæres factus sit.**
(VIN. COM. 756.)—A penal action does not lie
against the heir, unless indeed the heir is benefited
from the wrong.

34. **Actio personalis moritur cum persona.** (4
INST. 315.)—A personal action dies with the person.

35. **Actio quælibet in sua vita.** (JENK. CENT.
77.)—Every action proceeds in its own way.

36. **Actiones compositæ sunt, quibus inter
se homines disceptarent, quas actiones, ne
populus prout vellet institueret, certas solemn-
esque esse voluerunt.** (WHART. 20.)—Actions
are disposed by which men dispute among themselves, which actions are made definite and solemn,
lest the people proceed as they think proper.

37. **Actiones in personam, quæ adversus eum
intenduntur, qui ex contractu vel delicto obligatus est aliquid dare vel concedere.** (WHART.
20.)—Personal actions are those which are brought

against him who, from a contract or a tort, is obliged to give or allow something.

38. Actionum genera maxime sunt servanda. (LOFFT, 460.)—The correct form of action should be followed.

39. Actionum quædam sunt in rem, quædam in personam, et quædam mixtæ. (COKE, LITT. 284.)—Some actions are against the thing, others against the person, and others are mixed.

40. Actor qui contra regulam quid aduxit, non est audiendus. (2 BOUV. 116.)—A pleader should not be heard who advances a proposition, contrary to rules of law.

41. Actor sequitur forum rei. (HOME. L. T., 232.)—The plaintiff follows the forum of the thing in question.

42. Actore non probante reus absolvitur. (HOB. 103.)—The defendant is absolved if the plaintiff does not prove his case.

43. Acts indicate the intention. (8 COKE, 291).

44. Actori incumbit onus probandi. (HOB. 103.)—The burden of proof lies with the plaintiff.

45. Actus curiæ neminem gravabit. (JENK. CENT. 118.)—An act of the court injures no one.

46. Actus Dei nemini facit injuriam. (2 BLACK. COM. 122.)—An act of God injures no one.

47. Actus inceptus, cujus perfectio pendet voluntate partium, revocari potest; si autem

pendet ex voluntate tertiæ personæ, vel excontingenti, revocari non potest. (BACON.)—An act already begun, the completion of which depends upon the parties, may be recalled ; but, if it depend on the consent of a third person, or on a contingency, it cannot.

48. Actus judiciarius coram non judice irritus habetur; de ministeriali autem a quocunque provenit ratum esto. (LOFFT, 458.)—A judicial act done in excess of authority is not binding ; otherwise, if it be a ministerial act.

49. Actus legis nemini est damnosus. (2 INST. 287.)—An act of the law is prejudcialto no one.

50. Actus legis nemini facit injuriam. (5 COKE, 116.)—An act of the law injures no one.

51. Actus legitimi non recipiunt modum. (HOB. 153.)—Legitimate actions require no qualifications.

52. Actus me invito factus, non est meus actus. (BRACT. 101.)—An act done without my consent is not my act.

53. Actus non facit reum, nisi mens sit rea. (3 INST. 107.)—An act itself does not make one guilty, unless done with guilty intent.

54. Actus repugnum non potest in esse produci. (PLOW. 355.)—A repugnant act cannot be brought into being.

55. Actus servi in iis quibus opera ejus, cummunitur adhibita est, actus domini habetur.

(LOFFT, 227.)—The act of a servant in which he is usually employed, is considered the act of his master.

56. **Additio probat minoritatem.** (4. INST. 80.)—An addition proves inferiority.

57. **Ad ea quæ frequentius accidunt jura adaptantur.** (2. INST. 137.)—Laws are adapted to cases which most frequently occur.

58. **Adjournamentum est ad diem dicere seu diem dare.** (4. INST. 27.)—An adjournment is to appoint a day or to give a day.

59. **Admiralitas jurisdictionem non habet super iis quæ communi lege dirimuntur.** (LOFFT, 479.)—An admiralty court has no jurisdiction over those questions which are determined by the common law.

60. **Ad officium justiciariorum spectat, uni cuique coram eis placitanti justitiam exhibere.** (2. INST. 451.)—It is the duty of justices to administer justice to every one seeking it from him.

61. **Ad proximum antecedens fiat relatio, nisi impediatur sententia.** (JENK. CENT. 185.)—The antecedent refers to the next relative, unless it obstructs the sentence.

62. **Ad quæstionem facti non respondent judices; ad quæstionem juris non respondent juratores.** (COKE, LITT. 295.)—To questions of fact judges do not answer ; to questions of law the jury do not answer.

63. **Ad quæstiones legis judices, et non**

juratores respondent. (7 Mass. 279.)—Judges, and not juries, respond to questions of law.

64. Ad recte docendum oportet, primum inquirere nomina, quia rerum cognitio a nominibus rerum dependet. (Coke, Litt. 68.)—In order rightly to comprehend a thing, enquire first into the names, for a right knowledge of things depends upon their names.

65. Ad tristem partem strenua est suspicio. (Tayler, 4.)—Suspicion rests strongly on the unfortunate side.

66. Adversus periculum naturalis ratio permittit se defendere. (Lofft, 369.)—Natural reason allows one to defend himself against danger.

67. Ædificare in tuo proprio solo non licet quod alteri noceat. (3 Inst. 201.)—It is not lawful to build upon your own land so as to injure that of others.

68. Ædificatum solo, solo cedit. (Coke, Litt. 4. a.)—That which is built upon the land goes with the land.

69. Ædificia solo cedunt. (Fleta, 3. 2. 12.)—Buildings pass with a grant of land.

70. Æquitas agit in personam. (4. Bouv. Inst. n. 3733.)—Equity acts upon the person.

71. Æquitas casibus medetur. (Lofft, 499.)—Equity relieves against accidents.

72. Æquitas defectus supplet. (Lofft, 500.)—Equity supplies defects.

73. Æquitas erroribus medetur. (LOFFT, 498.) —Equity remedies errors.

74. Æquitas est correctio legis generaliter latæ, qua parte deficit. (PLOWD. 375.)—Equity is the correction of law, when too general, in the part in which it is defective.

75. Æquitas est correctio quædam legi adhibita, quia ab ea abest aliquid propter generalem sine exceptione comprehensionem. (PLOWD. 467.)—Equity is a certain correction applied to law, because on account of its general comprehensiveness, without an exception something is absent from it.

76. Æquitas est perfecta quædam ratio quæ jus scriptum interpretatur et emendat; nulla scriptura comprehensa, sed sola ratione consistens. (COKE, LITT. 24.)—Equity is a kind of perfect reason which interprets and amends the written law ; comprehended in no code, but consistent with reason alone.

77. Æquitas est quasi equalitas. (COKE, LITT. 24.)—Equity is as it were equality.

78. Æquitas ex lege generaliter lata aliquid excipit. (PLOWD. 362.)—Equity admits an exception from a generally enacted law.

79. Æquitas ignorantiæ opitulatur, oscitantiæ non item. (PLOWD. 84.)—Equity assists ignorance, but not carelessness.

80. Æquitas in eum qui vult summo jure agere, summum jus intendit. (PLOWD. 340.)—

Equity strains the utmost point of law toward the person who wishes to act according to the strictness of the law.

81. Æquitas in paribus causis paria jura desiderat. (PLOWD. 385.)—Equity in like cases requires like laws.

82. Æquitas jurisdictione non confundit. (PLOWD. 393.)—Jurisdiction is not confounded by equity.

83. Æquitas liberationi et seizinæ favet. (LOFFT, 536.)—Equity favors deliverance and seisin.

84. Æquitas naturam rei non mutat. (LOFFT, 536.)—Equity changes not the manner of things.

85. Æquitas neminem juvat cum injuria alterius. (LOFFT, 397.)—Equity assists no person to the injury of another.

86. Æquitas nil statuit, nisi in partes. (LOFFT, 383.)—Equity determines nothing except toward the parties.

87. Æquitas nomine pœnæ constitutis remedium ex æquo et bono præstat. (LOFFT, 495.)—Equity constitutes a remedy to things which have been appointed, under the name of punishment, agreeable to what is just and good.

88. Æquitas non facit jus, sed juri auxiliatur. (LOFFT, 379.)—Equity does not make law, but assists law.

89. Æquitas non medetur defectu eorum quæ jure positivo requisita alium. (LOFFT, 369.)—

Equity does not supply the defects of those things which are required by positive law.

90. Æquitas non sinit ut eandem rem duplici via simul quis persequatur. (FRANCIS, 11.)—Equity will not allow a double satisfaction to be given

91. Æquitas non supplet ea quæ in manu orantis esse possunt. (LOFFT, 391.)—Equity does not supply those things which are within the applicant's grasp.

92. Æquitas non tenetur adjuvare, ubi non est nodus dignus vindice. (LOFFT, 392.)—Equity will not assist unless the occasion renders it necessary.

93. Æquitas non vaga atque incerta est, sed terminos habet atque limites præfinitas. (LOFFT, 375.)—Equity is not vague and uncertain, but has determined boundaries and limits.

94. Æquitas non vult res novas atque inusitatas inducere. (LOFFT, 376.)—Equity does not incline to introduce new and unusual things.

95. Æquitas nunquam contravenit legis. —Equity never contradicts the law.

96. Æquitas nunquam liti ancillatur ubi remedium potest dare. (LOFFT, 501.)—Equity is not the handmaid of strife when she can give a remedy.

97. Æquitas opitulatur ubi pensationi damni locus est. (LOFFT, 503.)—Equity assists when there is room for a compensation of a loss.

98. Æquitas pars legis Angliæ. (LOFFT, 497.) Equity is a part of the English law.

99. Æquitas rei oppignoratæ redemptionibus favet. (LOFFT, 386.)—Equity favors the redemption of a thing in pawn.

100. Æquitas rem ipsam intuetur de forma et circumstantiis minus anxia. (FRANCIS, 13.)— Equity does not regard the form and circumstance, but rather the substance of the act.

101. Æquitas sequitur legem. (1 STORY, EQ. JUR. 64.)—Equity follows the law.

102. Æquitas supervacua odit. (LOFFT, 382.) Equity abhors superfluous things.

103. Æquitas uxoribus, liberis, creditoribus maxime favet. (LOFFT, 372.)—Equity favors wives, children, and creditors.

104. Æquitas veritatis filia, bonitatis et justitiæ soror. (LOFFT, 637.)—Equity is the daughter of truth, and the sister of goodness and justice.

105. Æquitas vult omnibus modis ad veritatem pervenire. (LOFFT, 380.)—Equity desires by all means to arrive at the truth.

106. Æquitas vult spoliatos, vel deceptos, vel lapsos ante omnia restitui. (LOFFT, 374.)— Equity desires the spoiled, the deceived, and the ruined, above all things, to have restitution.

107. Æquum et bonum, est lex legum. (HOB. 244.)—What is just and right is the law of laws.

108. Ær, lux, aqua profluens, feræ nulli pro-

pria, omnibus communia. (LOFFT, 179.)—Air, light, running water, and wild beasts, are the property of none, but are common to all.

109. Æs debitorem leve; graviorem inimicum facit. (TAYLER, 22.)—A small debt makes a debtor ; a large one an enemy.

110. Æstimatio præteriti delicti ex postremo facto nunquam crescit. (BAC. MAX. 8.)—The estimation of a committed crime never increases by a subsequent fact.

111. Affectio tua nomen imponit operi tuo. (COKE, LITT. 177.)—Your motive gives a name to your act.

112. Affectus punitur licet non sequatur effectus. (9 COKE, 57.)—The intention should be punished, although the consequence do not follow.

113. Affines mei affinis non est mihi affinis. (SHELFORD, M. & D., 174.)—A connection of my connection is not a connection of mine.

114. Affinitas dicitur, cum duæ cognationes, inter se divisæ, per nuptias copulantur, et altera ad alterius fines accedit. (COKE, LITT. 157.)— It is called affinity when two families, divided from one another, are united by marriage, and one of them approaches the confines of another.

115. Affirmanti, non neganti, incumbit probatio. (WHART. 30.)—He who affirms, not he who denies, must bear the burden of proof.

116. Affirmantis est probatio. (9 CUSH. 535.) —He who affirms must prove.

117. Affirmativum negativum implicat. (WHART. 30.)—An affirmative implies a negative.

118. Agentes et consentientes, pari poena plectentur. (5 COKE, 80.)—Parties both acting and consenting, are liable to the same punishment.

119. Agri ab universis per vices occupantur; arva per annos mutant. (TAYLER, 24.)—Commons are used by all in turn ; arable lands change with years.

120. Alea et ganea res turpissimæ. (LOFFT, 207.)—The dice and brothel are infamous things.

121. Alienatio rei præfertur juri accrescendi. (COKE, LITT. 185. a.)—Alienation is favored by the law rather than accumulation.

122. Alienation pending a suit is void. (1 JOHNS. CH. 566).

123. Aliquis non debet esse judex in propria causa, quia non potest esse judex et pars. (COKE, LITT. 141. a.)—A person ought not to be judge in his own cause, because he cannot be both a party and a judge.

124. Aliud est celare, aliud tacere. (3. BURR. 1910.)—To conceal is one thing, to be silent another.

125. Aliud est distinctio, aliud separatio. (15. BAC. 234.)—Distinction is one thing, separation another.

126. Aliud est possidere. aliud esse in possessione. (HOB. 163.)—It is one thing to possess, another to be in possession.

127. **Aliud est vendere, aliud vendenti consentire.** (DIG. 50. 17. 160.)—To sell is one thing, to give consent to him who sells is another.

128. **Allegans contraria non est audiendus.** (JENK. CENT. 16.)—He who alleges contradictory things is not to be heard.

129. **Allegans suam turpitudinem non est audiendus.** (4 INST. 279.)—One alleging his own infamy is not to be heard.

130. **Allegari non debuit quod probatum non relevat.** (1 CHAN. C., 45.)—That ought not to be alleged which, if proved, would not be relevant.

131. **Alterius circumventio alii non præbet actionem.** (DIG. 50. 17. 49.)—A deception practiced upon one person does not give a cause of action to another.

132. **Alternativa petitio non est audienda.** (5 COKE, 40.)—An alternative petition is not to be heard.

133. **A man cannot qualify his own act.** (NOY. 43). .

134. **Ambigua responsio contra proferentem est accipienda.** (10 COKE, 59.)—An ambiguous answer shall be construed against him who offers it.

135. **Ambiguis casibus semper præsumitur pro rege.** (LOFFT, 248.)—The presumption, in doubtful cases, always favors the king.

136. **Ambiguitas verborum latens, verifica-**

tione suppletur, nam quod ex facto oritur ambiguum verificatione facti tollitur. (BAC. MAX. 25.)—Latent ambiguity may be supplied by evidence ; for ambiguity arising upon the deed is removed by proof of the deed.

137. **Ambiguitas verborum patens nulla verificatione excluditur.** (LOFFT, 249.)—The evident ambiguity of words is excluded by verification.

138. **Ambiguum pactum contra venditorem interpretandum est.** (HALK. 11.)—Ambiguous agreements are to be interpreted against the seller.

139. **Ambiguum placitum interpretari debet contra proferentem.** (COKE, LITT. 303. b.)—An ambiguous pleading should be interpreted against the party offering it.

140. **Ambulatoria est voluntas defuncti usque ad vitæ supremum exitum.** (DIG. 34. 4. 4.)—The will of a decedent is ambulatory up to his last moments of life.

141. **Amici consilia credenda.** (TAYLER, 28.) —The advice of a friend should be regarded.

142. **Angliæ jura in omni casu libertati dant favorem.** (FORTESC. c. 42.)—The laws of England are favorable in every case to liberty.

143. **Animi motum vultus deteget.** (LOFFT, 19.)—The countenance is the index of the mind.

144. **Animus ad se omne jus ducit.** (2 BOU. 118.)—It is to the intention that all law applies.

145. **Animus hominis est anima scripti.** (3

BULS. 67.)—The intention of the man is the soul of the instrument.

146. **Animus non deponendus ob iniquum judicium.** (TAYLER, 29.)—The mind should not be cast down because of an unjust judgment.

147. **An intendment of the parties shall be ordered according to law.** (NOY, 46).

148. **Annua neo debitum judex non separat ipsum.** (8 COKE, 52.)—Even the judge divides not annuities or debt.

149. **Annus inceptus pro completo habetur.** (TRAY. 45.)—A year begun is held as completed.

150. **Apices juris non sunt jura.** (COKE, LITT. 304.)—Legal subtleties are not rights.

151. **Applicatio est vita regulæ.** (2 BULS. 79.)—Application is the life of a rule.

152. **Aqua cedit solo.** (COKE, LITT. 4. a.)—Water goes with the land. A grant of land carries the water upon it.

153. **Aqua currit, et debet currere, ut currere solebat.** (3. RAWLE, 84. 88.)—Water runs, and should run, as it has used to run.

154. **Arbitrimentum æquum tribuit cuique suum.** (NOY, 126.)—A just arbitration renders to every one his own.

155. **Arbitrio domini res æstimari debet.** (4. INST. 274.)—The owner of a thing should fix his price upon it.

156. **Arbitrium est judicium.** (JENK. CENT. 137.)—An award is a judgment.

157. **Arbitrium est judicium boni viri, secundum æquum et bonum.** (3 BULS. 64.)—An award is the judgment of a good man, according to goodness and justice.

158. **Arbor dum crescit; lignum dum crescere nescit.** (2 BULS. 82.)—A tree is so called whilst growing, but wood when it ceases to grow.

159. **Argumentum a divisione est fortissimum in jure.** (6 COKE, 60.)—An argument from division is of the greatest force in law.

160. **Argumentum a majori ad minus negative non valet; valet e converso.** (JENK. CENT. 281.) —An argument from the greater to the less is of no force negatively ; affirmatively it is.

161. **Argumentum a simili valet in lege.** (COKE, LITT. 191.)—An argument from a like case avails in law.

162. **Argumentum ab authoritate est fortissimum in lege.** (COKE, LITT. 254. a.)—An argument from authority is very strong in law.

163. **Argumentum ab impossibili plurimum valet in lege.** (COKE, LITT. 92.)—An argument deduced from an impossibility is of great weight in law.

164. **Argumentum ab inconvenienti plurimum valet in lege.** (COKE, LITT. 66. a.)—An argument from inconvenience avails much in law.

165. **Arma in armatos sumere jura sinunt.** (2 INST. 574.)—The laws permit the taking arms against the armed.

166. Assignatus utitur jure auctoris. (HALK. 14.)—An assignee acquires the rights of the assignor.

167. Audi alteram partem. (46 N. Y. 119.)— Hear the other side.

168. Auctoritates philosophorum, medicorum, et poetarum, sunt in causis allegandæ et tenendæ. (COKE, LITT. 264.)—The opinions of philosophers, physicians, and poets, are to be received and alleged in causes.

169. Aucupia verborum sunt judice indigna. (HOB. 343.)—A twisting of language is unworthy of a judge.

170. Augusta legibus soluta non est. (WHART. 69.)—The wife of the king is not exempted from the laws.

171. Authority to execute a deed must be given by deed. (1 HOLT, 141).

B.

172. Baratriam committit qui propter pecuniam justitiam baractat. (BELL, DIC.)—He is guilty of barratry who for money barters justice.

173. Bastardus non potest habere hæredem nisi de corpore suo legitime procreatum. (TRAY. 51.)—A bastard can have no heir unless it be one lawfully begotten of his own body.

174. Beatus qui leges juraque servat. (TAY-LER, 46.)—Blessed is the man who obeys the laws and ordinances.

175. Bello parta cedunt reipublicæ. (1 KENT, COM. 101.)—Things acquired in war go to the state.

176. Benedicta est expositio, quando res redimitur a destructione. (4 COKE, 26.)—Blessed is the exposition by which anything is saved from destruction.

177. Beneficium non datur nisi officii causa. (LOFFT, 489.)—A benefice is not given except for a service performed.

178. Beneficium non datum nisi propter officium. (HOB. 148.)—A remuneration is not given unless on account of a duty performed.

179. Beneficium principis debet esse mansurum. (JENK. CENT. 168.)—The benefit of a prince should be lasting.

180. Benigne faciendæ sunt interpretationes chartarum, ut res magis valeat quam pereat; et quælibet concessio fortissime contra donatorem interpretanda est. (4 MASS. 134.)—Liberal interpretations are to be made of deeds, to the end that more may stand than perish ; and all grants are to be taken most strongly against the grantor.

181. Benigne faciendæ sunt interpretationes, propter simplicitatem laicorum, ut res magis valeat quam pereat; et verba intentioni, non e contra, debent inservire. (COKE, LITT. 36. a.)—

Liberal construction is to be made of written instruments, on account of the simplicity of the laity, and with a view to carry out the intention of the parties ; and the words should be made subject, not contrary, to the intention.

182.   **Benignior sententia in verbis generalibus seu dubiis est præferenda.**   (4 COKE, 15.)—The more favorable construction is to be placed on general or doubtful expressions.

183.   **Benignius leges interpretandæ sunt quo voluntas earum conservetur.**   (DIG. 1. 3. 16.)— Laws should be so favorably interpreted that their intentions may be preserved.

184.   **Bis dat qui cito dat.**   (WHART. 21.)— He gives twice who gives quickly.

185.   **Bis idem exigi bona fides non patitur, et in satisfactionibus, non permittitur amplius fieri quam semel factum est.**   (9 COKE, 53.)— Good faith does not permit the same thing to be exacted twice ; and in giving satisfaction it is not permitted to give more than is given at once.

186.   **Bona fide possessor facit fructus perceptos et consumptus suos.**   (TRAY. 57.)—By good faith a possessor makes the goods which he has gathered and consumed his own.

187.   **Bona fides exigit ut quod convenit fiat.** (DIG. 19. 20. 21.)—Good faith demands that what is agreed upon shall be done.

188.   **Bona fides non patitur ut bis idem exigatur.**   (DIG. 50. 17. 57.)—Good faith does not

allow satisfaction to be exacted twice for the same thing.

189. **Bonæ fidei possessor, in id tantum quod ad se pervenerit tenetur.** (2 INST. 285.)—A possessor in good faith is only bound for that which he himself has obtained.

190. **Bonæ fidei venditorem, neo commodorum spem augere nec incommodorum conditionem obscurare oportet.** (TAYLER, 49.)—An honest vendor should neither conceal his anticipated profits, nor the disadvantageous condition of his goods.

191. **Boni judicis est ampliare jurisdictionem.** (CHAN. PREC. 329.)—A good judge will amplify his jurisdiction.

192. **Boni judicis est causas litium dirimere.** (2 INST. 304.)—It is the duty of a good judge to determine the course of litigations.

193. **Boni judicis est judicium sine dilatione mandare executioni.** (COKE, LITT. 289. b.)—It is the duty of a good judge to order judgment to be executed without delay.

194. **Boni judicis est lites dirimere.** (4 COKE, 15.)—It is the duty of a good judge to prevent litigations.

195. **Bonitas tota æstimabitur cum pars evincitur.** (TAYLER, 50.)—The goodness of the whole may be estimated when the condition of a part of a thing is proved.

196. **Bonum defendentis ex integra causa,**

malum ex quolibet defectu. (11 COKE, 68.)—
The good of a defendant arises from a .perfect
case, his harm from some defect.

197. **Bonum necessarium extra terminos necessitatis non est bonum.** (HOB. 144.)—Necessary
good is not good beyond the bounds of necessity.

198. **Bonus judex secundum æquum et bonum
judicat, et æquitatem stricto juri præfert.** (COKE,
LITT. 24. b.)—A good judge decides according to
justice and right, and prefers equity to strict
law.

199. **Breve judiciale debet sequi suum orig-
inale, et accessorium suum principale.** (JENK.
CENT. 292.)—A judicial writ ought to follow its
original, and an accessory its principal.

200. **Breve judiciale non cadit pro defectu
formæ.** (JENK. CENT. 43.)—A judicial writ fails
not through defect of form.

201. **Brevia, tam originalia quam judicialia,
patiuntur Anglica nomina.** (10 COKE, 133.)—Both
original and judicial writs bear English names.

202. **By an acquittance for the last payment,
all other arrearages are discharged.** (NOY. 40).

C.

203. **Carcer ad homines custodiendos, non ad
puniendos dari debet.** (COKE, LITT. 260. a.)—A

prison should be assigned to the custody, not the punishment of persons.

204. Caret periculo, qui etiam tutus, cavit. (TAYLER, 56.)—He is the most secure, who when safe, is on his guard.

205. Casus fortuitus non est sperandus, et nemo tenetur divinare. (4 COKE, 66.)—A fortuitus event is not to be foreseen ; and no person is understood to divine.

206. Casus omissus et oblivioni datus, dispositioni juris communis relinquitur. (5 COKE, 37.)—A case omitted and given to oblivion is left to the disposal of the common law.

207. Casus omissus habetur pro amisso. (WHART. 136.)—An omitted case is deemed as lost.

208. Catalla juste possessa amitti non possunt. (JENK. CENT. 28.)—Chattels justly possessed cannot be lost.

209. Catalla reputantur inter minima in lege. (JENK. CENT. 52.)—Chattels are considered in law among the minor things.

210. Causa causæ est causa causati. (FREE. 329.)—The cause of a cause is the cause of the effect.

211. Causæ dotis, vitæ, libertatis, fisci, sunt inter favorabilia in lege. (JENK. CENT. 284.)— Causes of dower, life, liberty, revenue, are among the favorable things in law.

212. Causæ ecclesiæ publicis causis æquipa-

rantur; et summa ratio est quæ pro religione facit. (COKE, LITT. 341. a.)—The cause of the Church is equal to public causes ; and for the best of reasons, it is the cause of religion.

213. Causa et origo est materia negotii. (1 COKE, 99.)—The cause and origin is the material of the thing.

214. Causa proxima, non remota, spectatur. (3 KENT, COM. 302.)—The near, and not the remote cause, is to be considered.

215. Causa publica vicarium non recipit. (LOFFT, 326.)—A public cause admits no substitute.

216. Causa vaga et incerta non est causa rationabilis. (5 COKE, 57.)—A vague and uncertain cause is not a rational one.

217. Cautionis in re plus est quam in persona. (LOFFT, 328)—There is more security in a thing than in a person.

218. Caveat emptor; qui ignorare non debuit quod jus alienum emit. (HOB. 99.)—Let the purchaser beware ; no one in ignorance should buy that which is the right of a third party.

219. Caveat venditor. (LOFFT, 328.)—Let the seller beware.

220. Caveat viator. (BR. 387. n.)—Let the traveler beware.

221. Certa debet esse intentio, et narratio, et certum fundamentum, et certa res quæ deducitur in judicium. (COKE, LITT. 303. a.)—The intention ought to be certain, and the count and foundation, and the thing which is brought to judgment.

222. **Certa res oportet in judicium deducantur.** (LOFFT, 35.)—It is often necessary to bring into court for trial a thing which is certain.

223. **Certum est quod certum reddi potest.** (9 COKE, 30.)—That is certain which can be made certain.

224. **Cessa regnare, si non vis judicare.** (HOB. 155.)—Cease to reign, if you do not wish to adjudicate.

225. **Cessante causa, cessat effectus.** (4 COKE, 38.)—When the cause ceases, the effect also ceases.

226. **Cessante primitivo, cessat derivativus.** (WHART. 145.)—The primitive ceasing, the derivative also ceases.

227. **Cessante ratione legis, cessat ipse lex.** (COKE, LITT. 70. b.)—The reason of the law ceasing, the law itself ceases.

228. **Cessante statu primitivo, cessat derivativus.** (8 COKE, 34.)—The original estate ceasing, the derivative ceases.

229. **C'est le crime qui fait la honte, et non pas l'echafaud.** (2 BOU. 119.)—It is the crime which makes the shame, and not the scaffold.

230. **Cestuy, que doit inheriter al pere, doit inheriter al fils.** (2 BLACK. COM. 239.)—He who would have been heir to the father of the deceased shall also be the heir of the son.

231. Chacea est ad communem legem. (REG. BREV. 80. b.)—A chace is by common law.

232. Charta de non ente non valet. (COKE, LITT. 36. a.)—A charter concerning a thing not in existence avails not.

233. Charta est legatus mentis. (COKE, LITT. 36. a.)—A charter is the legate of the mind.

234. Charta non est nisi vestimentum donationis. (COKE, LITT. 36. a.)—A charter is nothing else than the vestment of a gift.

235. Charters sont appelle "muniments" a "muniendo," quia muniunt et defendunt hæreditatem. (4 COKE, 153.)—Charters are called "muniments" from "muniendo," because they fortify and defend the inheritance.

236. Chirographum apud debitorem repertum præsumitur solutum. (HALK. 20.)—A deed or bond found with the debtor is presumed to be paid.

237. Circuitus est evitandus; et boni judicis est lites dirimere, ne lis ex lite oritur. (5 COKE, 31.)—Circuity is to be avoided ; and it is the duty of a good judge to determine litigations, lest one lawsuit arise out of another.

238. Civitas ea autem in libertate est posita qæ suis stat viribus, non ex alieno arbitrio pendet. (TAYLER, 68.)—That state alone is free which depends upon its own strength, and not upon the arbitrary will of another.

239. Civitas et urbs in hoc differunt, quod

incolæ dicuntur civitas, urbs vero complectitur
ædificia. (COKE, LITT. 109. b.)—A city and town
differ in this, that the inhabitants are called the
city, but town includes the buildings.

240. **Clam delinquens magis punitur quam
palam.** (8 COKE, 127.)—Those who sin secretly
are punished more severely than those who sin
openly.

241. **Clausula generalis de residuo non ea
complectitur quæ non ejusdem sint generis cum
iis quæ speciatim dicta fuerant.** (LOFFT, 419.)—
A general clause of remainder does not embrace
those things which are not of the same kind with
those which had been specially mentioned.

242. **Clausula generalis non refertur ad expressa.** (8 COKE, 154.)—A general clause does not
refer to things expressed.

243. **Clausula quæ abrogationem excludit (ab)
initio non valet.** (BAC. MAX. 19.)—A clause which
excludes abrogation avails not from the beginning.

244. **Clausulæ inconsuetæ semper inducunt
suspicionem.** (3 COKE, 81.)—Unusual clauses always excite suspicion.

245. **Clausula vel dispositio inutilis per præ-
sumtionem remotam vel causam ex post facto
non fulcitur.** (BAC. MAX. 21.)—A clause or useless disposition is not supported by a remote presumption or a cause from an after act.

246. **Clerici non penantur in officiis.** (COKE,

LITT. 96. b.)—The clergy cannot be compelled to serve temporal offices.

247. Clerici, vel monachi, ne sæcularibus negotiis se immisceant. (FER. ROM. HIST. 117.)—Clergymen or monks should not mix themselves in secular matters.

248. Clericus, et agricola, et mercator; tempore belli, ut oret que, colat, et commutet, pace fruuntur. (2 INST. 58.)—A clergyman, a husbandman, and a merchant, in order that they may preach, cultivate, and trade, enjoy peace in time of war.

249. Clericus non connumeretur in duabus ecclesiis. (1 ROL. 454.)—A clergyman should not be appointed to two churches.

250. Cogitationis pœnam nemo patitur. (BR. 311.)—No man is punished for his thoughts.

251. Cognomen majorum est ex sanguine tractum, hoc intrinsecum est; agnomen extrinsecum, ab eventu. (6 COKE, 65.)—The cognomen of ancestors is derived from the blood, and is intrinsic ; an agnomen arises from an event, and is extrinsic.

252. Cohæredes una persona censentur, propter unitatem juris quod habent. (COKE, LITT. 163. b.)—Co-heirs are deemed as one person on account of the unity of law which they possess.

253. Collegium est societas plurium corporum simul habitantium. (JENK. CENT. 229.)—A college is a society of several persons dwelling together.

254. **Collegium seu corpus corporatum nisi regiis constitutionibus non potest existere.** (LOFFT, 297.)—A college or incorporated body can only exist by consent of the sovereign.

255. **Commercium jure gentium commune esse debet, et non in monopolium et privatum paucorum quæstum convertendum.** (3 INST. 181.) —Commerce, by the law of nations, ought to be common, and not converted to monopoly and the private gain of a few.

256. **Commodum ex injuria sua nemo habere debet.** (JENK. CENT. 161.)—No man should derive any benefit from his own wrong.

257. **Communis error facit jus.** (4 INST. 240.) Common error makes right.

258. **Communis opiniones sunt bona in lege.** (COKE, LITT. 186. b.)—Common opinion is good authority in law.

259. **Communiter unum officium est excusatio alterius.** (HALK. 21.)—The performing of one duty excuses the non-performance of another.

260. **Compendia sunt dispendia.** (COKE, LITT. 305. b.)—Abridgments are hindrances.

261. **Compromissarii sunt judicis.** (JENK. CENT. 128.)—Arbitrators are judges.

262. **Compromissum ad similitudinem, judiciorum redigitur.** (9 CUSH. MASS. 571.)—A compromise is brought into relation with judgments.

263. **Conatus quid sit non definitur in lege.**

(2 BULS. 277.)—What an endeavor may be, is not defined in law.

264. Concessio per regem fieri debet de certitudine. (9 COKE, 46.)—A grant by the king ought to be made from certainty.

265. Concessio versus concedentem latam interpretationem habere debet. (JENK. CENT. 279.)—A concession ought to have a liberal interpretation against the party conceding.

266. Concordare leges legibus est optimus interpretandi modus. (HALK. 70.)—To make laws agree with laws is the best mode of interpreting them.

267. Concordia parvæ res crescunt, et opulentia lites. (4 INST. 74.)—Small means increase by concord and litigations by opulence.

268. Conditio beneficialis quæ statum construit, benigne secundum verborum intentionem est interpretanda; odiosa autem, quæ statum destruit stricte secundum verborum proprietatem accipienda. (8 COKE, 90.)—A beneficial condition which creates an estate ought to be construed favorably, according to the intention of the words; but a condition which destroys an estate is odious, and ought to be construed strictly according to the letter of the words.

269. Conditio dicitur, cum quid in casum incertum, qui potest tendere ad esse aut non esse, confertur. (COKE, LITT. 201. a.)—It is called a con-

dition, when that which can tend to be present or not, refers to an uncertain event.

270. Conditio illicita habetur pro non adjecta. (WHART. 188.)—A secret condition is deemed as not annexed.

271. Conditio ad liberum tenentum auferendum non nisi ex facto placitari debet. (LOFFT, 511.)—An argument for taking away a free tenure should not be pleaded, except from the deed.

272. Conditio liberum tenementum cassans non per nuda verba sine charta valebit. (LOFFT, 630.)—A condition making void a free tenement will be of no value by bare words without writing.

273. Conditio neminem juvabit nisi qui pars fuerit aut privus. (LOFFT, 629.)—An agreement avails no one unless he is a party or privy to it.

274. Conditio ex parte extincta ex toto extinguitur. (LOFFT, 510.)—A condition extinguished in part is totally extinguished.

275. Conditio (præcendens) adimpleri debet priusquam sequatur effectus. (COKE, LITT. 201. a.) —A condition precedent must be fulfilled before the effect can follow.

276. Conditionem testium tunc inspicere debemus cum signarent, non mortis tempore. (TAYLER, 74.)—The condition of witnesses must be considered when they sign, and not when they die.

277. Conditiones quælibet odiosæ; maxime autem contra matrimonium et commercium. (LOFFT, 644.)—Some agreements are odious, but mostly those against matrimony and commerce.

278. Confessio, facta in judicio, omni probatione major est. (JENK. CENT. 102.)—A confession made in judicial proceedings is of greater force than all proof.

279. Confessus in judicio pro judicato habetur, et quodammodo suo sententia damnatur. (11 COKE, 30.)—A person confessing a judgment is deemed as adjudged, and, in a manner, is condemned by his own sentence.

280. Confirmare est id quod firmum facere prius infirmum fuit. (COKE, LITT. 295. b.)—To confirm is to make firm that which was before infirm.

281. Confirmare nemo potest priusquam jus ei acciderit. (10 COKE, 48.)—No person can confirm a right before the right shall come to him.

282. Confirmat usum qui tollit abusum. (MOORE, 764.)—He confirms a use who removes an abuse.

283. Confirmatio est nulla ubi donum præcedens est invalidum. (COKE, LITT. 295. b.)—There is no confirmation where the preceding gift is invalid.

284. Confirmatio omnes supplet defectus, licet id quod actum est ab initio non valuit. (COKE, LITT. 295. b.)—Confirmation supplies all defects, through that which has been done at the beginning was not valid.

285. Conjunctio mariti et feminæ est de jure naturæ. (2 Bou. 120,)—The union of man and woman is of the law of nature.

286. Consanguineus est, quasi eadem sanguine natus. (Coke, Litt. 157. a.)—Consanguinity is, as it were, sprung from the same blood.

287. Conscientia legalis ex lege fundatur. (Lofft, 513.)—Legal conscience is founded upon the law.

288. Conscientia legi nunquam contravenit. (Lofft, 483.)—Conscience never contravenes the law.

289. Consensus est voluntas multorum, ad quos res pertinet, simul juncta. (Dav. 48.)— Consent is the united will of many persons interested in the same thing.

290. Consensus facit legem. (Branch. Pr.) Consent constitutes law.

291. Consensus, non concubitus, facit matrimonium. (6 Coke, 22.)—Consent, and not concubinage, constitutes marriage.

292. Consensus tollit errorem. (2 Inst. 123.) Consent takes away error.

293. Consentientes et agentes pari pœna plectentur. (5 Coke, 80.)—Those consenting and those perpetrating are embraced in the same punishment.

294. **Consentire est facere.** (WHART.)—To consent to a thing is to perform it.

295. **Consentire matrimonio non possunt infra annos nubiles.** (6 COKE, 22.)—To consent to marriage is not possible before marriageable years.

296. **Consequentiæ non est consequentia.** (BAC. APH. 16.)—A consequence should not be deduced from a consequence.

297. **Consilia multorum requiruntur in magnis.** (4 INST. 1.)—The counsels of many are required in great things.

298. **Constitutiones tempore posteriores sunt his quæ ipsas præcesserunt.** (BR. 28.)—The later provisions in a statute should prevail even though they fail to agree with the form.

299. **Constitutum esse eam domum unicuique nostrum debere existimari, ubi quisque sedes et tabulas haberet, suarumque rerum constitutionem fecisset.** (DIG. 50. 16. 203.)—It is settled that that is to be considered the home of each one of us where he may have his habitation and account-books, and where he may have made an establishment of his business.

300. **Constructio ad principia refertur rei.** (LOFFT, 516.)—Construction is referred to the principles of a thing.

301. **Constructio est secundum æquitatem.** (LOFFT, 519.)—Construction is according to equity.

302. **Constructio legis non facit injuriam.** (COKE, LITT. 183. a.)—The construction of law does not work any injury.

303. **Consuetudo alicujus loci lex est legis loci.** (LOFFT, 338.)—The custom of any place is the law of that place.

304. **Consuetudo contra ration'em introducta potius usurpatio quam consuetudo appellari debet.** (COKE, LITT. 113. a.)—A custom introduced against reason should rather be called an usurpation than a custom.

305. **Consuetudo debet esse certa; nam incerta pro nulla habentur.** (DAV. 90.)—A custom should be certain, for uncertain things are held as nothing.

306. **Consuetudo est altera lex.** (4 COKE, 21.) —Custom is a second law.

307. **Consuetudo est optimus interpres legum.** (2 INST. 18.)—Custom is the best expounder of the law.

308. **Consuetudo et communis assuetudo vincit legem non scriptam, si sit specialis; et in-, terpretatur legem scriptam, si lex sit generalis.** (JENK. CENT. 273.)—Custom and common usage overcome the unwritten law, if it be special ; and interpret the written law, if it be general.

309. **Consuetudo ex certa causa rationabili usitata privat communem legem.** (LITT. §169.)— A custom grounded on a certain reasonable cause, supersedes the common law.

310. Consuetudo loci est observanda. (6 COKE, 67.)—The custom of a place is to be observed.

311. Consuetudo, licet sit magnæ authoritatis nunquam tamen præjndicat manifestæ veritati. (4 COKE, 18.)—A custom, though it be of great authority, should never, however be prejudicial to manifest truth.

312. Consuetudo maneriorum domini voluntatem regit. (LOFFT, 339.)—The will of the master is ruled by the custom of the manor.

313. Consuetudo neque injuria oriri, neque tolli potest. (LOFFT, 340.)—A custom can neither arise nor be abolished by injury.

314. Consuetudo non habitur in consequentiam. (3 KEB. 499.)—Custom is not to be drawn into a precedent.

315. Consuetudo non præjudicat veritati. (LOFFT, 337.)—Custom is not prejudicial to truth.

316. Consuetudo populi Anglicani et communis lex libertas. (LOFFT, 341.)—The custom of the English people and the common law are free.

317. Consuetudo præscripta et legitima vincit legem. (COKE, LITT. 113. a.)—A prescriptive and legitimate custom overcomes the law.

318. Consuetudo pro lege servatur. (COKE. LITT. 113. a.)—Custom is observed for law.

319. Consuetudo regni Angliæ est lex Angliæ. (JENK. CENT. 119.)—The custom of England is the jaw of England.

320. Consuetudo regni est lex regni. (JENK. CENT. 118.)—The custom of a nation is the law of that nation.

321. Consuetudo semel reprobata non potest amplius induci. (DAV. 33.)—Custom once disallowed cannot be again alleged.

322. Consuetudo vincit communem legem. (COKE, LITT. 33. b.)—Custom overrules the common law.

323. Consuetudo volentes ducit, lex nolentes trahit. (JENK. CENT. 274.)—Custom leads the willing, law compels the unwilling.

324. Contemporanea consuetudo optimus interpres. (TAYLER, 77.)—Contemporary custom is the best interpreter.

325. Contemporanea expositio est optima et fortissima in lege. (2 INST. 11.)—A contemporaneous exposition is the best and most powerful in the law.

326. Contestatio litis eget terminos contradictarios. (JENK. CENT. 117.)—Joinder of issue in a lawsuit requires contradictory terms.

327. Contra fictionem non admittitur probatio. (TAYLER, 78.)—Against fiction proof is not to be admitted.

328. Contra legem facit qui id facit quod lex prohibet. (DIG. 1. 3. 29.)—He does contrary to the law who does what the law prohibits.

329. Contra negantem principia non est dis-

putandum. (COKE, LITT. 343. a.)—Against one
denying principles there is no disputing.

330. Contra non valentem agere nulla currit
præscriptio. (WHART. 208.)—Against one unable
to act runs no prescription.

331. Contra veritatem lex nunquam aliquid
permittit. (2 INST. 252.)—The law never permits
anything contrary to truth.

332. Contractus ad mentem partium verbis
notatam intelligendus. (LOFFT, 522.)—A contract should be understood according to the intention of the parties, expressed in words.

333. Contractus est quasi actus contra
actum. (2 COKE, 15.)—A contract is, as it were,
act against act.

334. Contractus ex turpi causa, vel contra
bonos mores nullus est. (HOB. 167.)—A contract with a base consideration or against good
morals is null.

335. Contractus infantis invalidus, si in damnum sui spectet. (LOFFT, 308.)—A contract of a
minor is invalid if it lead to his injury.

336. Contractus legem ex conventione accipiunt. (DIG. 16. 3. 1. 6.)—The agreement of the
parties makes the law of the contract.

337. Contrariorum contraria est ratio.
(HOB. 344.)—The reason of contrary things is
contrary.

338. Contraxisse unusquisquem in eo loco
intelligitur in quo ut solveret se obligavit.

(TAYLER, 78.)—Every person is understood to have contracted in that place in which he has bound himself to pay.

339. Contrectatio rei alienæ, animo furandi, est furtum. (JENK. CENT. 132.)—The touching of property not one's own, with intention to steal, is theft.

340. Conventio privatorum non potest publico juri derogare. (WING. 746.)—A convention of private persons cannot affect public right.

341. Conventio vincit legem. (6 TAUNT. 430.)—An agreement conquers law.

342. Convicia si irascaris, tua divulgas; spreta, exolescunt. (3 INST. 198.)—If you be angered by insults, you publish them ; if despised they are forgotten.

343. Convitium convitio tegere, est lutum luto porrigere. (1 BULS. 86.)—To cover reproach with reproach, is to heap mud upon mud.

344. Copulatio verborum indicat acceptationem in eodem sensu. (BAC. MAX. 3.)—The coupling of words shows that they are to be taken in the same sense.

345. Corporalis injuria non recipit æstimationem de futuro. (BAC. MAX. 6.)—A bodily injury receives no satisfaction from a future course of proceeding.

346. Corpus corporatum ex uno potest consistere. (LOFFT, 302.)—An incorporated body may consist of one person.

347. Corpus corporatum non habet hæredes neque executores; neque mori potest. (LOFFT, 299.)—An incorporated body has no heirs nor executors, nor can it die.

348. Corpus humanum non recipit æstimationem. (HOB. 59.)—A human body is not susceptible of appraisement.

349. Corruptio optimi est pessima. (WHART. 220.)—Corruption of the best is worst.

350. Creditor qui permittit rem venire pignus dimittit. (HALK. 32.)—A creditor who permits property to be sold gives up the pledge.

351. Crescente malitia crescere debet et pæna. (2 INST. 479.)—Vice increasing, punishment ought also to increase.

352. Crimen ex post facto non diluitur. (HALK. 32.)—A crime cannot be expiated by after deeds.

353. Crimen falsi dicitur, cum quis illicitur, cui non fuerit ad hæc data auctoritas, de sigillo regis rapto vel invento brevia, cartasve consignaverit. (FLETA, 1. 22. 8.)—The crime of forgery is when any one unlawfully, to whom power has not been given for such purposes, has signed writs or charters with the king's seal, which he has either stolen or found.

354. Crimen læsæ majestatis omnia alia crimina excedit quoad pœnam. (3 INST. 210.)—The crime of treason exceeds all other crimes as to its punishment.

355. Crimen omnia ex se nata vitiat. (5 HILL, N. Y. 523.)—Crime vitiates all things which spring from it.

356. Crimina morte extinguuntur. (2 BOU. 112.)—Crimes are extinguished by death.

357. Cruciatus legibus invisi. (ERSK. INST. 4. 3.)—Tortures are odious to the law.

358. Cui jurisdictio data est, ea quoque concessa esse videntur sine quibus jurisdictio explicari non potest. (DIG. 2. 1. 2.)—To whom jurisdiction is given, to him those things also are neid to be granted, without which the jurisdiction cannot be exercised.

359. Cui licet quod majus, non debet quod minus est non licere. (4 COKE, 23.)—He who has authority to do the more important act shall not be debarred from doing that of less importance.

360. Cui pater est populus non habet ille patrem. (COKE, LITT. 123. a.)—He to whom the people is father, has no father.

361. Cui plus licet quam par est, plus vult quam licet. (2 INST. 464.)—He to whom more is granted than is just, wants more than is granted.

362. Cuicunque aliquis quid concedit, concedere videtur et id sine quo res ipsa esse non potuit. (11 COKE, 52.)—The grantor of anything to another, grants that also without which the thing granted would be useless.

363. Cujus est commodum, ejus debet esse incommodum. (1 KAMES, EQ. 289.)—Whose is the advantage, his also should be the disadvantage.

364. Cujus est dare, ejus est disponere. (2 COKE, 71.)—Whose is to give, his is to dispose.

365. Cujus est divisio, alterius est electio. (COKE, LITT. 166. b.)—Whichever has the division, the other has the choice.

366. Cujus est donandi eidem et vendendi et concedendi jus est. (HALK. 33.)—Whose it is to give, his is also the right to sell and grant.

367. Cujus est instituere ejus est abrogare. (2 BOU. 122.)—Whose it is to institute, his it is to abrogate.

368. Cujus est solum, ejus est usque ad coelum; et ad inferos. (COKE, LITT. 4. a.)—Whose is the land, his is also that which is above and below it.

369. Cujus juris est principale, ejusdem juris erit accessorium. (2 INST. 493.)—He who has jurisdiction of the principal, has also jurisdiction of the accessory.

370. Cujus per errorem dati repetitio est, ejus consulto dati, donatio est. (DIG. 50. 17. 53.)—That which, when given through mistake, can be recovered back, when given with knowledge of the facts, becomes a gift.

371. Cujusque rei potissima pars principium est. (10 COKE, 49.)—Of everything the chief part is the beginning.

372. **Ouilibet in sua arte perito est credendum.** (COKE, LITT. 125. a.)—Whosoever is skilled in his profession is to be believed.

373. **Oulpa caret, qui scit sed prohibere non potest.** (DIG. 50. 17. 50.)—He is free from blame, who knows but cannot prevent.

374. **Oulpa est immiscere se rei ad se non pertinenti.** (2 INST. 444.)—It is a fault to meddle with what does not belong to you.

375. **Oulpa lata dolo æquiparatur.** (WHART. 234.)—Gross negligence is equivalent to fraud.

376. **Oulpæ poena par esto.** (BRANCH, PR.) —Let the punishment be measured by the extent of the crime.

377. **Oulpa tenet suos auctores.** (ERSK. INST. 4. 1. 14.)—A fault binds its own authors.

378. **Oulpa vel poena ex æquitate non intenditur.** (HALK. 84.)—Blame or punishment does not proceed from equity.

379. **Oum actio fuerit mere criminalis institui poterit ab initio criminaliter vel civiliter.** (BRACT. 102.)—When an action is only criminal, it may be established from the beginning either criminally or civilly.

380. **Oum adsunt testimonia rerum, quid opus est verbis.** (2 BULS. 53.)—Where the proofs of facts are present, what need is there of words?

381. **Oum confitente sponte mitius est agendum.** (4 INST. 66.)—One confessing willingly should be gently dealt with.

382. Cum de lucro duorum quæritur, melior est causa possidentis. (DIG. 50. 17. 126.)—When there is a question of gain between two, the cause of the possessor is the better.

383. Cum duo inter se pugnantia reperiuntur in testamento, ultimum ratum est. (COKE, LITT. 112. b.)—Where two clauses in a will are repugnant, one to the other, the last in order shall prevail.

384. Cum in testamento ambigue aut etiam perperam scriptum, est benigne interpretari, et secundum id quod credibile est cogitatum credendum est. (DIG. 34. 5. 24.)—Where ambiguities or absurdities occur in a will they should be liberally interpreted, and in accordance with the probable intention of the testator.

385. Cum legitimæ nuptiæ factæ sunt, patrem liberi sequuntur. (2 BOU. 122.)—The children born of a legitimate marriage follow the condition of the father.

386. Cum par delictum est duorum, semper oneratur petitor, et melior habetur possessoris causa. (DIG. 50. 17. 154.)—Where two claimants are at fault, the condition of the one in possession is the best.

387. Cum principalis causa non consistit ne ea quidem quæ sequuntur locum habent. (DIG. 50. 17. 129.)—Where the principal cause is not consistent, the things which follow have no place.

388. Curatus non habet titulum. (8 Buls. 310.)—A curate has no title.

389. Curia cancellariæ officina justitiæ. (2 Inst. 552.)—The court of chancery is the workshop of justice.

390. Curia cancellaria non nisi parliamento subdita. (Halk. 34.)—The court of chancery is not subject, except to parliament.

391. Curia ecclesiastica locum non habet super iis quæ juria sunt communis. (Halk. 35.)—An ecclesiastical court has no power over matters in common law.

392. Curia parliamenti suis propriis legibus subsistit. (4 Inst. 50.)—The court of parliament is governed by its own peculiar laws.

393. Curiosa et captiosa interpretatio in lege reprobatur. (1 Buls. 6.)—A curious and captious interpretation is reprobated in law.

394. Currit tempus contra desides et sui juris contemptores. (Bract. 100.)—Time runs against the slothful and those who neglect their rights.

395. Cursus curiæ est lex curiæ. (3 Buls. 53.)—The practice of the court is the law of the court.

396. Custom is the best interpreter of the law. (4 Inst. 75).

397. Custome serra prise stricte. (Jenk. Cent. 83.)—Custom should be taken strictly.

398. Custos corporis cujusque infantis est

is esto ad quem hæreditas nequeat pervenire. (HALK. 35.)—Let him be the guardian of the body of an infant to whom the inheritance cannot come.

399.   Custos statum hæredis in custodia existentis meliorem, non deteriorem, facere potest. (7 COKE, 7.)—A guardian can make the estate of an existing heir under his guardianship better, but not worse.

D.

400.   Da tua dum tua sunt; post mortem tunc tua non sunt.   (3 BULS. 18.)—Give your things while they are yours ; after death they are not yours.

401.   Damnum absque injuria esse potest. (HALK. 12.)—There may be damage without in-jury.

402.   Dans et retinens, nihil dat. (WHART. 242.)—He who gives and retains, gives nothing.

403.   De bonis defuncti primo deducenda sunt ea quæ sunt necessitatis; et postea, quæ sunt utilitatis; et ultimo, quæ sunt voluntatis. (TAY-LER, 110.)—From the goods of a deceased person, the first to be deducted are those which are of necessity, and afterward those which are of utility, and lastly those which are of bequest.

404. De fide et officio judicis non recipitur quæstio; sed de scientia, sive error sit juris aut facti. (BAC. MAX. 17.)—Of the good faith and intention of a judge, a question cannot be entertained ; but it is otherwise as to his knowledge or error, be it in law or in fact.

405. De gratia speciali, certa scientia, et mero motu, talis clausula non valet in his in quibus præsumitur principem esse ignorantem. (1 COKE, 53.)—Concerning special grace, certain knowledge, and mere motive, a clause does not prevail in those things in which the prince was presumed to be ignorant.

406. De grossis arboribus decimæ non dabuntur, sed de sylva cedura decimæ dabuntur. (2 ROL. 123.)—Of whole trees, tithes are not given ; but of wood used to be cut, tithes are given.

407. De jure decimarum, originem ducens de jure patronatus tunc cognitio spectat ad legem civilem, i.e., communem. (GODB. 63.)—Concerning the right of tithes, deducing its origin from the right of the patron, then the cognizance of them looks to the civil, that is to say the common, law.

408. De jure judices, de facto juratores, respondent. (COKE, LITT. 295. b.)—The judges answer to the law, the jury to the fact.

409. De jure naturæ cogitare per nos, atque

(4)

dicere debemus; de jure populi quæ relicta sunt et tradita. (TAYLER, 118.)—We may construe the laws of nature, we must consider, of ourselves ; but the common law we must accept the constructions that have descended to us.

410. De majori et minori non variant jura. (2 VER. 552.)—In regard to major and minor laws do not vary.

411. De minimis non curat lex. (CRO. ELIZ. 353.)—Of trifles the law does not concern · itself.

412. De minimis non curat prætor. (TRAY. 137.)—The judge does not concern himself about trifles.

413. De morte hominis nulla est cunctatio longa. (COKE, LITT. 134. b.)—Concerning the death of a man no delay is long.

414. De molendino de nova erecto non jacet prohibitio. (CRO. JAC. 429.)—A prohibition lies not against a newly erected mill.

415. De nomine proprio non est curandum cum in substantia non erretur; quia nomina mutabilia sunt, res autem immobiles. (6 COKE, 66.)—As to the proper name it is not to be regarded, where it errs not in substance ; because names are changeable, but things are immutable.

416. De non apparentibus, et non existentibus, eadem est ratio. (4 COKE, 47.)—Of things which do not appear, and things which do not exist, the rule in legal proceedings is the same.

417. **De nullo, quod est sua natura indivisibile, et divisionem non patitur, nullam partem habebit vidua; sed satisfaciat ei ad valentiam.** (COKE, LITT. 32. a.)—A widow shall have no part from that which in its own nature is indivisible and is not susceptible of division; but let her satisfy herself with an equivalent.

418. **De similibus ad similia eadem ratione procedendum est.** (BRANCH, PR.)—From similars to similars we are to proceed by the same rule.

419. **De similibus idem est judicium.** (7 COKE, 18.)—Concerning similars the judgment is the same.

420. **Debet esse finis litium.** (JENK. CENT. 61.)—There should be an end of law suits.

421. **Debet quis juri subjacere, ubi delinquit.** (3 INST. 34.)—Everyone should be subject to the law of the place where he commits an offence.

422. **Debet sua cuique domus esse perfugium tutissimum.** (12 JOHNS. N. Y. 54.)—Every man's house should be a perfectly safe refuge.

423. **Debile fundamentum fallit opus.** (NOY, 12.)—A weak foundation destroys the superstructure.

424. **Debita sequuntur personam debitoris.** (2 KENT. COM. 429.)—Debts follow the person of the debtor.

425. Debitor non præsumitur donare. (1 KAME's, EQ. 212.)—A debtor is not presumed to give.

426. Debitorum pactionibus, creditorum petitio nec tolli, nec minui potest. (POTHIER, OB 87.)—The right to sue of creditors can neither be taken away nor diminished by the contracts of their debtors.

427. Debitum et contractus sunt nullius loci. (7 COKE, 3.)—Debt and contract are of no place.

428. Debitum in præsenti solvendum in futuro. (2 BARB. N. Y. 457.)—A debt due at present to be paid at a future time.

429. Deceptis, non decipientibus, jura subveniunt. (HALK. 36.)—Laws assist the deceived, not the deceiving.

430. Decet tamen principem servare leges, quibus, ipse salutus est. (WHART. 249.)—It behooves indeed the prince to keep the laws by which he himself is preserved.

431. Decimæ de decimatis solvi non debent. (WHART. 249.)—Tithes should not be paid from what is given for tithes.

432. Decimæ non debent solvi ubi non est annua renovatio; et ex annuatis renovantibus simul semel. (CRO. JAC. 42.)—Tithes should not be paid, where there is not an annual renovation, and from annual renovations once altogether.

433. Decipi quam fallere est tutius. (LOFFT, 396.)—It is more safe to be deceived than to deceive.

434. Decreta conciliorum non ligant reges nostros. (WHART. 251.)—The decrees of councils do not bind our kings.

435. Decretum est sententia lata super legem. (WHART. 252.)—A decree is a sentence laid upon the law.

436. Deficiente uno sanguine non potest esse hæres. (3 COKE, 41.)—One wanting blood, cannot be an heir.

437. Delegata potestas non potest delegari. (2 INST. 597.)—A delegated power cannot be delegated.

438. Delegatus debitor est odiosus in lege. (2 BULS. 148.)—A delegated debtor is odious in law.

439. Delegatus non potest delegare. (BR. 839.)—A delegate cannot delegate.

440. Deliberandum est diu quod statuendum est semel. (12 COKE, .74.)—That which is to be resolved once for all, should be long deliberated upon.

441. Delinquens per iram provocatus puniri debet mitius. (3 INST. 55.)—A delinquent provoked by anger should be punished more mildly.

442. Denominatio fieri debet a dignioribus.

(WHART. 267.)—Denomination should be made for the more worthy.

443. Derivative potestas non potest esse major primitiva. (NOY, 8.)—The power derived cannot be greater than that from which it is derived.

444. Derogatur legi; cum pars detrahitur; abrogatur legi, cum prorsus tollitur. (DIG. 50. 16. 102.)—To derogate from a law is to take away part of it; to abrogate a law is to abolish it entirely.

445. Designatio justiciarorum est a rege; jurisdictio vero ordinaria a lege. (4 INST. 74.) —The appointment of justices is by the king; but ordinary jurisdiction is by the law.

446. Designatio unius est exclusio alterius, et expressum facit cessare tacitum. (COKE, LITT. 210. a.)—The appointment of one is the exclusion of another; and that expressed makes that which is understood to cease.

447. Deus solus hæredem facere potest non homo. (COKE, LITT. 7. b.)—God alone, and not man, can make an heir.

448. Dies Dominicus non est juridicus. (NOY, 2.)—The Lord's day (Sunday) is not juridical, or a day for legal proceedings.

449. Dies inceptus pro completo habetur. (WHART. 274.)—A day begun is held as complete.

450. Dies incertus pro conditione habetur.

(BELL, DIC.)—An uncertain day is held as a condition.

451. **Dies interpellat pro homine.** (BELL, DIC.)—A day demands as a man.

452. **Difficile est ut unus homo vicem duorum sustineat.** (4 COKE, 118.)—It is difficult for one man to fill the place of two.

453. **Dignitas supponit officium et curam, et non est partibilis.** (LOFFT, 334.)—Dignity supposes office and charge, and is not divisible.

454. **Dignitates rex dat virtus conservat, delicta auferunt.** (LOFFT, 833.)—The king gives honors, virtue preserves them, transgressions take them away.

455. **Dignus mercede operarius.** (LOFFT, 262.)—The laborer is worthy of his hire.

456. **Dilatio quæ pro justitia faciat acceptissima; quæ contra justitiam maxime invisa.** (HALK. 38.)—Delay for the sake of justice is most acceptable; but contrary to justice is very odious.

457. **Dilationes in lege sunt odiosæ.** (BRANCH, PR.)—Delays in law are odious.

458. **Discontinuare nihil aliud significat quam intermittere, desuescere, interrumpere.** (COKE, LITT. 825. a.)—To discontinue signifies nothing else than to intermit, to disuse, to interrupt.

459. **Discretio est scire, per legem, quid**

sit justum. (10 COKE, 140.)—Discretion is to know through law what is just.

460. Disparata non debent jungi. (JENK. CENT. 24.)—Dissimilar things should not be joined.

461. Dispensatio est mali prohibiti provida relaxatio, utilitate seu necessitate pensata; et est de jure domino regi concessa, propter impossibilitatem prævidendi de omnibus particularibus. (10 COKE, 88.)—A dispensation is the provident relaxation of a prohibited evil, weighed from utility or necessity; and it is conceded by law to the king, on account of the impossibility of foreknowledge concerning all particulars.

462. Dispensatio est vulnus, quod vulnerat jus commune. (DAV. 69.)—A dispensation is a wound, which wounds common right.

463. Disseisinam satis facit, qui uti non permittit possessorem, vel minus commode, licet omnino non expellat. (COKE, LITT. 331. b.)— He makes disseisin enough who does not permit the possessor to enjoy, or makes his enjoyment less commodious, though he does not expel altogether.

464. Dissimilium dissimiles est ratio. (COKE, LITT. 191. a.)—Of dissimilars the rule is dissimilar.

465. Dissimulatione tollitur injuria. (ERSK. INST. 4. 4. 108.)—Injury is removed by reconciliation.

466. Distinguenda sunt tempora; aliud est facere, aliud perficere. (1 COKE, 24.)—Times are to be distinguished; it is one thing to do, another to complete.

467. Distinguenda sunt tempora; distingue tempora, et concordabis legis. (1 COKE, 24.) —Times are to be distinguished; distinguish times, and you will make the laws agree.

468. Districtio non potest esse, nisi pro certis servitiis. (HALK. 39.)—Goods cannot be distrained except for certain services.

469. Divide et impera, cum radix et vertex imperii in obedientium consensu rata sunt. (4 INST. 35.)—Divide and govern, since the foundation and crown of empire are established in the consent of the obedient.

470. Divinatio non interpretatio est, quæ omnino recedit a litera. (BAC. MAX. 3.)—It is guessing, not interpretation which altogether differs from the letter.

471. Divisibilis in semper divisibilia. (WHART. 288.)—A thing divisible, may always be divided.

472. Dolo facit qui petit quod redditurus est. (BR. 346.)—He seeks with guile who seeks what he should return.

473. Dolo malo pactum se non servaturum. (BR. 731.)—By fraud or dole a contract perishes.

474. Dolosus versatur in generalibus. (3 COKE, 81.)—A deceiver deals in generalities.

475. Dolum ex indiciis perspicuis probari convenit. (CODE, 2. 21. 6.)—Fraud should be proved by the clearest evidence.

476. Dolus auctoris non nocet successori. (WHART. 289.)—The fraud of a predecessor does not prejudice the successor.

477. Dolus circuitu non purgatur. (BAC. MAX. 1.)—Fraud is not purged by circuity.

478. Dolus est machinatio cum aliud, dissimulat aliud agit. (LANE, 47.)—Deceit is an artifice, since it pretends one thing and does another.

479. Dolus et fraus nemini patrocinentur. (3 COKE, 79.)—Deceit and fraud shall excuse or benefit no man.

480. Dolus et fraus una in parte sanari debent. (NOY, 83.)—Deceit and fraud should always be remedied.

481. Dolus præsumitur contra versantem in illicito. (TRAY. 162.)—Wrongful intention is presumed against one engaged in an unlawful act.

482. Dominium non potest esse in pendenti. (TRAY. 163.)—The right of property cannot be in abeyance.

483. Dominus aliquando non potest alienare. (WHART. 291.)—A lord sometimes cannot alienate.

484. Dominus capitalis loco hæredes habetur quoties per defectum vel delictum extinguitur

sanguis sui tenentis. (COKE, LITT. 13. a.)—
The supreme lord takes the place of the heir,
as often as the blood of the tenant is extinct
through deficiency or crime.

485. **Dominus non maritabit pupillum nisi
semel.** (COKE, LITT. 79. b.)—A lord cannot
give a ward in marriage but once.

486. **Dominus omnium in regno terrarum
rex habendus; et ab eo omnes tenent ita tamen,
ut suum cuique sit.** (HALK. 40.)—The sovereign is first seized of all lands; of him all others
hold, so that everyone has his own.

487. **Dominus rex nullum habere potest
parem, multo minus surperiorem.**—The king
can have no equal, much less a superior.

488. **Dominus vel causam servi vel personam inculpatio defendet, etiam ubi alii non
liceret.** (HALK. 40.)—A master may defend the
cause of his servant, even when it is not lawful
for another.

489. **Domum suam unicuique reficere licet,
dum non officiat invito alteri in quo jus non
habet.** (HALK. 40.)—It is lawful for every
man to repair his own house, provided he does
it not to the injury of another over whom he
has no rights.

490. **Domus sua cuique est tutissimum refu-
gium.** (5 COKE, 92.)—To everyone his house is
his surest refuge; or, every man's house is his
castle.

491. Dona clandestina sunt semper suspiciosa. (3 COKE, 81.)—Clandestine gifts are always suspicious.

492. Donari videtur quod nulli jure cogente conceditur. (DIG. 50. 17. 82.)—That is considered to be given which is granted when no law compels.

493. Donatio non præsumitur. (JENK. CENT. 109.)—A gift is not presumed.

494. Donatio perficitur possessione accipientis. (JENK. CENT. 109.)—A gift is perfected by the possession thereof by the donee.

495. Donatio principes intelligitur sine præjudicio tertii. (DAV. 75.)—A gift of a prince is understood to be without the prejudice of a third party.

496. Donatio quælibet ex vi legis sortitur effectum. (HALK. 41.)—A donation obtains its effect by force of the law.

497. Donationum alia perfecta, alia incepta et non perfecta; ut si donatio lecta fuit et concessa, ac traditio nondum fuerit subsecuto. (COKE, LITT. 56. b.)—Some gifts are perfect, others incipient or not perfect; as if a gift were read and agreed to, but delivery had not then followed.

498. Donator nunquam desinit possidere antequam donatarius incipiat possidere. (DYER, 281.)—He who gives never ceases to possess before that the receiver begins to possess.

499. Dormiunt aliquando leges, nunquam moriuntur. (2 Inst. 161.)—The laws sometimes sleep, never die.

500. Dos de dote peti non debet. (4 Coke, 122.)—Dower ought not to be sought from dower.

501. Doti lex favet; præmium pudoris est, ideo parcatur. (Coke, Litt. 31. a.)—The law favors dower; it is the reward of chastity, therefore is to be preserved.

502. Droit ne done pluis que soit demande. (2 Inst. 286.)—The law gives no more than is demanded.

503. Droit ne poet pas morier. (Jenk. Cent. 100.)—Right cannot die.

504. Duas uxores eadem tempore habere non licet. (Tayler, 142.)—It is not lawful to have two wives at the same time.

505. Duo non possunt in solido unam rem possidere. (Coke, Litt. 268. b.)—Two persons cannot possess one thing in entirety.

506. Duo sunt instrumenta ad omnes res aut confirmandas aut impugnandas—ratio et auctoritas. (8 Coke, 16.)—There are two instruments either to confirm or impugn all things—reason and authority.

507. Duorum in solidum dominium vel possessio esse non potest. (Dig. 18. 6. 5. 15.)—Ownership or possession in entirety cannot be in two of the same thing.

508. **Duplex placitum non admittitur.** (HALK. 41.)—A double decree cannot be regarded.

509. **Duplicationem possibilitatis lex non patitur.** (1 ROL. 321.)—The law does not permit a duplication of possibilities.

510. **Durum est per divinationem a verbis recedere.** (HALK. 41.)—It is hard by conjecture to depart from the meaning of words.

E.

511. **Ea est accipienda interpretatio quæ vitio caret.** (BAC. MAX. 3.)—That interpretation is to be received which is free from fault.

512. **Ea quæ, commendandi causa, in venditionibus dicuntur, si palam appareant, venditorem non obligant.** (DIG. 18. 1. 43.)—Those things which, by way of commendation, are stated at sales, if they are openly apparent, do not bind the seller.

513. **Ea quæ dari impossibilia sunt, vel quæ in rerum natura non sunt, pro non adjectis habentur.** (DIG. 50. 17. 135.)—Those things which cannot be given, or which have no existence in the nature of things, are held as not expressed.

514. **Ea quæ in curia nostra rite acta sunt, debitæ executioni demandari debent.** (COKE, LITT. 289. a.)—Those things which are properly

transacted in our court should be committed to due execution.

515. **Ea quæ raro accidunt, non temere in agendis negotiis computantur.** (DIG. 50. 17. 64.) —Those things which rarely happen are not to be rashly computed in transacting business.

516. **Ea sola deportationis sententia aufert quæ ad fiscum perveniret.** (HALK. 42.)—A sentence of transportation deprives of monetary consideration.

517. **Eadem causa diversis rationibus coram judicibus ecclesiasticis et secularibus ventilatur.** (2 INST. 622.)—The same cause is argued from different principles before ecclesiastical and secular judges.

518. **Eadem mens præsumitur regis quæ est juris et quæ esse debet, præsertim in dubiis.** (HOB. 154.)—The mind of the sovereign is presumed to be coincident with that of the law, and that which it ought to be, especially in ambiguous matters.

519. **Ecce modum mirum! quod fœmina fert breve regis non nominando virum, conjunctum robore legis.** (COKE, LITT. 132. b.)—Behold, indeed, a wonder! that a woman has the king's writ without naming her husband, who is related to her by law.

520. **Ecclesia ecclesiæ decimas solvere non debet.** (CRO. ELIZ. 479.)—A church ought not to pay tithes to a church.

521. **Ecclesia est domus mansionalis omnipotentis Dei.** (2 INST. 164.)—The church is the mansion house of the omnipotent God.

522. **Ecclesia est infra aetatem, et in custodia domini regis, qui tenetur jura et haereditates ejusdem manutenere et defendere.** (11 COKE, 49.)—The church is under age, and in the custody of the king, who is bound to uphold and defend its rights and inheritances.

523. **Ecclesia fungitur vice minoris: meliorem conditionem suam facere potest, deteriorem nequaquam.** (COKE, LITT. 341. a.)—The church enjoys the privilege of a minor: it can make its own condition better, but not worse.

524. **Ecclesia meliori, non deteriori, potest.** (2 EDEN, 313.)—The church may grow better, but cannot grow worse.

525. **Ecclesia non moritur.** (2 INST. 3.)—The church does not die.

526. **Ecclesia semper in regis est tutela.** (LOFFT, 309.)—The church is always under protection of the king.

527. **Ecclesiae magis favendum est quam personae.** (GODB. 172.)—The church is to be more favored than a person.

528. **Edicta magistratum constitutio principis.** (TAYLER, 155.)—The manifesto of the constitution is the decree of the ruler.

529. **Effectus sequitur causam.** (WING. 226.)—The effect follows the cause.

530. Ei incumbit probatio qui dicit, non qui negat. (DIG. 22. 3. 2.)—The proof lies upon him who affirms, not upon him who denies.

531. Ei nihil turpe, cui nihil satis. (4 INST. 53.)—Nothing is base, to whom nothing is sufficient.

532. Ejus est interpretari cujus est condere. (BR. 148.)—It is for the power that imposed the law to interpret the law.

533. Ejus est non nolle qui potest velle. (DIG. 50. 17. 3.)—It is not for him to refuse who is able to be willing.

534. Ejus est periculum, cujus est dominium aut commodum. (WHART. 328.)—He has the risk who has the dominion or advantage.

535. Ejus nulla culpa est cui parere necesse sit. (DIG. 50. 17. 169.)—No guilt attaches to him who is compelled to obey.

536. Electa una via, non datur recursus ad alteram. (3 BOU. 124.)—Where there is concurrence of means, he who has elected one cannot have recourse to another.

537. Electio est interna, libera et spontanea separatio unius rei ab alia, sine compulsione, consistens in animo et voluntate. (DYER, 281.) Election is an internal, free, and spontaneous separation of one thing from another, without compulsion, consistent in mind and will.

538. Electio semel facta, et placitum tes-

(5)

tatum non patitur regressum. (COKE, LITT. 146. a.)—Election once made, and plea witnessed, suffers no recall.

539. Electiones fiant rite et libere sine interruptione aliqua. (2 INST. 169.)—Elections should be made rightly and freely, without any inter·ruption.

540. Emptio et venditio contrahitur simulat que de pretio convenerit. (HALK. 43.)—The buying and selling is complete at the time the price is agreed upon.

541. Emptor emit quam minimo potest; venditor vendit quam maximo potest. (2 KENT. COM. 486.)—A buyer buys for as little as possible; a seller sells for as much as possible.

542. En eschange il covient que les estates soient egales. (COKE, LITT. 50. b.)—In an exchange it is necessary that the estates be equal.

543. Enitia pars semper præferanda est, propter privilegium ætatis. (COKE, LITT. 166. b.)—The part of the elder sister is always to be preferred, on account of the privilege of age.

544. Enumeratio infirmat regulam in casibus non enumeratis. (BAC. APH. 17.)—Enumeration disaffirms the rule in cases not enumerated.

545. Enumeratio unius est exclusio alterius. (4 JOHNS, CH. N. Y. 106. 114.)—Specification of one thing is an exclusion of the rest.

546. Eodem modo quo oritur, eodem modo

dissolvitur. (CRO. ELIZ. 697.)—A thing is discharged in the same way in which it arises.

547. Eodem modo quo quid constituitur, eodem modo destruitur. (6 COKE, 53.)—In the same way in which anything is constituted, it may be destroyed.

548. Ephemeris annua pars legis Anglicanæ. (HALK. 43.)—An annual diary is a part of the English law. (The law takes notice of the calendar).

549. Episcopus alterius mandato quam regis non tenetur obtemperare. (COKE, LITT. 134. b.) —A bishop need not obey any mandate save the king's.

550. Episcopus teneat placitum, in curia Christianitatis, de iis quæ mere sunt spiritualia. (12 COKE, 44.)—A bishop may hold plea in a Christian court, of things merely spiritual.

551. Equality is equity. (1 STORY, EQ. JUR. 64).

552. Equity delights to do justice, and that not by halves. (5 BARB. N. Y. 277. 280).

553. Equity looks upon that as done, which ought to be done. (4 BOU. INST. 3729).

554. Equity prevents a multiplicity of suits. (FRANCIS, 9).

555. Equity prevents mischief. (FRANCIS, 8).

556. Equity regards length of time. (FRANCIS, 10).

557. Equity suffers not a right without a remedy. (4 Bou. Inst. 3726).

558. Equity suffers not advantage to be taken of a penalty or a forfeiture where compensation can be made. (Francis, 12).

559. Error fucatus nuda veritate in multis est probabilior; et sæpenumero rationibus vincit veritatem error. (2 Coke, 73.)—Painted error appears in many things more probable than naked truth; and very frequently conquers truth by reasoning.

560. Error juris nocet. (1 Story, Eq. Jur. 139.)—An error of law is injurious.

561. Error nominis nunquam nocet, si de identitate rei constat. (1 Duer, on Ins. 171.)—A mistake in the name never injures, if there is no doubt as to the identity of the thing.

562. Error placitandi æquitatem non tollit. (Lofft, 577.)—A clerical error does not take away equity.

563. Error qui non resistitur, approbatur. (Doct. & Stud. 70.)—An error which is not resisted, is approved.

564. Errores ad sua principia referre, est refellere. (3 Inst. 15.)—To refer errors to their principles, is to refute them.

565. Errores scribentis nocere non debet. (Jenk. Cent. 324.)—The mistakes of one writing ought not to harm.

566. Erubescit lex filios castigare parentes.

(8 COKE, 116.)—The law blushes when children correct their parents.

567. Est aliquid quod non oportet etiam si licet; quicquid vero non licet certe non oportet. (HOB. 159.)—There is that which is not proper, even though permitted; but whatever is not permitted, is certainly not proper.

568. Est autem jus publicum et privatum quod ex naturalibus præceptis aut gentium, aut civilibus est collectum; et quod in jure scripto jus appellatur, id in lege Angliæ rectum esse dicitur. (COKE, LITT. 558. a.)—Public and private law is that which is collected from natural precepts, on the one hand of nations, on the other of citizens; and that which in the civil law is called JUS, that in the law of England is said to be right.

569. Est autem vis legem simulans. (2 BOU. 125.)—Violence may also put on the mask of the law.

570. Est boni judicis ampliare jurisdictionem. (GILB. 14.)—It is the part of a good judge to extend the jurisdiction.

571. Est ipsorum legislatorum tanquam viva vox; rebus et non verbis legem imponimus. (10 COKE, 101.)—The utterance of legislators themselves is like the living voice; we impose law upon things not upon words.

572. Est quiddam perfectius in rebus licitis.

(Hob. 159.)—There is something more than perfect in things allowed.

573. **Estoveria sunt ardendi, arundi, construendi, et claudendi.** (13 Coke, 68.)—Estovers are for burning, ploughing, building and inclosing.

574. **Est une maxime en nostre ley parols ont plea.**—There is a maxim in our law, words make the plea.

575. **Et est pactio duorum plurumque in idem placitum consensus.** (Halk. 43.)—The meeting of the minds of two or more in an agreement makes a contract.

576. **Eum qui nocentem infamat, non est æquum et bonum ob eam rem condemnari; delicta enim nocentium nota esse oportet et expedit.** (Dig. 47. 10. 17.)—It is not just and proper that he who speaks ill of a bad man should be condemned on that account; for it is fitting and expedient that the crimes of bad men should be known.

577. **Eventus est qui ex causa sequitur, et dicitur eventus quia ex causis evenit.** (9 Coke, 81.)—An event is that which follows from the cause; and is called an event because it arises from causes.

578. **Eventus varios res nova semper habet.** (Coke, Litt. 379. a.)—A new matter always induces various results.

579. **Every man is presumed to intend the

natural and probable consequences of his own voluntary acts. (1 GR. Ev. 18).

580. **Ex abusu non arguitur ad usum.** (BR. 42.)—No argument can be drawn against the use of a thing from its abuse.

581. **Ex antecedentibus et consequentibus fit optima interpretatio.** (2 INST. 317.)—From that which goes before, and from that which follows, is derived the best interpretation.

582. **Ex delicto, non ex supplicio, emergit infamia.** (WHART. 357.)—Infamy arises from the crime, not from the punishment.

583. **Ex diuturnitate temporis omnia præsumuntur esse solennitur acta.** (COKE, LITT. 6. b.)—From lapse of time, all things are presumed to have been done properly.

584. **Ex dolo malo non oritur actio.** (COWP. 343.)—From fraud a right of action does not arise.

585. **Ex facto jus oritur.** (2 INST. 479.)—The law arises from the deed.

586. **Ex frequenti delicto augetur pœna.** (2 INST. 479.)—Punishment increases with increasing crime.

587. **Ex judicorum publicorum admissis, non alias traneunt adversus hæredes pœnæ bonorum ademptionis quam si lis contesta et condemnatio fuerit secuta excepto majestatis judicio.** (HALK. 44.)—In an arraignment for high treason, a confession in open court is equal

to a verdict of conviction and confiscation of goods, upon trial after plea of not guilty.

588. Ex maleficio non oritur contractus. (WHART. 366.)—From a wrong no contract can arise.

589. Ex malis moribus bonæ leges natæ sunt. (2 INST. 161.)—Good laws arise from evil manners.

590. Ex multitudine signorum colligitur identitas vera. (BAC. MAX. 24.)—From a number of signs true identity is collected.

591. Ex nihilo nihil fit. (13 WEND. N. Y. 178. 221.)—From nothing nothing comes.

592. Ex nuda submissione non oritur actio. (LOFFT, 506.)—From a naked submission no action arises.

593. Ex nudo pacto non oritur actio. (NOY, 24.)—From a nude contract, i.e., a contract without consideration, an action does not arise.

594. Ex pacto illicito non oritur actio. (BR. 666.)—No action can arise from an illegal contract.

595. Ex paucis dictis intendere plurima possis. (LITT. §384.)—From few expressions you may imply many things.

596. Ex paucis plurima concipit ingenium. (LITT. §550.)—From few things the mind conceives many.

597. Ex procedentibus et consequentibus optima fit interpretatio. (1 ROL. 375.)—The best interpretation is made from that which precedes and follows.

598. Ex qua persona quis lucrum capit ejus factum præstare debet. (HALK. 45.)—He who derives advantage from anyone should bear that person's obligations.

599. Ex tota materia emergat resolutio. (WING. 238.)—The explanation should arise from the whole subject matter.

600. Ex turpi causa non oritur actio. (WHART. 371.)—An action does not arise from a base cause.

601. Ex turpi contractu non oritur actio. (2 KENT. COM. 466.)—No action arises from an immoral contract.

602. Ex uno disces omnes. (2 BOU. 126.)—From one thing you can discern all.

603. Excambium naturaliter vult in se warrantium. (22 VIN. ABR. 26.)—An exchange naturally creates a warranty.

604. Excambium non potest inter tres partes datur. (HALK. 43.)—An exchange cannot exist among three parties.

605. Exceptio ejus rei cujus petitur dissolutio nulla est. (JENK. CENT. 37.)—There is no exception of that thing of which the dissolution is sought.

606. Exceptio falsi omnium ultima. (WHART. 353.)—A false plea is the basest of all things.

607. Exceptio firmat regulam in contrari-

um. (BAC. APH. 17.)—The exception affirms the rule to be the contrary.

608. Exceptio nulla est versus actionem quæ exceptionem perimit. (JENK. CENT. 106.) —There is no plea against an action which entirely destroys the plea.

609. Exceptio probat regulam de rebus exceptio. (11 COKE, 41.)—An exception proves the rule concerning things not excepted.

610. Exceptio quæ firmat legem, exponit legem. (2 BULS. 189.)—An exception which confirms the law, expounds the law.

611. Exceptio quoque regulam declarat. (BAC. APH. 17.)—The exception also declares the rule.

612. Exceptio semper ultima ponenda est. (9 COKE, 53.)—An exception is always to be put last.

613. Excessit ex ephebis est persona. (RILEY, 114.)—He who comes out of his minority becomes legally a person.

614. Excessivum in jure reprobatur. Excessus in re qualibet jure reprobatur communi. (11 COKE, 44.)—Excess in law is reprehended. Excess in anything is reprehended in common law.

615. Excessus non petita excusatio manifesta fit. (   )—He who excuses before he is accused establishes his own guilt.

616. Excommunicatio minor est, per quam

quis a sacramentorum participatione conscientia vel sententia arceatur; major est, quæ non solum a sacramentorum verum etiam fidelium communione excludit, et ab omni actu legitimo separat aut dividit. (COKE, LITT. 133. a.) —The LESSER excommunication is that by which a man, either by conscience or sentence is expelled from participation in the sacraments; the GREATER is where he is not only excluded from participation in the sacraments, but from all community with the faithful, and from every legitimate act.

617. **Excommunicato interdicitur omnes actus legitimus, ita quod agere non potest, neo aliquem convenire, licet ipse ab aliis passit convenire.** (COKE, LITT. 133. a.)—Every legitimate act is forbidden an excommunicated person; he cannot act or sue by any person, although he himself may be sued by others.

618. **Excusat aut extenuat delictum in capitalibus, quod non operatur idem in civilibus.** (BAC. MAX. 7.)—A wrong, in capital cases, is excused or palliated, which would not be so treated in civil cases.

619. **Excusatur quis quod clameum non apposuerit, ut si toto tempore litigii fuit ultra mare quacunque occasione.** (COKE, LITT. 260. a.)—He is excused who does not bring his claim, if, during the whole period in which it

should have been brought, he has been beyond sea on any occasion.

620. Executio est executio juris secundum judicium. (3 INST. 212.)—Execution is the execution of the law according to the judgment.

621. Executio est finis et fructus legis. (COKE, LITT. 289. b.)—Execution is the end and fruit of the laws.

622. Executio juris non facit injuriam. (2 ROL. 301.)—The execution of the process of the law does no injury.

623. Exempla illustrant, non restringunt, legem. (COKE, LITT. 24. a.)—Examples illustrate, not restrain, the law.

624. Exempla non restringunt regulam, sed loquuntur de casibus crebrioribus. (TRAY. 201.) —Examples do not restrict the rule, but speak of the cases which most frequently occur.

625. Exilium est patriæ privatio, natalis soli mutatio, legum nativarum amissio. (7 COKE, 20.)—Exile is a privation of country, a change of natal soil, a loss of native laws.

626. Exitus acta probat; finis, non pugna coronat. (WHART. 366.)—The conclusion proves the fact; the termination, not the fight, crowns the victory.

627. Expedit reipublicæ ne sua re quis male utatur. (2 BOU. 126.)—It is for the interest of the state that no one should misuse his own possessions.

628. Expedit reipublicæ ut sit finis litium. (COKE, LITT. 303. b.)—It is for the public good that there be an end of litigation.

629. Experientia per varios actus legem facit. Magistra rerum experientia. (COKE, LITT. 60. a.)—Experience by various acts makes law. Experience is the mistress of things.

630. Expertorum dictum nunquam transit in rem judicatam. (BON. TR. PR. §74.)—The testimony of experts should not be disregarded in judicial proceedings.

631. Expositio, quæ ex visceribus causæ nascitur, est aptissima et fortissima in lege. (10 COKE, 24.)—That exposition which springs from the vitals of a cause, is the fittest and most powerful in law.

632. Expressa nocent, non expressa non nocent. (CAL. LEX.)—Things expressed do harm; things not expressed do no harm.

633. Expressa non prosunt quæ non expressa proderunt. (4 COKE, 73.)—Things expressed do no good, which, not expressed, do no harm.

634. Expressio eorum quæ tacite insunt, nihil operatur. (4 COKE, 73.)—The expressing of those things which are implied, operates nothing.

635. Expressio unius personæ vel rei est exclusio alterius. (COKE, LITT. 210. a.)—The express mention of one person or thing is the exclusion of another.

636.   Expressum   facit   cessare   tacitum. (COKE, LITT. 210. a.)—What is expressed makes what is silent to cease.

637.   Expressum   servitium   regat   vel   declaret tacitum.   (15 BAC. 73.)—Let service expressed rule or declare what is silent.

638.   Externus non habet terras, habet res suas, et vitam et libertatem.   (LOFFT, 153.)— A foreigner has no lands, but only his personal effects, and life, and liberty.

639.   Extinguitur obligatio que rite constiteret si in eum casum inciderit a quo incipere non potuit.   (HALK. 46.)—An obligation which has been sealed in due form, is extinguished if it fall into that state from which it cannot arise.

640.   Extortio est crimen quando quis colore officii extorquet quod non est debitum, vel supra debitum, vel ante tempus quod est debitum.   (10 COKE, 102.)—Extortion is a crime, when, by color of office, any person extorts that which is not due, or above due, or before the time when it is due.

641.   Extra legem positus est civiliter mortuus.   (COKE, LITT. 130. a.)—An outlaw is civilly dead.

642.   Extra territorium jus dicenti non paretur impune.   (10 COKE, 77.)—The command of one speaking beyond his territory cannot be obeyed with impunity.

643. Extraneus est subditus qui extra terram, i.e., potestatem regis, natus est. (7 COKE, 16.)—A foreigner is one who is born out of the territory, that is, the government of the king.

644. Extrema potius pati quam turpia facere. (LOFFT, 213.)—Better suffer extremities than do things infamous.

645. Extremis probatis, præsumuntur media. (TRAY. 207.)—Extremes being proved, the medium things are presumed.

F.

646. Faciles est lapsus juventutis. (JENK. CENT. 47.)—Youth is liable to err.

647. Facinus quos inquinat æquat. (WHART. 371.)—Guilt makes equal those whom it stains.

648. Facta sunt potentiora verbis. (2 BOU. 126.)—Facts are more powerful than words.

649. Facta tenet multa quæ fieri prohibentur. (12 COKE, 125.)—Deeds contain many things which are prohibited to be done.

650. Factum a judice quod ad ejus officium non spectat, non ratum est. (DIG. 50. 17. 170.)—An action of a judge, which relates not to his office, is of no force.

651. **Factum cuique suum, non adversario, nocere debet.** (DIG. 50. 17. 155.)—A man's actions should injure himself, not his adversary.

652. **Factum infectum fieri nequit.** (1 KAMES, EQ. 96. 259.)—That which is done cannot be undone.

653. **Factum negantis nulla probatio.** (2 BOU. 126.)—No proof is incumbent upon him who denies a fact.

654. **Factum non dicitur quod non perseverat.** (5 COKE, 96.)—That is not called a deed which does not continue in force.

655. **Factum unius alteri nocere non debet.** (COKE, LITT. 152. b.)—The deed of one should not hurt another.

656. **Facultas probationum non est angustanda.** (4 INST. 279.)—The faculty of proofs is not to be narrowed.

657. **Falsa demonstratio non nocet.** (6 HILL, N. Y. 616.)—A false description does not vitiate a document.

658. **Falsa demonstratione legatum non perim.** (INST. 2. 20. 30.)—A legacy is not destroyed by a false description.

659. **Falsa orthographia, sive falsa grammatica non vitiat concessionem.** (9 COKE, 48.)—Neither false spelling nor false grammar will vitiate a grant.

660. **Falsus in uno, falsus in omnibus.** (2

Bou. 126.)—False in one thing, false in all things.

661. Fama, fides, et oculus non patiuntur ludum. (3 Buls. 226.)—Fame, faith, and eyesight do not suffer deceit.

662. Fatetur facinus qui judicium fugit. (5 Coke, 109.)—He who flees judgment confesses his guilt.

663. Fatuus præsumitur qui in proprio nomine errat. (5 Johns. Ch. 148. 161.)—A man is presumed to be simple who makes a mistake in his own name.

664. Favorabilia in lege sunt fiscus, dos, vita, libertas. (Jenk. Cent. 94.)—Things favorably considered in law are, the treasury, dower, life, and liberty.

665. Favorabilores rei potius quam actores habentur. (Dig. 50. 17. 125.)—Defendants are rather to be favored than plaintiffs.

666. Favorabiliores sunt executiones aliis processibus quibuscunque. (Coke, Litt. 289. b.) —Executions are preferred to all other processes whatever.

667. Favorabiliores tam auctores rei potuis auctores quam interveniores habentur. (Riley, 47.)—Accusers are held more favorably than intervenors.

668. Favores ampliandi sunt; odia restringenda. (Jenk. Cent. 186.)—Favors are to be enlarged; things odious are to be restrained.

(6)

669. Felix est qui potuit rerum cognoscere causas. (COKE, LITT. 231. a.)—Happy is he who has been able to understand the causes of things.

670. Felonia, ex vi termini, significat quodlibet capitale crimen felleo animo perpetratum. (COKE, LITT. 391. a.)—Felony, by force of the term, signifies some capital crime perpetrated with malicious intent.

671. Felonia implicatur in qualibet proditione. (3 INST. 15.)—Felony is implied in every treason.

672. Feodum est quod quis tenet ex quacunque causa, sive sit tenementum sive redditus. (COKE, LITT. 1. a.)—A fee is that which one holds from any cause, whether tenement or rent.

673. Feodum simplex ex feodo simplici pendere non potest. (HALK. 47.)—A simple fee cannot depend upon a simple fee.

674. Fere in omnibus pœnalibus judiciis, et ætati et imprudentiæ succuritur. (HALK. 47.)—In all criminal trials, let allowance be made for youth and imprudence.

675. Festinatio justitiæ est noverca infortunii. (HOB. 97.)—The speeding of justice is the stepmother of misfortune.

676. Feuda ad instar patrimonium sunt reducta. (TRAY. 213.)—Lands held in fee are reduced to the nature of a patrimony.

677. Fiat jus, ruat justitia. (WHART.)—Let law prevail, though justice fail.

678. Fiat justitia, ruat cœlum. (DYER, 385.) —Let justice be done though the heavens fall.

679. Fiat prout fieri consuerit; nil temere novandum. (JENK. CENT. 116.)—Let it be done even as it is accustomed to be done; let nothing be innovated rashly.

680. Fictio cedit veritati; fictio juris non est ubi veritas. (WHART. 386.)—Fiction yields to truth; where there is truth fiction of law does not exist.

681. Fictio est contra veritatem; sed pro veritate habetur. (2 BOU. 127.)—Fiction is against the truth; but it is to be esteemed truth.

682. Fictio legis inique operatur alicui damnum vel injuriam. (3 COKE, 36.)—A feigning of law iniquitously works loss or injury to some one.

683. Fictio legis neminem lædit. (3 BLACK. COM. 43.)—A fiction of law injures no one.

684. Fidelitas. De nullo tenemento, quod tenetur ad terminum, fit homagii; fit tamen inde fidelitatis sacramentum. (COKE, LITT. 67. b.)—Fealty. For no tenement which is held for a term, is the oath of homage made; but the oath of fealty is made.

685. Fides est obligatio conscientiæ alicujus ad intentionem alterius. (WHART. 387.)—Faith is an obligation of conscience of one to the will of another.

686. Fides servanda. (3 BARB. N. Y. 828. 830.)—Good faith must be observed.

687. Fides servanda est; simplicitas juris gentium prævaleat. (2 Bou. 127.)—Good faith should be preserved; the simplicity of the law of nations should prevail.

688. Fieri non debet, sed factum valet. (5 Coke, 38.)—It ought not to be done, but once done it is valid.

689. Filiatio non potest probari. (Coke, Litt. 126. a.)—Filiation cannot be proved.

690. Filius constat esse in familia patris, et non matris. (Tray. 218.)—A son appears to be in the family of the father, and not of the mother.

691. Filius est nomen naturæ, sed hæres nomen juris. (1 Sid. 193.)—Son is a name of nature, but heir is a name of law.

692. Filius in utero matris est pars viscerum matris. (7 Coke, 8.)—A son in the mother's womb is a part of the mother's vitals.

693. Fines mandatorum domini regis per rescripta sua (scil. brevia) diligentur sunt observandi. (5 Coke, 87.)—The limits of the king's mandates in his rescripts (i.e., writs) are to be diligently observed.

694. Finis finem litibus imponit. (3 Coke, 78.)—A fine puts an end to litigation.

695. Finis rei attendendus est. (3 Inst. 51.)—The end of a thing is to be attended to.

696. Finis talis concordia finalis dicitur eo quod finem imponit negotio, adeo quod

neutra pars litigantium, ab eo de cætero potest recedere. (COKE, LITT. 121. a.)—A final concord is that which puts an end to the business, so that neither side of the litigation can recede from one thing to another.

697. **Finis unius diei est principium alterius.** (2 BULS. 305.)—The end of one day is the beginning of another.

698. **Firmior et potentior est operatio legis quam dispositio hominis.** (COKE, LITT. 102. a.) —The operation of the law is firmer and more powerful than the disposition of man.

699. **Flumina et portus publica sunt, ideoque jus piscandi omnibus commune est.** (DAV. 150.) —Rivers and ports are public, therefore the right of fishing is common to all.

700. **Fœminæ ab omnibus officiis civibus vel publicis remotæ sunt.** (DIG. 50. 17. 2.)— Women are excluded from all civil and public offices.

701. **Fœminæ non sunt capaces de publicis officiis.** (JENK. CENT. 237.)—Women are not qualified for public offices.

702. **Forma dat esse.** (2 EDEN, 99.)—Form gives being.

703. **Forma legalis forma essentialis.** (10 COKE, 100.)—Legal form is essential form.

704. **Forma non observata infertu adnullatio actus.** (12 COKE, 7.)—Form not being observed, a nullity of the act is inferred.

705. **Forstellarius est pauperum depressor, et totius communitatis et patriæ publicus inimicus.** (3 INST. 196.)—A forestaller is an oppressor of the poor, and a public enemy of the whole community and country.

·706. **Fortior est custodia legis quam hominis.** (2 ROL. 325.)—The custody of the law is stronger than that of man.

707. **Fortior et æquior est dispositio legis quam hominis.** (COKE, LITT. 234. a.)—The disposition of the law is stronger and more equal than that of man.

708. **Fortunam faciunt judicem.** (COKE, LITT. 167. a.)—Fortune is made judge.

709. **Fractionem diei non recipit lex.** (LOFFT, 572.)—The law does not regard a part of a day.

710. **Frangenti fidem fides frangatur eidem.** (WHART. 403.)—Let faith be broken to him who breaks faith.

711. **Frater fratri uterino non succedet in hæreditate paterna.** (WHART. 403.)—A brother shall not succeed a uterine brother in the paternal inheritance.

712. **Fraudis interpretatio semper in jure civilii, non ex eventu duntaxat, sed ex concilio quoque desideratur.** (HALK. 49.)—The civil law always interprets the intention, rather than the event, as material in inferring fraud.

713. **Fraus adstringit, non dissolvit, per-**

juriam. (LOFFT, 624.)—Fraud binds, but does not dissolve, perjury.

714. **Fraus æquitate præjudicat.** (HALK. 49.) —Fraud judges from equity.

715. **Fraus auctoris non nocet successori.** (TRAY. 222.)—The fraud of the ancestor does not harm his successor.

716. **Fraus est celare fraudem.** (1 VER. 270.) —It is a fraud to conceal a fraud.

717. **Fraus est odiosa et non præsumenda.** (CRO. CAR. 550.)—Fraud is odious and not to be presumed.

718. **Fraus et dolus nemini patrocinari debent.** (3 COKE, 78.)—Fraud and deceit should benefit no one.

719. **Fraus et jus nunquam cohabitant.** (WING. 680.)—Fraud and justice never dwell together.

720. **Fraus latet in generalibus.** (WHART. 407.)—Fraud lies hidden in general expressions.

721. **Fraus legibus invisissima.** (LOFFT, 89.) —Fraud is most hateful to law.

722. **Fraus meretur fraudem.** (PLOWD. 100.) —Fraud deserves fraud.

723. **Freight is the mother of wages.** (3 KENT, COM. 196).

724. **Frequentia actus multum operatur.** (4 COKE, 78.)—The frequency of an act effects much.

725. Fructus augeat hæreditatem. (2 Bou. 127.)—Fruits enhance an inheritance.

726. Fructus pendentes pars fundi videntur. (Dig. 6. 1. 44.)—Hanging fruits make part of the farm.

727. Fructus perceptos villæ non esse constat. (Dig. 19. 1. 17. 1.)—Gathered fruits do not constitute a part of the farm.

728. Frumenta quæ sata sunt solo cedere intelliguntur. (Inst. 2. 1. 32.)—Grain which is sown is understood to be part of the soil.

729. Frustra agit qui judicium prosequi nequit cum effectu. (Fleta, 6. 37. 9.)—He sues in vain, who cannot prosecute his judgment with effect.

730. Frustra est potentia quæ nunquam venit in actum. (2 Coke, 51.)—That power is in vain that never comes into act.

731. Frustra expectatur eventus cujus effectus nullus sequitur. (2 Bou. 128.)—An event is vainly expected whose effect does not follow.

732. Frustra feruntur leges nisi subditis et obedientibus. (7 Coke, 13.)—Laws are made in vain unless to those subject and obedient.

733. Frustra fit per plura quod fieri potest per pauciora. (Jenk. Cent. 68.)—That is done in vain by the many that might be done by the few.

734. Frustra legis auxilium quærit qui in legem committit. (Fleta, 4. 2. 8.)—He who offends against the law seeks in vain the help of the law.

735. Frustra petis quod statim alteri reddere cogeris. (JENK. CENT. 256.)—Vainly you ask that which you may immediately be forced to restore to another.

736. Frustra probatur quod probatum non relevat. (WHART. 409.)—It is vain to prove that which when proved is not relevant.

737. Furiosi nulla voluntas est. (DIG. 50. 17. 40.)—A madman has no will.

738. Furiosus absentis loco est. (DIG. 50. 17. 24. 1.)—A madman is considered absent.

739. Furiosus nullum negotium contrahere potest. (DIG. 50. 17. 5.)—A madman cannot contract any business.

740. Furiosus solo furore punitur. (COKE, LITT. 247. b.)—A madman is punished by his insanity alone.

741. Furiosus stipulari non potest, nec aliquid negotium agere, qui non intelligit quid agit. (4 COKE, 126.)—An insane person who knows not what he does, cannot make a bargain, nor transact any business.

742. Furor contrahi matrimonium non sinit, quia consensu opus est. (1 BLACK. COM. 439.)—Insanity prevents the contracting of marriage, because consent is necessary.

743. Furtum est contrectatio rei alienae fraudulenta, cum animo furandi, invito illo domino

cujus res illa fuerat. (3 INST. 107.(—A theft is
the fraudulent handling of another's property,
with the intention of stealing; the proprietor,
whose property it was, not bidding it.

**744. Furtum non est ubi initium habet de-
tentionis per dominum rei.** (3 INST. 107.)—
It is not theft where the commencement of the
detention arises through the act of the owner.

G.

**745. Generale dictum generaliter est inter-
pretandum; generalia verba sunt generaliter
intelligenda.** (3 INST. 76.)—A general saying
is to be interpreted generally. General words
are to be interpreted generally.

746. Generale nihil certum implicat. (2
COKE, 83.)—A general expression implies nothing
certain.

**747. Generale tantum valet in generalibus
quantum singulare in singulis.** (11 COKE. 59.)
—What is general is worth as much among things
general, as what is particular among things particular.

**748. Generalia præcedunt, specialia seguun-
tur.** (REG. BREV.)—Things general precede;
things special follow.

749. Generalia specialibus non derogant.

(JENK. CENT. 120.)—Things general are not derogatory to things special.

750. **Generalia sunt praeponenda singularibus.** (BRANCH, PR.)—Things general are to be put before things particular.

751. **Generalibus specialia derogant.** (BRANCH, PR.)—Things special affect things general.

752. **Generalis clausula non porrigitur ad ea quae antea specialiter sunt comprehensa.** (8 COKE, 154.)—A general clause does not extend to those things which are previously specially provided for.

753. **Generalis gratia proditionem et homicidium non excipit poena.** (LOFFT, 351.)—General favor does not exempt treason and homicide from punishment.

754. **Generalis regula generaliter est intelligenda.** (6 COKE, 64.)—A general rule is to be understood generally.

755. **Glossa viperina est quae corrodit viscera textus.** (10 COKE, 70.)—It is a poisonous gloss which corrodes the vitals of the text.

756. **Grammatica falsa non vitiat chartam.** (9 COKE, 48.)—False grammar does not vitiate a deed.

757. **Gravioris injuriae species est quae scripta fit, quia diutius in conspectu hominum perseverat; vocis enim facile obliviscimur, ad litera scripta manet; et per manus multorum longe, lateque vagatur.** (TAYLER, 218.)—Writing

words is a species of more serious injury than speaking them, for we easily forget spoken words; but what is written remains, and passes through the hands of many, far and near.

758. Gravius est alternam quam temporalem lædere majestatem. (HALK. 52.)—It is more grievous to injure an alternate than a temporary authority.

759. Gravius est divinam quam temporalem lædere majestatem. (11 COKE, 29.)—It is more serious to injure divine than temporal majesty.

H.

760. Habemus optimum testem confitentem reum. (FOSTER, CR. LAW, 243.)—We have the best witness, a confessing defendant.

761. Habendum in charta vel auget restringit; sed non novum inducit. (HALK. 52.)—The habendum in a deed either increases or restricts; but induces nothing new.

762. Hæredem Deus facit, non homo. (COKE, LITT. 7. b.)—God, not man, makes the heir.

763. Hæredem ejusdem potestatis jurisque esse cujus fuit defunctis constat. (HALK. 54.)— The heir has all the powers and privileges of him to whom he is heir.

764. Hæredes succoresque sui cuique liberi,

et nullum testamentum. (TAYLER, 220.)—The children of each man are his heirs and successors, when there is no will.

765. Hæredi favetur. (HALK. 52.)—An heir is to be favored.

766. Hæredi magis parcendum est. (DIG. 31. 1. 47.)—Much is to be overlooked in an heir.

767. Hæredipetæ suo propinquo vel extraneo periculoso sane custodi nullus committatur. (COKE, LITT. 88. b.)—To the next heir, whether a relation or a stranger, certainly an unsafe guardian, let no one be committed.

768. Hæreditas, alia corporalis, alia incorporalis: corporalis est, quæ tangi potest et videri; incorporalis quæ tangi non potest nec videri. (COKE, LITT. 9. a.)—Inheritance, some corporeal, others incorporeal: corporeal is that which can be touched and seen; incorporeal, that which can be. neither touched nor seen.

769. Hæreditas est successio in universum jus quod defunctus habuerat. (COKE, LITT. 287. b.)—Inheritance is the succession to every right possessed by the deceased person.

770. Hæreditas ex dimidio sanguine non datur. (LOFFT, 853.)—Inheritance from half blood is not granted.

771. Hæreditas, n'est pas tant solement entendue lou home ad terres ou tenements per discent d'enheritage, mes auxi chescun fee

simple ou tail que home ad per son purchase puit estre dit enheritance, pur ceo que ses heirs luy purront enheriter. (COKE, LITT. 26. b.) —Inheritance not only comprehends all the lands and tenements which a man has by descent from his ancestors, but also every fee-simple or fee-tail which he has by purchase, because his heir can inherit it from him.

772. Hæreditas nihil aliud est, quam successio in universum jus quod defunctus habuerat. (DIG. 50. 17. 62.)—An inheritance is nothing else than the faculty of succeeding to all the rights of the deceased.

773. Hæreditas nunquam ascendit. (2 BLACK. COM. 212.)—The right of inheritance never lineally ascends.

774. Hæredum appellatione veniunt hæredes hæredum in infinitum. (COKE, LITT. 9. a.)— By the title of heirs, come the heirs of heirs, in infinity.

775. Hæres est alter ipse et filius est pars patris. (3 COKE, 12.)—An heir is another self, and a son is part of the father.

776. Hæres est aut jure proprietatis, aut jure representionis. (3 COKE, 40.)—One is an heir either by right of property, or right of representation.

777. Hæres est nomen collectivum. (1 VENT. 215.)—Heir is a collective name.

778. Hæres est nomen juris, filius est nomen

naturæ. (BAC. MAX. 11.)—Heir is a name of law; son is a name of nature.

779. Hæres est pars antecessoris. (COKE, LITT. 22. b.)—The heir is a part of the ancestor.

780. Hæres hæredis mei est meus hæres. (WHART. 434.)—The heir of my heir is my heir.

781. Hæres legitimus est quem nuptiæ demonstrant. (COKE, LITT. 7. b.)—He is the lawful heir, whom wedlock demonstrates.

782. Hæres minor uno et viginti annis non respondebit, nisi in casu dotis. (MOORE, 348.)—An heir under twenty-one years is not answerable, except in the case of dower.

783. Hæres non tenetur in Anglia ad debita antecessoris reddenda, nisi per antecessorem ad hoc fuerit obligatus præterquam debita regis tantum. (COKE, LITT. 386. a.)—In England' the heir is not bound to pay his ancestor's debts, except debts due to the king, unless he be bound to it by his ancestor.

784. He ne es othes worthes yt es enes gylty of oth broken. (TAYLER, 222.)—He is not worthy of oaths that is guilty of an oath broken.

785. Hermaphroditus tam masculo quam fœminæ comparatnr, secundum prævalentiam sexus incalescentis. (COKE, LITT. 8. a.)—An hermaphrodite is to be considered male or female, according to the predominance of the prevailing sex.

786. He who is the prior in time is stronger in right. (2 BARB. CHY. 338. 854).

787. He who claims a thing by a superior title shall neither gain nor lose by it. (NOY, 11).

788. He who has committed iniquity shall not have equity. (FRANCIS, 2).

789. He who will have equity done to him must do equity to the same person. (4 BOU. INST. 3723)

790. Hoc servabitur quod initio convenit. (DIG. 50. 17. 23.)—This shall be preserved which is useful in the beginning.

791. Homagium non per procuratores nec per literas fieri potuit, sed in propria persona. (COKE, LITT. 68. a.)—Homage cannot be done by proxy, nor by letters, but in person.

792. Homagium repellit perquisitum. (GILB. 152.)—Homage repels perquisition.

793 Home ne sera puny pur suer des briefes en court le roy, soit il a droit ou a tort. (2 INST. 228.)—A man shall not be punished for suing out writs in the king's court, whether he be right or wrong.

794. Homicidium vel hominis cædium, est hominis occisio ab homine facta. (3 INST. 54.)—Homicide is the killing of a man, done by a man.

795. Hominum causa jus constitutum est. (2 Bou. 129.)—Law is constituted for the benefit of man.

796. Homo potest esse habilis et inhabilis diversis temporibus. (5 Coke, 98.)—A man may be both capable, and incapable, at different times.

797. Homo vocabulum est naturæ; persona juris civilis. (Cal. Lex.)—Man is a term of nature; person, of the civil law.

798. Hora non est multum de substantia negotii, licet in apello de ea aliquando fiat mentio. (1 Buls. 82.)—The hour is not of much consequence as to the substance of business, although in appeal it may be sometimes mentioned.

799. Hostes sunt qui nobis vel quibus nos bellum decernimus, cæteri proditores vel prædones sunt. (7 Coke, 24.)—Enemies are those against whom we declare war, or who declare it against us; all others are traitors or pirates.

I.

800. Ibi semper debet fieri triatio, ubi juratores meliorem possunt habere notitiam. (7

(6)

Coke, 1.)—A trial should always be had where the jury may get the best information.

801. **Id perfectum est quod ex omnibus suis partibus constat; et nihil perfectum est dum aliquid restat agendum.** (9 Coke, 9.)—That is perfect which is complete in all its parts, and nothing is perfect while anything remains to be done.

802. **Id possumus quod de jure possumus.** (Lane, 116.)—We may do that which we can do by law.

803. **Id quod est magis remotum, non trahit ad se quod est magis junctum, sed e contrario in omni casu.** (Coke, Litt. 164. a.)—That which is more remote does not draw to itself that which is nearer, but the contrary in every case.

804. **Id quod nostrum est sine facto nostro ad alium transferre non potest.** (Dig. 50. 17. 11.) —That which is ours cannot, without our deed, be transferred to another.

805. **Idem agens et patiens esse non potest.** (Jenk. Cent. 40.)—It is not possible to be at once the person acting, and the person acted upon.

806. **Idem est facere et non prohibere cum possis; et qui non prohibet cum prohibere possit in culpa est.** (3 Inst. 158.)—It is the same thing to commit and not to prohibit when in one's power, and he who does not prohibit a thing when he can prohibit it, is in fault.

807. Idem est nihil dicere et insufficienter dicere. (2 INST. 178.)—To speak insufficiently is the same thing as to say nothing.

808. Idem est non -esse et non apparere. (JENK. CENT. 207.)—Not to exist, and not to appear, are the same thing.

809. Idem est non probari et non esse; non deficit jus, sed probatio. (2 BOU. 129.)—What does not appear, and what does not exist are the same; it is not the defect of the law, but want of proof.

810. Idem est scire aut scire debet aut potuisse. (2 BOU. 129.)—To be able to know is the same as to be obliged to know.

811. Idem semper antecedenti proximo refertur. (COKE, LITT. 385. b.)—THE SAME always relates to its next antecedent.

812. Identitas vera colligitur ex multitudine signorum. (BAC. MAX. 24.)—The true identity is collected from a multitude of signs.

813. If an affirmative statute, which introduces a new law, direct a thing to be done in a certain manner, that thing shall not, even though there are no negative words, be done in any other manner. (12 ABB. P. R. 35. 36).

814. Ignorantia eorum quæ quis scire tenetur non excusat. (HALE, PL. CR. 42.)—Ignorance of those things which one is bound to know does not excuse.

815. Ignorantia facti excusat; ignorantia juris

non excusat. (2 COKE, 3.)—Ignorance of fact excuses; ignorance of law does not excuse.

816. Ignorantia judicis est calamitas innocentis. (2 INST. 591.)—The ignorance of the judge is the misfortune of the innocent.

817. Ignorantia juris sui non praejudicat juri. (LOFFT, 552.)—Ignorance of one's own law is not prejudicial to that law.

818. Ignorantia legum neminem excusat; omnes enim praesumuntur eas nosse quibus omnes consentiant. (LOFFT, 10.)—Ignorance of the law excuses no one; for all are presumed to know those things to which all consent.

819. Ignorantis terminis ignoratur et ars. (COKE, LITT. 2. a.)—The terms being unknown, the act is also unknown.

820. Ignoscitur ei qui sanguinem suum qualiter redemptum voluit. (1 BLACK. COM. 131.)—The law holds him excused, who chose that his blood should be redeemed in any way.

821. Il n'est pars permis decouferer, ou de negocier avec les enemis de l'etat. (TAYLER, 238.)—It is not permitted to disclose secrets, or to negotiate with the enemies of the state.

822. Ille honore dignus est, qui se, suae legibus patriae, et non sine magno labore et industria, reddidit versatum. (TAYLER, 237.)—He deserves honor, who has with much labor and industry rendered himself familiar with the laws of the country.

823. **Illud quod alias licitum non est, necessitas facit licitum, et necessitas inducit privilegium quod jure privatur.** (10 COKE, 61.)—That which is not otherwise lawful, necessity makes lawful, and necessity makes a privilege which supersedes law.

824. **Illud quod alteri unitur extinguitur neque amplius per se vacare licet.** (GODOLPH 169.)—That which is united to another is extinguished, nor can it be any more independent.

825. **Imaginaria venditio non est pretio accedente.** (HALK. 57.)—It is not an imaginary sale at which the price is paid.

826. **Immobilia situm sequuntur.** (2 KENT, COM. 67.)—Immovables follow the law of the place where they are situated.

827. **Imperii majestas est tutelae salus.** (COKE, LITT. 64. b.)—The majesty of the empire is its safety and protection.

828. **Imperitia culpae aenumerantur.** (DIG. 50. 17. 132.)—By ignorance failures are increased.

829. **Imperitia est maxima mechanicorum poena.** (11 COKE, 54.)—Lack of skill is the greatest punishment of mechanics.

830. **Impersonalitas non concludit nec ligat.** (COKE, LITT. 352. b.)—Impersonality neither concludes nor binds.

831. **Impius et crudelis judicandus est qui libertati non favet.** (COKE, LITT. 124. b.)—He

is to be judged impious and cruel who does not favor liberty.

832. Impossibilium nulla obligatio est. (DIG. 50. 18. 185.)—There is no obligation to perform impossibilities.

833. Impotentia excusat legem. (COKE, LITT. 29. a.)—Impossibility is an excuse in law.

834. Improbi rumores dissipati sunt rebellionis prodromi. (2 INST. 226.)—Wicked rumors spread abroad are the forerunners of rebellion.

835. Impunitas continuum affectum tribuit delinquenti. (4 COKE, 45.)—Impunity offers a continual bait to the delinquent.

836. Impunitas semper ad deteriora invitat. (5 COKE, 109.)—Impunity invites to greater crimes.

837. Impuris manibus nemo accedat curiam. (TAYLER, 239.)—No one may come into court with unclean hands.

838. In actis publicis collegii sive corporis alicujus corporati consensus est voluntas multorum ad quos res pertinet simul juncta. (LOFFT, 634.)—In public acts of a college, or any incorporated body the united will of the majority to whom the matter belongs, is the consent.

839. In aedificiis lapis male positus non est removendus. (11 COKE, 69.)—In buildings a stone badly placed is not to be removed.

840. In aequali jure melior est conditio possidentis. (PLOWD. 296.)—In equal rights the condition of the possessor is the better.

841. In alta proditione nullus potest esse accessorius, sed principalis solummodo. (3 INST. 138.)—In high treason there is no accessory, but principal alone.

842. In alternatives electio est debitoris. (WHART. 474.)—In alternatives the debtor has the election.

843. In ambigua voce legis ea potius accipienda est significatio, quæ vitio caret; præsertim cum etiam voluntas legis ex hoc colligi possit. (2 INST. 173.)—When ambiguities, or faults of expression render the meaning of the law doubtful, that interpretation should be preferred which is most consonant to equity, especially where it is in conformity with the general design of the legislature.

844. In ambiguis casibus semper præsumitur pro rege. (WHART. 474.)—In doubtful cases the presumption is always in favor of the king.

845. In ambiguis orationibus maxime sententia spectanda est ejus qui eas protulisset. (DIG. 50. 17. 96.)—In ambiguous speeches the intention of him who uttered them is chiefly to be regarded.

846. In Anglia non est interregnum. (JENK. CENT. 205.)—In England there is no interregnum.

847. In atrocioribus delictis punitur affectus licet non sequatur effectus. (2 ROL. 89.)—In more atrocious crimes, the intent is punished, though an effect does not follow.

848. **In capitalibus sufficit generalis malitia, cum facto paris gradus.** (LOFFT, 400.)—In capital cases general malice suffices, with the fact of an equal degree of guilt.

849. **In casu extremæ necessitatis omnia sunt communia.** (HALE, PL. CR. 54.)—In cases of extreme necessity, everything is common.

850. **In civilibus ministerium excusat, in criminalibus non item.** (LOFFT, 228.)—Agency excuses in civil, but not in criminal matters.

851. **In civilibus proxima et directa præstare quis tenetur; in criminalibus etiam consequentia.** (LOFFT, 429.)—In civil cases one is bound to perform the nearest and direct things; but in criminal cases, even consequent things.

852. **In civilibus voluntas pro facto reputabitur.** (LOFFT, 132.)—In civil cases the will is sometimes taken for the deed.

853. **In claris non est locus conjecturis.** (WHART. 475.)—In things obvious there is no room for conjecture.

854. **In commodato hæc pactio, ne dolus præstetur, rata non est.** (DIG. 13. 7. 17.)—If, in a contract for a loan, a clause is inserted that fraud should not be accounted of, such clause is void.

855. **In conjunctivis oportet utramque partem esse veram.** (WING. 13.)—In things conjunctive each part must be true.

856. **In consimili casu, consimile debet esse**

remedium. (HARD. 65.)—In similar cases the remedy should be the same.

857. In consuetudinibus non diuturnitas temporis sed soliditas rationis est consideranda. (COKE, LITT. 141. a.)—In customs, not the length of time but the strength of the reasons should be considered.

858. In contractibus, benigna; in testamentis, benignior; in restitutionibus, benignissima interpretatio facienda est. (COKE, LITT. 112. b.) —In contracts the interpretation should be liberal; in wills more liberal; and in restitutions most liberal.

859. In contractis tacite insunt quæ sunt moris et consuetudinis. (WHART. 475.)—In contracts those things which are of custom and usage are tacitly implied.

860. In contrahenda venditione, ambiguum pactum contra venditorem interpretandum est. (DIG. 50. 17. 172.)—In contracting a sale, an ambiguous agreement is to be interpreted against the seller.

861. In conventionibus contrahentium voluntatem potius quam verba spectari placuit. (DIG. 50. 16. 219.)—In agreements the rule is to regard the intention of the contracting parties rather than their words.

862. In criminalibus non est argumentandum a pari ultra casum a lege definitum. (TRAY. 247.)—Penal statutes cannot be extended, by

argument from analogy, to cases not provided for by law.

863. In criminalibus probationes debent esse luce clariores. (3 INST. 210.)—In criminal cases the proofs ought to be clearer than the light.

864. In criminalibus silentum præsentis consensum præsumit; in civilibus nonnunquam vel absentis et ubi ejus interest etiam ignorantis. —In criminal cases the silence of a person present presumes consent; in civil cases sometimes that of the person absent, and even ignorant where his interest lies, does the same.

865. In criminalibus sufficit generalis malitia intentionis cum facto paris gradus. (BAC. MAX. 15.)—In criminal cases a general malicious intention is sufficient, with an act of equal degree.

866. In criminalibus voluntas reputabatur pro facto. (3 INST. 106.)—In criminal acts the will is to be taken for the deed.

867. In disjunctivis sufficit alteram partem esse veram. (WING. 13.)—In things disjunctive, it is sufficient should either part be true.

868. In dubiis benigniora præferenda sunt. (DIG. 50 17. 56.)—In doubtful cases, the more favorable are to be preferred.

869. In dubiis magis dignum est accipiendum. (BRANCH, PR.)—In doubtful cases the more worthy is to be taken.

870. In dubiis non præsumitur pro testa-

mento. (CRO. CAR. 51.)—In doubtful cases there is no presumption in favor of a will.

871. **In dubio hæc legis constructio quam verba ostendunt.** (BRANCH, PR.)—In a doubtful case, that is the construction of the law which the words point out.

872. **In dubio pars mitior est sequenda.** (WHART. 477.)—In doubt, the milder course is to be followed.

873. **In dubio pro dote, libertate, innocentia, possessore, debitore, reo, respondendum est.** (BROWN, LAW DIC.)—In doubt the response is in favor of dower, liberty, innocence, of the possessor, of the debtor, and of the defendant.

874. **In dubio pro innocentia respondendum est.** (TRAY. 249.)—In a doubtful case the decision should be in favor of innocence.

875. **In dubio sequendum quod tutius est.** (WHART. 477.)—In doubt, the safer course should be adopted.

876. **In eo quod plus sit semper inest et minus.** (DIG. 50. 17. 110.)—The less is always included in the greater.

877. **In eo quod vel is qui petit, vel is a quo petitur a lucri factus est, durior causa est petitoris.** (HALK. 62.)—In that which either he who seeks, or he from whom it is sought for the sake of gain, the cause of the applicant is the harder.

878. **In executione sententiæ, alibi latæ,**

servare jus loci in quo fit executio; non ubi res judicata. (TAYLER, 243.)—In executing a sentence otherwise extensive, the law of the place must prevail, where the execution takes effect, not where the matter was adjudged.

879. In expositione instrumentorum, mala grammatica, quod fieri potest, vitanda est. (6 COKE, 39.)—In constructing instruments, bad grammar is to be avoided as much as possible.

880. In facto quod se habet ad bonum et malum, magis de bono quam de malo lex intendit. (COKE, LITT. 78. b.)—In a deed which addresses itself to good and bad, the law looks more to the good than to the bad.

881. In favorabilibus annus incoeptus pro completo habetur. (BROWN, LAW DIC.)—In things favored the year begun is held as completed.

882. In favorabilibus magis attenditur quod prodest quam quod nocet. (BAC. MAX. 12.)—In things favorable what does good is more to be regarded than what does harm.

883. In favorem vitæ, libertatis, et innocentiæ omnia præsumuntur. (LOFFT, 125.)—In favor of life, liberty, and innocence, all things are to be presumed.

884. In fictione juris semper æquitas existit. (11 COKE, 51.)—In a legal fiction equity always exists.

885. In fraudem vero qui, salvis verbis legis,

sententiam ejus circumvenit.—He truly acts fraudulently who, observing the letter of the law, eludes its spirit.

886. **In generalibus versatur error.** (3 Sum. C. C. 290.)—Error dwells in general expressions.

887. **In genere quicunque aliquid dicit, sive actor sive reus, necesse est ut probat.** (Best, Ev. 497.)—In general whoever says anything, whether plaintiff or defendant, must prove it.

888. **In hæredes non solent transire actiones quæ pœnales ex maleficio sunt.** (2 Inst. 442.) —Penal actions arising from anything of a criminal nature do not pass to heirs.

889. **In hiis enim quæ sunt favorabilia animæ, quamvis sunt damnosa rebus, fiat aliquando extentio statuti.** (10 Coke, 101.)—In things favorable to the spirit, though injurious to property, an extension of the statute should be sometimes made.

890. **In hiis quæ de jure communi omnibus conceduntur, consuetudo alicujus patriæ vel loci non est alleganda.** (11 Coke, 85.)—In those things which by common right are conceded to all, the custom of a particular country or place is not to be alleged.

891. **In iis quæ sunt meræ facultatis nunquam præscribitur.** (Tray. 253.)—Prescription does not run in favor of a mere faculty of acting.

892. **In judicio non creditur nisi juratis.**

(Cro. Car. 64.)—In law no one is credited unless he is sworn.

893.   In judiciis minori ætati succurritur. (Jenk. Cent. 89.)—In judicial affairs the minor is protected.

894.   In lege omnia semper in præsenti stare censentur. (Lofft, 487.)—In law all things are always judged from their present condition.

895.   In loco facti imprestabilis subest damnum et interesse.   (Tray. 256.)—Damages come in place of an act not performed.

896.   In majore summa continetur minor. (5 Coke, 15.)—In the greater sum is contained the less.

897.   In maleficiis voluntas spectatur non exitus. (Dig. 48. 8. 14.)—In criminal matters, the intention is regarded, not the event.

898.   In maxima potentia minima licentia. (Lofft, 504.)—In the greatest power there is the least license.

899.   In mercibus illicitis non sit commercium.   (3 Kent, Com. 263.)—There should be no commerce in illicit goods.

900.   In nostra lege una comma evertit totum placitum.   (Tayler, 247.)—In our law, one comma upsets the entire plea.

901.   In novo casu, novum remedium apponendum est. (2 Inst. 3.)—In a new case a new remedy is to be applied.

902.   In obscura voluntate manumittentis

favendum est libertati. (DIG. 50. 17. 179.)—
When the expression of the will of one who
seeks to manumit a slave, is obscure, liberty is
to be favored.

903. In obscuris inspici solere quod veri-
similius est, aut quod plerumque fieri solet.
(DIG. 50. 17. 114.)—In cases of obscurity we
usually regard what is probable, and what is
generally done.

904. In obscuris quod minimum est sequimur. (DIG. 50. 17. 9.)—In obscure cases we follow
that which is least so.

905. In odium spoliatoris omnia præsumuntur. (1 VER. 19.)—Against a despoiler all things
are presumed.

906. In omni actione ubi duæ concurrunt
districtiones, videlicit in rem et in personam,
illa districtio tenenda est quæ magis timetur et
magis ligat. (BRACT. 372.)—In every action where
two distresses concur, as those against a thing,
and those against a person, that should be chosen
which is most dreaded, and which binds most
firmly.

907. In omni re nascitur res quæ ipsam rem
exterminat. (2 INST. 15.)—In everything the
thing is born which destroys that thing itself.

908. In omnibus causis pro facto accipitur
id, in quo per alium moræ sit, quo minus fiat.
(HALK. 69.)—In all causes that may be accepted
as a fact in which by means of another, it may
be prevented from being done.

909. **In omnibus contractibus sive nominatis, sive innominatis, permutatio continetur.** (2 BLACK. COM. 444.)—In all contracts whether named or not, an exchange is understood.

910. **In omnibus fere minori ætati succurritur.** (HALK. 64.)—In all cases aid should be given to minors.

911. **In omnibus imperatoris excipitur fortuna, cui ipsas leges Deus subjecit.** (TAYLER, 248.) —God subjects in all things, the fortunes of emperors to the laws of the land.

912. **In omnibus obligationibus in quibus dies non ponitur, præsenti die debetur.** (DIG. 50. 17. 14.)—In all obligations in which a day is not fixed for payment, it is due on the present day.

913. **In omnibus pœnalibus judiciis et ætati et imprudentiæ succurritur.** (DIG. 50. 17. 108.) —In all trials for penal offences, allowance is made for youth and want of discretion.

914. **In omnibus quidem, maxime tamen in jure, æquitas spectanda sit.** (DIG. 50. 17. 90.) —Equity is to be regarded in all things, but particularly in law.

915. **In one thing all things following shall be concluded as granting, demanding, or prohibiting.** (NOY, 42).

916. **In pari causa possessor potior haberi debet.** (DIG. 50. 17. 128.)—In an equal cause, the possessor has the advantage.

917. In pari delicto, potior est conditio possidentis. (2 BURR. 926.)—In equal fault the condition of the possessor is the better.

918. In pœnalibus causis benignius interpretandum est. (DIG. 50. 17. 155. 2.)—In penal cases the more favorable interpretation should be made.

919. In præparatoriis ad judicium favetur actori. (2 INST. 57.)—In things preceding judgment the plaintiff is favored.

920. In præsentia majoris cessat potentia minoris. (JENK. CENT. 214.)—In presence of the major the minor power ceases.

921. In pretio emptionis et venditionis naturaliter licet contrahentibus se circumvenire. (1 STORY, CONT. 606.)—In the price of buying and selling, it is naturally allowed to the contracting parties to overreach each other.

922. In propria causa nemo judex. (12 COKE, 13.)—No one can be judge in his own cause.

923. In quo quis delinquit, in eo de jure est puniendus. (COKE, LITT. 233. b.)—In whatever one offends, in that, according to law he should be punished.

924. In re communi melior est conditio prohibentis. (TRAY. 263.)—In common property the condition of the one prohibiting is the better.

925. In re communi neminem dominorum

jure facere quicquam, invito altero, posse. (DIG. 10. 3. 28.)—One co-proprietor can exercise no authority over the common property against the will of the other.

926. In re dubia benigniorem interpretationem sequi, non minus justius est, quam tutius. (DIG. 50. 17. 192.)—In a doubtful case, to follow the milder interpretation is not less the more just, than it is the safer way.

927. In re dubia magis inficiatio quam affirmatio intelligenda. (GODB. 42.)—In a doubtful case the negative, rather than the affirmative, is to be understood.

928. In re lupanari, testes lupanares admittentur. (6 BARB. N. Y. 320. 324.)—In a case concerning a brothel, prostitutes are admitted as witnesses.

929. In re obscura melius est favere repetitioni quam adventitio lucro. (HALK. 65.)—In an obscure case it is better to favor repetition than adventitious gain.

930. In re pari, potiorem causam esse prohibentis constat. (DIG. 10. 3. 28.)—Where a thing is owned in common, the cause of him prohibiting its use is the stronger.

931. In rebus manifestus errat qui authoritates legum allegat; quia perspicue vera non sunt probanda. (5 COKE, 67.)—In things manifest he errs who alleges the authorities of law; because obvious truths need not be proved.

932. In rebus novis constituendis evidens esse inutiles debet, ut recedatus ab eo jure, quod diu æquam visum est. (HALK. 65.)—In settling new affairs, the utility must be evident, in order to justify a departure from laws long seen to be salutary.

933. In rebus quæ snnt favorabilia animæ, quamvis sunt damnosa rebus, fiat aliquando extensio statuti. (10 COKE, 101.)—In things that are favorable to the spirit, though injurious to the things, an extension of the statute may sometimes be made.

934. In rem actio est per quam rem nostram quæ ab alio possidetur potimus, et semper adversus eum est qui rem possidet. (DIG. 44 7. 25.)—The action IN REM is that by which we seek our property which is possessed by another, and is always against him who possesses the property.

935. In republica maxime conservanda sunt jura belli. (2 INST. 58.)—In the state, the laws of war are especially to be preserved.

936. In restitutionem, non in pœnam, hæres succedit. (2 INST. 198.)—The heir succeeds to the restitution, not to the penalty.

937. In rex non potest conjunctim tenere cum alio. (HALK. 66.)—One king cannot hold conjointly with another.

938. In satisfactionibus non permittitur amplius fieri quam semel factum est. (9 COKE,

53.)—In damages, more must not be received, than has been once received.

939. In stipulationibus cum quæritur quid actum si. verba contra stipulatorem interpretanda sunt. (DiG. 45. 1. 38. 18.)—In contracts, when the question is what was agreed upon, the words of the agreement are to be interpreted against the questioner.

940. In stipulationibus id tempus spectatur quo contrahimus. (DIG. 50. 17. 144. 1.)—In contracts reference should be had to the time at which they were made.

941. In suo hætenus facere licet quatenus, nih'l in alienum immittit. (TRAY. 267.)—One may do with his own as he pleases, if he does not invade the rights of others.

942. In suo quisque negotio hebetior est quam in aliena. (COKE, LITT. 377. a)—Everyone is more dull in his own business than in that of another.

943. In testamentis plenius testatoris intentionem scrutamur. (3 BULS. 103.)—In testaments the intention of the testator should be most fully inquired into.

944. In testamentis plenius voluntates testantium interpretantur. (DIG. 50. 17. 12)—In testaments the will of the testator should be liberally construed.

945. In testamentis ratio tacita non debet considerari sed verba solum spectari debent.

(WHART. 508.)—In wills an unexpressed meaning ought not to be considered, but the words alone should be looked to.

946. In theatrum, cum commune sit, recti tamen dici potest ejus esse cum locum quisque occupavit.—In a theatre, for the time being, it may be correctly said that each one owns the seat that he occupies.

947. In toto et pars continetur. (DIG. 50. 17. 113.)—A part is included in the whole.

948. In traditionibus scriptorum chartarum non quod dictum est, sed quod gestum factum est, inspicitur. (9 COKE, 137.)—In the delivery of writings or deeds, not what is said, but what is done is to be regarded.

949. In veram quantitatem fidejussor teneatur nisi pro certa quantitate accessit. (17 MASS. 597.)—Let the surety be holden for the true quantity unless he agreed for a certain quantity.

950. In verbis non verba sed res et ratio quaerenda est. (JENK. CENT. 132.)—In words, not the words only, but the thing and the meaning should be inquired into.

951. In vocibus videndum non a quo sed ad quid sumatur. (ELLES. POST. 62.)—In discourses it is to be seen not from what, but to what, it is advanced.

952. Incaute factum pro non facto habetur. (DIG. 28. 4. 1.)—An unforeseen fact is held for no fact.

953. Incendium ære alieno non exuit debitorum. (CODE, 4. 2. 11.)—A fire does not release a debtor from his debt.

954. Incerta pro nullis habentur. (LOFFT, 555.)—Things uncertain are reckoned as nothing.

955. Incerta quantitas vitiat actum. (1 ROL. 465.)—An uncertain quantity vitiates the act.

956. Incertum ex incerto pendens lege reprobatur. (LOFFT, 521.)—An uncertainty depending upon an uncertainty is reprobated by law.

957. Incidentia nolunt separari. (HALK. 67.) —Incidents cannot be separated.

958. Incidentia rei tacite sequuntur. (LOFFT, 556.)—The incidents of a thing follow tacitly.

959. Incivile est, nisi tota lege prospecta, una aliqua particula ejus proposita, judicare, vel respondere. (DIG. 1. 3. 24.)—It is improper, unless the whole law be examined, to give judgment or advice upon a view of a single clause of it.

960. Incivile est nisi tota sententia inspecta de aliqua parte judicare. (HOB. 171.)—It is unlawful to judge of any part unless the whole sentence be examined.

961. Inclusio unius est exclusio alterius. (11 COKE, 59.)—The inclusion of one is the exclusion of another.

962. Incolas domicilium facit. (1 JOHNS. CAS. N. Y. 363. 366.)—Residence creates domicile.

963. Incommodum non solvit argumentum.

(WHART. 475.)—An inconvenience does not de-stroy an argument.

964. Incorporalia bello non adquiruntur. (6 MAULE & S. 104.)—Incorporeal things are not acquired by law.

965. Inde datæ leges ne fortior omnia posset. (DAV. 36.)—Laws are made lest the stronger party should possess all.

966. Indefinitum equipollet universali. (1 VENT. 368.)—The indefinite is equivalent to the universal.

967. Independenter se habet assecuratio a viaggio navis. (3 KENT, COM. 318.)—The voyage insured is an independent thing from the sh:p.

968. Index animi sernio. (WHART. 476.)—Speech is the index of the mind.

969. Inesse potest donationi modus, conditio, sive causa: ut, modus est; si, conditio; quia, causa. (DYER, 138.)—In a gift there may be a manner, condition, or cause: as, (UT,) introduces a manner; if, (SI,) a condition; because, (QUID,) a cause.

970. Infans est qui, propter defectum ætatis, pro se fari nequeat. (LOFFT, 307.)—He is an infant who, on account of defect of age cannot speak for himself.

971. Infans non multum a furioso distat. (1 STORY, EQ. JUR. 223. 242.)—An infant does not differ much from a lunatic.

972. Infantes de damno præstare tenetur, de

pœna non item. (LOFFT, 274.)—Infants are sometimes obliged to performances involving loss, but not punishment.

973. Infinitum in jure reprobatur. (12 COKE, 24.)—Infinity in law is reprehensible.

974. Iniquissima pax est anteponenda justissimo bello. (18 WEND. N. Y. 257. 305.)—The most unjust peace should be preferred to the most just war.

975. Iniquum est alios permittere, alios inhibere mercaturam. (3 INST. 181.)—It is unjust to permit some, and to prohibit others, to trade.

976. Iniquum est aliquem rei sui esse judicem. (12 COKE, 13.)—It is unjust for anyone to be a judge in his own cause.

977. Iniquum est ingenuis hominibus non esse liberam rerum suarum alienationem. (COKE, LITT. 223. a.)—It is unjust for freemen not to have the free disposal of their own property.

978. Initia magistratuum meliora firma; finis inclinat. (TAYLER, 246.)—Public offices are more vigorous in the beginning; but weaken toward the close.

979. Injuria fit ei cui convicium dictum est vel de eo factum carmen famosum. (9 COKE, 60.)—An injury is done to him of whom a reproachful thing is said, or an obscene song is made.

980. Injuria illata judici, seu locum tenenti regis, videtur ipsi regi illata, maxime si fiat

in exercentem officii. (3 INST. 1.)—An injury
offered to a judge or person representing the king,
is considered as offered to the king himself, especially if it be done in the exercise of his
office.

981. Injuria non excusat injuriam. (15 Q. B.
276.)—An injury does not excuse an injury.

982. Injuria non præsumitur. (COKE, LITT.
232. b.)—A wrong is not to be presumed.

983. Injuria propria non cadet in beneficium
facientis. (BRANCH, PR.)—A man should not
be benefited by his own wrong doing.

984. Injuria servi dominum pertingit. (LOFFT,
229.)—The master is liable for injury done by
his servant.

985. Insanus est qui, abjecta ratione, omnia
cum impetu et furore facit. (4 COKE, 128.)—
He is insane who, reason being thrown away,
does everything with violence and rage.

986. Instans est finis unius temporis et principium alterius. (COKE, LITT. 185. b.)—An instant is the end of one period of time, and the
beginning of another.

987. Instrumenta domestica, seu ad notatio,
si non aliis quoque ad minicis adjuventur, ad
probationem sola non sufficiunt. (TAYLER, 251.)
—Family documents, or memoranda, when not
sustained by other evidence, are not of themselves
sufficient proof.

988. Intentio cæca mala. (2 BULS. 179.)—A hidden intention is bad.

989. Intentio inservire, debet legibus, non leges intentioni. (COKE, LITT. 314. b.)—Intention ought to be subservient to the laws, not the laws to the intention.

990. Intentio legitime cognita et legibus consentanea maxime habenda. (HALK. 68.)—An intention legitimately known, and in accordance with the laws, should be especially regarded.

991. Intentio mea imponit nomen operi meo. (HOB. 123.)—My intent gives a name to my act.

992. Inter alias causas acquisitiones magna, celebris, et famosa est causa donationis. (BRACT. 11.)—Among other modes of acquiring property, a great, celebrated and famous method is that of gift.

993. Inter alios res gestas aliis non posse præjudicium facere sæpe constitutum est. (CODE, 7. 60. 1. 2.)—It has often been settled that affairs between other parties should not prejudice.

994. Inter cuncta leges et percunctabere doctos. (COKE, LITT. 232. b.)—Among many things, you will even question laws and learned men.

995. Inter pares non est potestas. (TAYLER, 253.)—Among equals no one is the more powerful.

996. Interdum evenit ut exceptio quæ prima facie justa videatur, tamen inique noceat. (INST. 4. 14.)—It sometimes happens that a plea which at first seems just, is nevertheless injurious and unequal.

997. Interest reipublicæ ne maleficia remaneant impunita. (JENK. CENT. 31.)—It is to the interest of the state that crimes should not remain unpunished.

998. Interest reipublicæ ne quis ne sua male utatur. (6 COKE, 37.)—It is to the interest of the state that no man shall use his own improperly.

999. Interest reipublicæ quod homines conserventur. (12 COKE, 62.)—It is to the interest of the commonwealth that human lives be preserved.

1000. Interest reipublicæ res judicatas non rescindi. (2 INST. 360.)—It is to the interest of the state that things adjudged be not rescinded.

1001. Interest reipublicæ suprema hominum testamenta rata haberi. (COKE, LITT. 236. a.) —It is to the interest of the state that the last wills of its citizens be sustained.

1002. Interest reipublicæ ut bonis bene sit, et male malis, et suum cuique. (LOFFT, 162.) —It is to the interest of the state that it may be well with the good, ill with the wicked, and that everyone may have his own.

1003. Interest reipublicæ ut carceres sint in tuto. (2 INST. 589.)—It is to the interest of the state that prisons be secure.

1004. Interest reipublicæ ut pax in regno conservetur, et quæcunque paci adversentur provide declinentur. (2 INST. 158.)—It is to the interest of the state that peace be preserved in the kingdom, and that whatever is adverse to it be prudently declined.

1005. Interest republicaæ ut sit finis litium. (COKE, LITT. 303. b.)—It is to the interest of the state that there be a limit to litigation.

1006. Interpretare et concordare legis legibus est optimus interpretandi modus. (8 COKE, 169.) —To interpret and to reconcile the laws to laws, is the best mode of interpretation.

1007. Interpretatio fienda est ut res magis valeat quam pereat. (JENK. CENT. 198.)—That interpretation is to be made that the thing may stand rather than fall.

1008. Interpretatio talis in ambiguis semper fienda est, ut evitetur inconveniens et absurdum. (4 INST. 328.)—In ambiguous cases that interpretation is to be made, that what is inconvenient and absurd is to be avoided.

1009. Interruptio multiplex non tollit præscriptionem semel obtentum. (2 INST. 654.)— Frequent interruption does not take away a prescription once secured.

1010. Intestatus decedit, qui aut omnino

testamentum non fecit aut non juri fecit, aut id quod fecerat ruptum irritumve factum est, aut nemo ex eo hæres exstitit. (DIG. 38. 16. 1.) —He dies intestate who either has made no will at all; or has not made it legally; or if the will he has made be annulled or rendered useless; or from whom there is no living heir.

1011. Inutiles labor, et sine fructu, non est effectus legis. (COKE, LITT. 127. b.)—Useless labor, and without fruit, is not the effect of law.

1012. Inveniens libellum famosum et non corrumpens punitur. (MOORE, 813.)—He who finds a notorious libel, and does not destroy it, is punished.

1013. Invitat culpam qui peccatum præterit. (HALK. 70.)—He encourages a fault who overlooks a transgression.

1014. Invito beneficium non datur. (DIG. 50. 17. 69.)—A benefit is not bestowed upon one unwilling to receive it.

1015. Invitus nemo rem cogitur defendere. —No one is compelled against his will to defend his own property.

1016. Ipsæ leges cupiunt ut jure regantur. (COKE, LITT. 174. b.)—The laws themselves require that they should be governed by right.

1017. Ira furor brevis est. (4 WEND. N. Y. 336. 355.)—Anger is a brief insanity.

1018. Ira hominis non implet justitiam Dei.

(LOFFT, 484.)—The anger of a man does not fulfil the justice of God.

1019. Is damnum dat qui jubet dare; ejus vero nulla culpa est cui parere necesse est. (HALK. 71.)—He occasions a loss who gives orders to cause it; but no blame is attached to him who is obliged to obey.

1020. Is qui dolo male desiit possidere pro possessore habetur. (TRAY. 279.)—He who has fraudulently ceased to possess, is still held to be a possessor.

1021. Is quid actionem habet ad rem recuperandam ipsam rem habere videtur. (HALK. 71.)—He is considered as having possession of a thing who has an action to recover it.

1022. It is equity that he should have satisfaction who sustained the loss. (FRANCIS, 5).

1023. It is equity that he should make satisfaction who received the benefit. (FRANCIS, 4).

1024. Ita lex scripta est. (DIG. 40. 9. 12.)—The law is so written.

1025. Ita semper fiat relatio ut valeat dispositio. (6 COKE, 76.)—Let the relation be so made that the disposition may stand.

1026. Ita tuo utere ut alienum ne lædas. (LOFFT, 180.)—So use your own as not to injure your neighbor's property.

1027. Iter est jus eundi, ambulandi hominis;

non etiam jumentum agendi vel vehiculum.
(COKE, LITT. 56. a.)—ITER is the right of going
or walking, and does not include the right of
driving a beast of burden or a carriage.

J.

1028. Jacere telum voluntatis est; ferire
quem nolueris fortunæ. (TRAY. 280.)—To throw
a dart is a matter of will ; that it strikes one
whom you do not wish to injure is a matter of
chance.

1029. Judex æquitatem semper spectare
debet. (JENK. CENT. 45.)—A judge ought always
to regard equity.

1030. Judex ante oculos æquitatem semper
habere debet. (JENK. CENT. 58.)—A judge ought
always to have equity before his eyes.

1031. Judex bonus nihil ex arbitrio suo faciat,
nec propositione domesticæ voluntatis, sed juxta
leges et jura pronunciet. (7 COKE, 27.)—A good
judge may do nothing from his judgment, or
from a dictate of private will; but he should
pronounce according to law and justice.

1032. Judex damnatur cum nocens absolvitur. (2 BOU. 133.)—The judge is condemned
when the guilty are acquitted.

1033. Judex de pace civium constituitur.

(TAYLER, 264.)—The judge is appointed for the peace of the citizens.

1034. Judex debet judicare secundum allegata et probata. (2 BOU. 133.)—The judge should decide according to the allegations and the proofs.

1035. Judex est lex loquens. (7 COKE, 4.)— The judge is the law speaking.

1036. Judex habere debet duos sales; salem sapientiæ, ne sit insipidus, et salem conscientiæ, ne sit diabolus. (3 INST. 147.)—A judge should have two salts; the salt of wisdom, lest he be insipid; and the salt of conscience, lest he be devilish.

1037. Judex non potest esse testis in propria causa. (4 INST. 279.)—A judge cannot be a witness in his own cause.

1038. Judex non potest injuriam sibi datam punire. (12 COKE, 114.)—A judge cannot punish a wrong done to himself.

1039. Judex non reddit plus quam quod petens ipse requirit. (2 INST. 286.)—A judge does not give more than the plaintiff demands.

1040. Judicandum est legibus, non exemplis. (4 COKE, 33.)—We are to judge by the laws, not by examples.

1041. Judices non tenentur exprimere causam sententiæ suæ. (JENK. CENT. 75.)—Judges are not bound to explain the reason of their sentence.

1042. Judices recenter et subtiliter excogitatis minime favent contra communem legem. (LOFFT, 561.)—Judges by no means favor things raised recently and subtilely against common law.

1043. Judici officium suum excedenti non paretur. (JENK. CENT. 139.)—To a judge who exceeds his office no obedience is due.

1044. Judici satis pœna est quod Deum habet ultorem. (1 LEON. 295.)—It is sufficient punishment for a judge that he has God for his avenger.

1045. Judicia in curia regis non adnihilentur, sed stent in robore suo quousque per errorem aut attinctam adnullentur. (2 INST. 360.)—Judgments in the king's courts are not to be annihilated, but to remain in force until annulled by error or attaint.

1046. Judicia in deliberationibus crebro maturescunt in accelerato processu nunquam. (3 INST. 210.)—Judgments become frequently matured by deliberation, never by hurried process.

1047. Judicia posteriora sunt in lege fortiora. (8 COKE, 97.)—The later decisions are the stronger in law.

1048. Judicia sunt tunquam juris dicta, et pro veritate accipiuntur. (2 INST. 537.)—Judgments are, as it were, the sayings of the law, and are received as truth.

1049. Judiciis posterioribus fides est adhibenda. (13 COKE, 14.)—Credit is to be given to the later decisions.

1050. Judicis est in pronuntiando sequi regulam, exceptione non probata. (2 BOU. 133.)— The judge in his decision should follow the rule, when the exception is not proved.

1051. Judicis est judicare, secundum allegata et probata. (DYER, 12.)—It is the duty of a judge to decide according to the facts alleged and proved.

1052. Judicis est jus dicere non dare. (LOFFT, 42.)—It is the duty of a judge to declare, not to make the law.

1053. Judicis officium est opus diei in die suo perficere. (2 INST. 256.)—It is the duty of a judge to finish the work of each day within that day.

1054. Judicis officium est ut res ita tempora rerum quærere; quæsito tempore tutus eris. (COKE, LITT. 171. a.)—It is the duty of a judge to inquire as well into the time of things as into things themselves; by inquiring into the time you will be safe.

1055. Judicium a non suo judice datum nullius est momenti. (10 COKE, 76.)—A judgment given by an improper judge is of no moment.

1056. Judicium duodecem proborum et legalium hominum veritates dictum esse per com-

munem **Angliæ legem censetur.** (Lofft, 47.)
—The decision of twelve good and upright men
is thought by the common law of England to
be the dictate of truth.

1057. **Judicium est iis quæ religione faciant
faveri, etsi verba desint.** (Lofft, 560.)—It is a
decision to favor those things that favor religion,
though words be wanting.

1058. **Judicium est juris dictum, et per judicium jus est novitur revelatum quod diu fuit
velatum.** (10 Coke, 42.)—Adjudication is the
utterance of the law, and by it the law which
long lay concealed is newly revealed.

1059. **Judicium est quasi juris dictum.** (Coke,
Litt. 168. a.)—Judgment is, as it were, a saying
of the law.

1060. **Judicium non debet esse illusorium;
suum effectum habere debent.** (2 Inst. 841.)
—A judgment ought not to be illusory; it should
have its own effect.

1061. **Judicium redditur in invitum, in præsumptione legis.** (Coke, Litt. 248. b.)—Judgment, in presumption of law, is given contrary
to inclination.

1062. **Judicium semper pro veritate accipitur.** (2 Inst. 380.)—A judgment is always to
be taken for truth.

1063. **Jura debet esse omni exceptione major.**
(Halk. 74.)—Laws should be greater than any
exception.

1064. Juncta juvant. (11 EAST, 220.)—Things joined have effect.

1065. Jura ecclesiastica limitata sunt infra limites separatos. (3 BULS. 53.)—Ecclesiastical laws are limited within separate bounds.

1066. Jura eodem modo destruuntur quo constituuntur. (WHART. 524.)—Laws are repealed by the same means by which they were made.

1067. Jura naturæ sunt immutabilia. (LOFFT, 563.)—The laws of nature are unchangeable.

1068. Jura publica anteferenda privatis. (COKE, LITT. 180. a.)—Public rights are to be preferred to private rights.

1069. Jura publica ex privato promiscue decidi non debent. (COKE, LITT. 181. b.)—Public rights should not be promiscuously decided out of a private transaction.

1070. Jura regis specialia non conceduntur per generalia verba. (JENK. CENT. 103.)—The special rights of the king are not granted by general words.

1071. Jura sanguinis nullo jure civili dirimi possunt. (BAC. MAX. 11.)—The right of blood cannot be taken away by any civil law.

1072. Juramentum est indivisibile, et non est admittendum in parte verum et in parte falsum. (4 INST. 279.)—An oath is indivisible, and is not to be admitted as partly true, and partly false.

1073. Jurare est Deum in testem vocare,

et est actus divini cultus. (3 INST. 165.)—To swear, is to call God to witness, and is an act of religion.

1074. Jurato creditur in judicio. (3 INST. 79.)—In judgment credit is to be given to the swearer.

1075. Juratores debent esse vicini, sufficientes, et minus suspecti. (JENK. CENT. 140.) —Jurors ought to be neighbors, of sufficient estate, and free from suspicion.

1076. Juratores sunt judices facti. (JENK. CENT. 68.)—Jurors are the judges of the facts.

1077. Jure naturæ æquum est neminem cum alterius detrimento et injuria fieri locupletiorum. (DIG. 50. 17. 200.)—By the law of nature it is just that no one become more rich by the detriment and injury of another.

1078. Juri non est consonum quod aliquis accessorius in curia regis convincatur antequam aliquis de facto fuerit attinctus. (2 INST. 183.)— It is not consonant to justice that any accessory should be convicted in the king's court before any one has been attainted of the fact.

1079. Juri sanguinis nunquam præscribitur. (TRAY. 287.)—Against a right by blood no prescription runs.

1080. Juris effectus in executione consistit. (COKE, LITT. 289. b.)—The effect of law consists in execution.

1081. Jurisdictio est potestas de publico

introducta, cum necessitate juris dicendi. (10 COKE, 73.)—Jurisdiction is a power introduced for the public good, on account of the necessity of expounding the law.

1082. **Jurisprudentia est divinarum atque humanarum rerum notitia; justi atque injusti scientia.** (DIG. 1. 1. 10. 2.)—Jurisprudence is the knowledge of things divine and human; the science of the just and the unjust.

1083. **Jurisprudentia legis communis Angliæ est scientia socialis et copiosa.** (7 COKE, 28.) —The jurisprudence of the common law of England is a science, sociable and copious.

1084. **Jus accrescendi inter mercatores, pro beneficio commercii, locum non habet.** (COKE, LITT. 182. a.)—The right of survivorship does not exist among merchants for the benefit of commerce.

1085. **Jus accrescendi præfertur oneribus.** (COKE, LITT. 185. a.)—The right of survivorship is preferred to incumbrances.

1086. **Jus accrescendi præfertur ultimæ voluntati.** (COKE, LITT. 185. b.)—The right of survivorship is preferred to a last will.

1087. **Jus civile est quod quisque sibi populus constituit.** (INST. 1. 2. 1.)—Civil law is that which each nation has established for itself.

1088. **Jus constitui oportet in his quæ ut plurimum accidunt, non quæ ex inopinato.**— The law ought to be established to meet those cases which most frequently happen, not those which occur unexpectedly.

1089. Jus descendit, et non terra. (COKE, LITT. 345. a.)—A right descends, not the land.

1090. Jus dicere et non jus dare. (2 EDEN, 39.)—To declare the law is not to make it.

1091. Jus est ars boni et æqui. (DIG. 1. 1. 1. 1.)—Law is the science of the good and the just.

1092. Jus est norma recti; et quicquid est contra normam recti est injuria. (3 BULS. 313.) —Law is a rule of right, and whatever is contrary to the rule of right, is an injury.

1093. Jus et fraus nunquam cohabitant. (10 COKE, 45.)—Right and fraud never dwell together.

1094. Jus ex injuria non oritur. (4 BING. 639.)—A right does not arise from a wrong.

1095. Jus in re inhærit ossibus usufructuarii. (WHART. 530.)—A life-tenant inherits in person a right in the thing.

1096. Jus naturale est quod apud omnes homines eandem habet potentiam. (7 COKE, 12.) —Natural right is that which has the same power among all men.

1097. Jus naturæ proprie est dictamen rectæ rationis, quo scimus quid turpe, quid honestum, quid faciendum, quid fugiendum. (TAYLER, 270.) —The law of nature is properly the dictate of right reason, by which we know what is dishonest and what is honest; what should be done and what avoided.

1098. Jus nec inflecti gratia, nec frangi potentia, nec adulterari pecunia potest. (CICERO.) —Favor ought not to be able to bend justice, power to warp it, nor money to corrupt it.

1099. Jus non habenti, tute non paretur. (HOB. 146.)—It is not safe to obey him who has no right.

1100. Jus non patitur ut idem bis solvatur. (WHART. 530.)—The law does not suffer the same thing to be paid twice.

1101. Jus non scriptum tacito et illiterato hominum consensu, et moribus expressum. (TAYLER, 270.)—The unwritten law is expressed by the tacit and ignorant consent and customs of the people.

1102. Jus publicum et privatum quod ex naturalibus præceptis aut gentium, aut civilibus est collectum, et quod in jure scripto. (COKE, LITT. 158. b.)—Public and private law is that which is collected from natura· principles, either of nations or in states, and what is in written law.

1103. Jus publicnm privatorum pactis mutari non potest. (DIG. 2. 14. 38.)—A public law cannot be changed by the agreement of private parties.

1104. Jus quo universitates utuntur, est idem quod habent privati. (16 MASS. 44.)—

The law which governs corporations is the same which governs individuals.

1105. **Jus respicit aequitatem.** (COKE, LITT. 24. b.)—Law regards equity.

1106. **Jus sanguinis, quod in legitimus successoribus, spectatur ipso nativitatis tempore questium est.** (HALK. 76.)—The right of blood which in legitimate succession is considered, is sought for at the time of birth.

1107. **Jus summum saepe summa est malitia.** (TAYLER, 272.)—Law too severe does the most harm.

1108. **Jus superveniens auctori accrescit successori.** (HALK. 76.)—A right growing to a person accrues to the successor.

1109. **Jus testamentorum pertinet ordinario.** (WHART. 530.)—The right of testaments belongs to the ordinary.

1110. **Jus triplex est; proprietatis, possessionis, et possibilitatis.** (WHART. 530.)—Right is three-fold; of property, of possession, and of possibility.

1111. **Jus vendit quod usus approbavit.** (ELLES. POST. 35.)—The law dispenses what use has approved.

1112. **Jusjurandi forma verbis differt, re convenit; hunc enim sensum habere debet, ut Deus invocetur.** (GROTIUS, 2. 13. 10.)—The form of taking an oath differs in words, yet agrees in meaning; for it ought to have this sense, that the Deity be invoked.

1113. Jusjurandum inter alios factum neo nocere neo prodesse debet. (4 Inst. 279.)—An oath made among others should neither harm nor profit.

1114. Justitia debet esse libera, quia nihil iniquius venali justitia; plena, quia justitia non debet claudicare; et celeris, quia dilatio est quædam negatio. (2 Inst. 56.)—Justice ought to be unbought, because nothing is more hateful than venal justice; free, for justice should not shut out; and quick, for delay is a sort of denial.

1115. Justitia est constans et perpetua voluntas jus suum cuique tribuendi. (Inst. 1. 1.)—Justice is the constant and perpetual desire to give to everyone his due.

1116. Justitia est duplex; viz., severe puniens et vere præveniens. (3 Inst. Epil.)—Justice is double; punishing with severity, and preventing with lenity.

1117. Justitia est libertate priore. (Halk. 77.)—Justice is prior to liberty.

1118. Justitia est virtus excellens et Altissimo complacens. (4 Inst. 58.)—Justice is an excellent virtue, and pleasing to the Most High.

1119. Justitia firmatur solium. (3 Inst. 140.)—By justice the throne is strengthened.

1120. Justitia nemini neganda est. (Jenk. Cent. 178.)—Justice should be denied to no one.

1121. Justitia non est neganda, non differenda.

(JENK. CENT. 93.)—Justice is not to be denied,
nor delayed.

1122. Justitia non novit patrem nec matrem;
solam veritatem spectat justitia. (1 BULS. 199.)
—Justice knows neither father nor mother; justice regards truth alone.

1123. Justitiæ soror fides. (HALK. 77.)—
Justice is the sister of faith.

1124. Justum non est aliquem antenatum
mortuum facere bastardum qui pro tota vita
sua pro legitimo habetur. (8 COKE, 101.)—
It is not just to make a man a bastard after
his death, who all his life has been held legitimate.

L.

1125. L'obligation sans cause, ou sur une
fausse cause, ou sur cause illicite, ne peut
avoir aucun effet. (CODE, 3. 3. 4.)—An obligation without cause, or upon a false cause, or
upon an unlawful cause, can have no effect.

1126. L'ou le ley done chose, la ceo done
remedy a vener a ceo. (2 ROL. 17.)—Where the
law gives a thing, it gives a remedy to recover.

1127. La conscience est la plus changeante
de regles. (2 BOU. 135.)—Conscience is the most
changeable of rules.

1128. **La ley favour la vie d'un home.** (YEAR B. HEN. VI. 51.)—The law favors the life of a man.

1129. **La ley favour l'inheritance d'un home.** (YEAR B. HEN. VI. 51.)—The law favors a man's inheritance.

1130. **La ley voit plus tost suffer un mischiefe que un inconvenience.** (LITT. §231.)—The law would rather suffer a mischief than an inconvenience.

1131. **La propriete des choses mobliares est acquisi a l'enemi moment qu'elles sont en puissance; et si il leo vend chez nation neutres, le premiere proprietater n'est point endroit de les re eprendre.** (TAYLER, 285.)—Property in things personal is acquired by an enemy at the moment they are in his power; and if he sell them among neutral nations, the first proprietor has no right to retake them.

1132. **Lata culpa dolo æquiparatur.** (2 BOU. 135.)—Wilful negligence is equal to deceit.

1133. **Laudaturque domus congros qui prospicit agros.** (9 COKE, 58.)—The house is admired which commands an extensive view of the fields.

1134. **Law construeth every act to be lawful, when it standeth indifferent whether it be lawful or not.** (WING. 194).

1135. **Law construeth things according to common possibility or intendment.** (WING. 189).

1136. **Law construeth things to the best.** (WING. 193).

1137. Law construeth things with equity and moderation. (WING. 183).

1138. Law disfavoreth impossibilities. (WING. 155).

1139. Law disfavoreth improbabilities. (WING. 161).

1140. Law favoreth charity. (WING. 135).

1141. Law favoreth common right. (WING. 144).

1142. Law favoreth diligence, and therefore hateth folly and negligence. (FINCH, LAW. 1. 3. 70).

1143. Law favoreth honor and order. (WING. 199).

1144. Law favoreth justice and right. (WING. 141).

1145. Law favoreth life, liberty, and dower. (14 BAC. 345).

1146. Law favoreth mutual recompense. (FINCH, LAW. 1. 3. 42).

1147. Law favoreth possession where the right is equal. (FINCH, LAW. 1. 3. 36).

1148. Law favoreth public commerce. (WING. 198).

1149. Law favoreth public quiet. (WING. 200).

1150. Law favoreth speeding of men's causes. (WING. 175).

1151. Law favoreth things for the commonwealth. (WING. 197).

1152. **Law favoreth truth, faith, and certainty.** (WING. 154).

1153. **Law hateth delays.** (FINCH, LAW. 1. 3. 71).

1154. **Law hateth new inventions and innovations.** (WING. 204).

1155. **Law hateth wrong.** (FINCH, LAW. 1. 3. 62).

1156. **Law itself prejudiceth no man.** (FINCH, LAW. 1. 3. 63).

1157. **Law respecteth matter* of substance more than matter of circumstance.** (FINCH, LAW. 1. 3. 39).

1158. **Law respecteth possibility of things.** (FINCH, LAW. 1. 3. 40).

1159. **Law respecteth the bonds of nature.** (FINCH, LAW. 1. 3. 29).

1160. **Le contrat fait la loi.** (2 BOU. 135.) —The contract makes the law.

1161. **Le ley de Dieu et le ley de terre sont tout un, et l'un et l'autre preferre et favour le common et publique bien del terre.** (KEIL. 191.)—The law of God and the law of the land are all one; and both prefer and favor the common and public good of the land.

1162. **Le ley est le plus haut enheritance que le roy ad, car par le ley, il mesme et touts ses sujets sont rules, et si le ley ne fuit, nul roy ne nul enheritance serra.** (2 BOU. 135.)— The law is the highest inheritance that the king has, for by the law both he and all his subjects are ruled, and if there were no law, there would be neither king nor inheritance.

1163. **Le salut du peuple est la supreme loi.** (BR. 1.)—The safety of the people is the supreme law.

1164. **Legatos violare contra jus gentium est.** (WHART. 561.)—To do violence to ambassadors is contrary to the law of nations.

1165. **Legatum morte testatoris tantum confirmatur, sicut donatio inter vivos traditione sola.** (DYER, 143.)—A legacy is confirmed by the death of the testator, as much as a gift from a living person is by delivery alone.

1166. **Legatus regis viçe fungitur a quo destinatur, et honorandus est sicut ille cujus vicem gerit.** (12 COKE, 17.)—An ambassador fills the place of the king by whom he is sent, and is to be honored as he whose place he fills.

1167. **Legem enim contractus dat.** (22 WEND. N. Y. 215. 233.)—The contract makes the law.

1168. **Legem terræ amittentes perpetuam in famiæ notam inde merito incurrunt.** (3 INST. 221.)—Those who do not keep the law of the land, thence justly incur the perpetual brand of infamy.

1169. **Leges Angliæ sunt tripartitæ: jus commune consuetudines, ac decreta comitiorum.** (2 BOU. 135.)—The laws of England are three-fold: common law, customs, and decrees of parliament.

1170. Leges et constitutiones futuris certum est dare formam negotiis non ad facta præterita revocare, nisi nominatim. (TAYLER, 287.)—Laws and constitutions are made, to give form to future transactions, and may not be referred to matters already past and terminated.

1171. Leges figendi et refigendi consuetudo est periculosissima. (4 COKE, PREF.)—The custom of making and unmaking laws is most dangerous.

1172. Leges humanæ nascuntur, vivunt, et moriuntur. (7 COKE, 25.)—Human laws are born, live, and die.

1173. Leges naturæ perfectissimæ sunt, et immutabiles; humani vero juris conditio semper in infinitum decurrit, et nihil est in eo quod perpetuo stare possit. (7 COKE, 25.)—The laws of nature are perfect and immutable; but the condition of human law tends always to infinity, and there is nothing in it that can continue perpetually.

1174. Leges non verbis sed rebus sunt impositæ. (10 COKE, 101.)—Laws are imposed on things, not on words.

1175. Leges posteriores priores contrarias abrogant. (2 ROL. 410.)—Later laws abrogate prior contrary laws.

1176. Leges quæ retrospiciunt raro, et magna cum cautione sunt adhibendæ. (TAYLER, 288.)

—Retrospective laws are rare, and should be received with great caution.

1177. Leges suum ligent latorem. (FLETA, 1. 17. 11.)—Laws should bind those who make them.

1178. Leges vigilantibus, non dormientibus subveniunt. (5 JOHNS. CH. 122. 145.)—Laws aid the vigilant, not the negligent.

1179. Legibus sumptis desinentibus, lege naturæ utendum est. (2 ROL. 298.)—Laws imposed by the state failing, we must act by the law of nature.

1180. Legis constructio non facit injuriam. (COKE, LITT. 183. a.)—The construction of the law does no harm.

1181. Legis minister non tenetur, in executione officii sui, fugere aut retrocedere. (BRANCH, PR.)—The minister of the law is bound in the execution of his office, neither to flee nor retreat.

1182. Legis virtus hæc est; imperare, vetare, permittere, punire. (CAL. LEX.)—The virtue of the law is this; to command, forbid, permit, and punish.

1183. Legislatorum est viva vox, rebus et non verbis, legem imponere. (10 COKE, 101.) —The voice of legislators is a living voice, to impose laws on things, not on words.

1184. Legitime imperanti parere necesse est.

(10)

(JENK. CENT. 120.)—It is necessary to obey one who legitimately commands.

1185. **Legum omnes servi sumus, ut liberi esse possumus.** (TAYLER, 289.)—We are all slaves to the law, in order that we may become free.

1186. **Les fictions naissent de la loi, et non la loi des fictions.** (2 BOU. 136.)—Fictions arise from the law, and not the law from fictions.

1187. **Les lois extremes dans le bien font naitre le mal extreme.** (TAYLER, 290.)—Laws extreme in good, produce extreme in evil.

1188. **Les lois ne se chargent de punir que les actions exterieures.** (MONTES. ES. DES LOIS, 12. 11.)—Laws do not undertake to punish other than outward actions.

1189. **Lestestm doivent rien team fors ceo que ils soient de certein, s. ceo que ils veront ou oyront.** (BEST, EV. 865.)—Witnesses should testify to nothing unless they are certain of it, that is, unless they have seen or heard it.

1190. **Levis exceptio excusat a spolio.** (TRAY. 808.)—A slight defense excuses from the consequences of a plunder.

1191. **Lex aequitate gaudet; appetit perfectum; est norma recti.** (JENK. CENT. 36.)—The law delights in equity; it covets perfection; it is a rule of right.

1192. **Lex aliquando sequitur aequitatem.** (3 WILS. 119.)—Law sometimes follows equity.

1193. **Lex Angliæ est lex misericordiæ.** (2 INST. 315.)—The law of England is a law of mercy.

1194. **Lex Angliæ nunquam matris sed semper patris conditionem imitari partum judicat.** (COKE, LITT. 123. a.)—The law of England rules that the offspring shall always follow the condition of the father; never that of the mother.

1195. **Lex Angliæ nunquam sine parliamento mutare non potest.** (2 INST. 219.)—The law of England cannot be changed except by parliament.

1196. **Lex Angliæ non patitur absurdum.** (9 COKE, 22.)—The law of England does not suffer an absurdity.

1197. **Lex beneficialis rei consimili remedium præstat.** (2 INST. 689.)—A beneficial law affords a remedy in a similar case.

1198. **Lex certa esto pœna certa et crimini idonea, et legibus præfinita.** (LOFFT, 117.)—Let the law be certain; let the punishment be certain, and adequate to the crime, and previously decided by the laws.

1199. **Lex citius tolerare vult privatum damnum quam publicum malum.** (COKE, LITT. 152. b.)—The law should rather tolerate a private loss than a public evil.

1200. **Lex contra id quod præsumit, probationem non recipit.** (LOFFT, 573.)—The law admits no proof against that which it presumes.

1201. **Lex de futuro, judex de præterito.** (2 Bou. 136.)—The law provides for the future; the judge for the past.

1202. **Lex deficere non potest in justitia exhibenda.** (Coke, Litt. 197. b.)—The law ought not to fail in dispensing justice.

1203. **Lex dilationes semper exhorret.** (2 Inst. 240.)—The law always abhors delays.

1204. **Lex est ab æterno.** (Jenk. Cent. 34.) —The law is from the everlasting.

1205. **Lex est anima regis, et rex est anima legis.** (Branch, Pr.)—The law is the soul of the king, and the king is the soul of the law.

1206. **Lex est dictamen rationis.** (Jenk. Cent. 117.)—Law is the dictate of reason.

1207. **Lex est exercitus judicum tutissimus ductor.** (2 Inst. 526.)—The law is the safest leader of the army of judges.

1208. **Lex est norma recti.** (2 Bou. 136.)— Law is a rule of right.

1209. **Lex est ratio summa, quæ jubet quæ sunt utilia et necessaria, et contraria prohibet.** (Coke, Litt. 319. b.)—Law is the highest reason, which commands those things that are useful and necessary, and forbids what is contrary thereto.

1210. **Lex est sanctio sancta, jubens honesta, et prohibens contraria.** (2 Inst. 587.)—The law is a sacred sanction, commanding what is honorable, and forbidding what is contrary.

1211. **Lex est tutissima cassis; sub clypeo legis nemo decipitur.** (2 INST. 56.)—Law is the safest helmet; under the shield of the law no one is deceived.

1212. **Lex facit regem.** (LOFFT, 8.)—Law makes the king.

1213. **Lex favet doti.** (JENK. CENT. 50.)—The law favors dower.

1214. **Lex fingit ubi subsistit æquitas.** (BRANCH, PR.)—The law feigns where equity subsists.

1215. **Lex fingit ubi substitit æquitas.** (HALK. 80.)—The law feigns where equity withstands.

1216. **Lex hæreditates liberas esse vult non in perpetuum astrictas.** (LOFFT, 642.)—The law wishes inheritance to be free to those not strictly bound for all time.

1217. **Lex injusta non est lex.** (LOFFT, 98.)—An unjust law is not a law.

1218. **Lex intendit vicinum vicini facta scire.** (COKE, LITT. 78. b.)—The law presumes one neighbor to know the actions of another.

1219. **Lex judicat de rebus necessario faciendis quasi re ipsa factis.** (WHART. 570.)—The law judges of those things which must necessarily be done, as if actually done.

1220. **Lex mercatoria est lex terræ.** (TAYLER, 294.)—The mercantile law is the law of the land.

1221. **Lex necessitatis est lex temporis, i.e., instantis.** (HOB. 159.)—The law of necessity is the law of time, that is, of the present.

1222. **Lex neminem cogit ad vana seu inutilia peragenda.** (5 COKE, 21.)—The law forces no one to do vain or useless things.

1223. **Lex neminem cogit ostendere quod nescere præsumitur.** (LOFFT, 569.)—The law obliges no one to show what he is presumed not to know.

1224. **Lex nemini operatur iniquum, nemini facit injuriam.** (JENK. CENT. 22.)—The law works harm to no one, and does no one an injury.

1225. **Lex nil facit frustra; nil jubet frustra.** (3 BULS. 279.)—The law does nothing vainly; commands nothing vainly.

1226. **Lex non a rege est violanda.** (JENK. CENT. 7.)—The law should not be violated by the king.

1227. **Lex non cogit ad impossibilia.** (COKE, LITT. 92. a.)—The law forces not to impossibilities.

1228. **Lex non consilia nuda, sed actus apertos respicit.** (LOFFT, 123.)—The law regards not mere intentions, but open acts.

1229. **Lex non deficit in justitia exhibenda.** (JENK. CENT. 31.)—The law does not fail in showing justice.

1230. **Lex non exacte definit, sed arbitrio boni viri permittit.** (TAYLER, 294.)—The law does not define exactly, but leaves to the decision of a good man.

1231. **Lex non favet delicatorum votis.** (9 COKE, 58.)—The law favors not the wishes of the dainty.

1232. **Lex non intendit aliquid impossibile.** (12 COKE, 89.)—The law does not intend anything impossible.

1233. **Lex non patitur fractiones et divisiones statutum.** (BRANCH, PR.)—The law suffers no fractions and divisions of statutes.

1234. **Lex non præcipit inutilia; quia inutilis labor stultus.** (COKE, LITT. 197. b.)—The law commands not useless things; because useless labor is foolish.

1235. **Lex non requirit verificare quod apparet curiæ.** (9 COKE, 54.)—The law does not require that which is apparent to the court to be verified.

1236. **Lex orbis, insanis, et pauperibus pro tutore atque parente est.** (LOFFT, 352.)—The law is the guardian and father of orphans, the insane, and the poor.

1237. **Lex plus laudatur quando ratione probata.** (LITT. EPIL.)—The law is the more praised when it is consonant to reason.

1238. **Lex posterior derogat priori.** (MACK. CIV. LAW, 5.)—The later law annuls the earlier.

1239. **Lex prospicit, non respicit.** (JENK. CENT. 284.)—The law looks forward, not backward.

1240. **Lex** punit mendacium. (JENK. CENT. 15.)—The law punishes a lie.

1241. **Lex** pure pœnalis obligat tantum ad pœnam, non item ad culpam; lex pœnalis mixta et ad culpam obligat, et ad pœnam. (TAYLER, 294.)—The merely penal law binds only as to penalty, not as to fault; the mixed penal law binds both to fault and to penalty.

1242. **Lex** rejicit superflua, pugnantia, incongrua. (JENK. CENT. 133.)—The law rejects superfluous, contradictory, and incongruous things.

1243. **Lex** respicit æquitatem. (14 Q. B. 504. 511. 512.)—Law regards equity.

1244. **Lex** scripta si cesset id custodiri oportet quod moribus et consuetudine inductum est et si qua in re hoc defecerit tunc id quod proximum et consequens ei est, et si id non appareat tunc jus quo urbs Romana utitur servari oportet. (7 COKE, 19.)—If the written law be silent, that which is drawn from manners and customs should be observed; and if in that anything is defective, then that which is next and analogous to it; and if that does not appear, then that law which Rome used should be followed.

1245. **Lex** semper dabit remedium. (3 BOU. INST. 2411.)—Law will always give a remedy.

1246. **Lex** semper intendit quod convenit rationi. (COKE, LITT. 78. b.)—The law always intends what is agreeable to reason.

1247. **Lex spectat naturæ ordinem.** (COKE, LITT. 197. b.)—The law regards the order of nature.

1248. **Lex succurrit ignoranti.** (JENK. CENT. 15.)—The law assists the ignorant.

1249. **Lex uno ore omnes alloquitur.** (2 INST. 184.)—The law speaks to all with one mouth.

1250. **Lex vigilantibus non dormientibus subvenit.** (1 STORY, CONTR. 502.)—Law assists the wakeful, not the sleeping.

1251. **Lex vult potius malum quam inconveniens.** (LOFFT, 574.)—The law designs rather punishment than inconvenience.

1252. **Liberata pecunia non liberat offerentem.** (COKE, LITT. 207. a.)—Money being restored does not set free the party offering.

1253. **Liberi parentibus qui nequeant victum tolerare opitulantor.** (LOFFT, 224.)—Children should assist their parents, if they are unable to support themselves.

1254. **Libertas est cum quisque quod velit faciat modo secundum leges, bonas, communi consensu latas, certas præfinitas, apertas.** (LOFFT, 342.)—Liberty is the privilege of doing what one pleases, subject to certain good, predetermined laws, enacted by common consent.

1255. **Libertas est naturalis facultas ejus quid cuique facere libet, nisi quod de jure aut vi prohibetur.** (COKE, LITT. 116. b.)—Liberty is that natural faculty which allows everyone to do anything he pleases, except that which is prohibited by law or force.

1256. **Libertas est potestas faciendi id quod jure liceat.** (TAYLER, 296.)—Liberty is the power of doing what is allowed by law.

1257. **Libertas est res inestimabilis.** (JENK. CENT. 52.)—Liberty is an inestimable thing.

1258. **Libertas est sui quemque juris dimittendi ao retinendi esse dominum.** (HALK. 83.) —Liberty is the right to alienate or restrain one's own right.

1259. **Libertas non recipit aestimationem.** (BRACT. 14.)—Liberty does not admit of valuation.

1260. **Libertas nullo pretio pensabilis.** (LOFFT, 345.)—Liberty has no price.

1261. **Libertas omnibus rebus favorabilior est.** (DIG. 50. 17. 122.)—Liberty is more favored than all things.

1262. **Libertates regales ad coronam spectantes ex concessione regum a corona exierunt.** (2 INST. 496.)—Royal franchises relating to the crown, depart from the crown, by consent of the sovereign.

1263. **Libertinum ingratum leges civiles in pristinam servitutem redigunt; sed leges Angliae semel manumissum semper liberum judicant.** (COKE, LITT. 137. b.)—The civil laws reduce an ungrateful freeman to his original slavery; but the laws of England regard a man once manumitted as ever after free.

1264. Liberum corpus aestimationem non recipit. (DIG. 9. 3. 9.)—The body of a freeman does not admit of a valuation.

1265. Liberum est cuique apud se explorare, an expediat sibi consilium. (6 JOHNS. N. Y. 181. 184.)—Everyone is free to ascertain for himself, or to have recourse to counsel.

1266. Librorum appellatione continentur omnia volumina, sive in charta, sive in membrana sint, sive in quavis alia materia. (DIG. 32. 52. PR.)—Under the name of books are contained all volumes, whether upon paper or parchment, or any other material.

1267. Licet dispositio de interesse futuro sit inutilis tamen potest fieri declaratio praecedens quae sortiatur effectum interveniente novo actu. (BAC. MAX. 14.)—Although a disposition of a future interest be void, yet a precedent declaration may be made, which, a new act intervening, may chance to have an effect.

1268. Liceat eos exhaeredare quos occidere licebat. (TAYLER, 297.)—It is lawful to disinherit those whom it is lawful to deprive of life.

1269. Licita bene miscentur, formula nisi juris obstet. (BAC. MAX. 23.)—Lawful acts may well be united in one unless some form of law oppose.

1270. Ligeantia est quasi legis essentia; est

vinculum fidei. (COKE, LITT. 129. a.)—Allegiance is, as it were, the essence of law; it is the chain of faith.

1271. **Ligeantia naturalis, nullis claustris coercetur, nullis metis refrænatur, nullis finibus premitur.** (7 COKE, 10.)—Natural allegiance is restrained by no barriers, curbed by no bounds, compressed by no limits.

1272. **Ligna et lapides sub armorum appellatione non continentur.** (BRACT. 144.)—Sticks and stones are not contained under the name of arms.

1273. **Linea recta est index sui et obliqui; lex est linea recti.** (COKE, LITT. 158. b.)—A right line is an index of itself and of an oblique; law is a line of right.

1274. **Linea recta semper præfertur transversali.** (COKE, LITT. 10. b.)—The right line is always preferred to the collateral.

1275. **Literæ patentes regis non erunt vacuæ.** (1 BULS. 6.)—Letters-patent of the king shall not be void.

1276. **Litibus imponit finis finem.** (3 INST. 78.)—A fine puts an end to litigation.

1277. **Litis nomen, omnem actionem significat, sive in rem, sive in personam sit.** (COKE, LITT. 292. a.)—The name of lawsuit signifies every action, whether it be for the thing, or against the person.

1278. **Litus est quousque maximus fluctus a**

mari pervenit. (DIG. 50. 16. 96.)—The shore is where the highest wave from the sea has reached.

1279. **Locus contractus regit actum.** (2 KENT, COM. 458.)—The place of the contract governs the act.

1280. **Locus pro solutione reditus aut pecuniæ secundum conditionem dimissionis aut obligationis, est stricte observandus.** (4 COKE, 73.)— A place for the payment of rent or money, according to the condition of a lease or bond, should be strictly observed.

1281. **Longa patientia trahitur ad consensum.** (FLETA, 4. 26.)—Long sufferance is construed as consent.

1282. **Longa possessio est pacis jus.** (COKE, LITT. 6. b.)—Long possession is the law of peace.

1283. **Longa possessio parit jus possidendi, et tollit actionem vero domino.** (COKE, LITT. 110. b.)—Long possession produces the right of possession, and takes away an action from the true owner.

1284. **Longum est iter per precepta; breve et efficax per statuta.**—The way is long that is marked out by precepts; short and certain when indicated by statutes.

1285. **Longum tempus et longus usus, qui excedit memoriam hominum, sufficit pro jure.** (COKE, LITT. 115. a.)—Long time and long use, which exceeds the memory of man, suffices in law.

1286. Loquendum ut vulgus; sentiendum ut docti. (7 COKE, 11.)—Speak as the ordinary people; think as the learned.

1287. Luat in corpore, si non habet in loculo. (TAYLER, 299.)—He must suffer in body, if he has nothing in his purse.

1288. Lubricum linguæ non facile trahendum est in pœnam. (CRO. CAR. 117.)—A slip of the tongue should not lightly be given to punishment.

1289. Lucet ipsa per se æquitas. (RILEY, 11.) —Equity shines by her own light.

1290. Lucrum facere ex pupilli tutela tutor non debet. (1 JOHNS. CH. N. Y. 527. 535.)— A guardian ought not to make money out of the guardianship of his ward.

1291. Lunaticus qui gaudet in lucidis intervallis. (4 COKE, 124.)—He is a lunatic who enjoys lucid intervals.

M.

1292. Magis dignum trahit ad se minus dignum. (YEAR, B. 20 HEN. VI. 2 ARG.)—The more worthy draws to itself the less worthy.

1293. Magister rerum usus; magistra rerum

experientia. (COKE, LITT. 229. b.)—Use is the master of things; experience is the mistress of things.

1294. **Magna Charta et Charta de Foresta sont appeles les deux grandes charters.** (2 INST. 570.)—Magna Charta and the Charter of the Forest are called the·two great charters.

1295. **Magna culpa dolus est.** (DIG. 50. 16. 226.)—Great neglect is equivalent to fraud.

1296. **Magna fuit quondam magna reverentiæ chartæ.** (2 INST. PROEM.)—Reverence for the great charter in old times was great.

1297. **Magna negligentia culpa est.** (DIG. 50. 16. 226.)—Gross negligence is a fault.

1298. **Maihemium est homicidium inchoatum.** (3 INST. 118.)—Mayhem is incipient homicide.

1299. **Maihemium est inter crimina majora minimum et inter minora maximum.** (COKE, LITT. 127. a.)—Mayhem is the least of great crimes, and the greatest of small crimes.

1300. **Maihemium, est membri mutilatio; et dici poterit, ubi aliquis in aliqua parte sui corporis effectus sit inutilis ad pugnandum.** (COKE, LITT. 126. b.)—Mayhem is the mutilation of a limb; and is so called when anyone is so hurt in his body, that a member used in fight is rendered useless.

1301. **Major hæreditas venit uniouique nostrum a jure et legibus quam a·parentibus.** (2 INST. 56.)—A greater inheritance comes to every one of us from right and the laws than from parents.

1302. **Major numerus in se continet minorem.** BRACT. 16.)—The greater number contains in itself the less.

1303. **Majore pœna affectus quam legibus statuta est, non est infamis.** (4 INST. 66.)—One affected with a greater punishment than is provided by law is not infamous.

1304. **Majus est delictum seipsum occidere quam alium.** (3 INST. 54.)—It is a greater crime to kill one's self than to kill another.

1305. **Mala grammatica non vitiat chartam. Sed in expositione instrumentorum mala grammatica quoad fieri possit evitanda est.** (6 COKE, 39.)—Bad grammar does not vitiate a deed. But in the exposition of instruments, bad grammar, as far as possible, is to be avoided.

1306. **Male res se habet cum quo virtute effici debeat a tentatur pecunia.** (LOFFT, 617.)— That is a bad case wherein one tries to accomplish with money that which should be prompted by virtue.

1307. **Maledicta expositio est quæ corrumpit textum.** (4 COKE, 35.)—It is a bad exposition that corrupts the text.

1308. **Maleficia non debent remanere impunita; et impunitas continuum affectum tribuit delinquendi.** (4 COKE, 45.)—Evil deeds should not remain unpunished; and impunity affords continual incitement to the delinquent.

1309. **Maleficia propositis distinguuntur.**
(JENK. CENT. 290.)—Evil deeds are distinguished
from evil purposes.

1310. **Malitia est acida, est mali animi affectus.** (2 BULS. 49.)—Malice is sour; it is the
quality of a bad mind.

1311. **Malitia supplet ætatem.** (DYER, 104.)
—Malice makes up for age.

1312. **Malitiis hominum est obviandum.** (4
COKE, 15.)—The malice of men should be avoided.

1313. **Malitiis hominum non est indulgendam.**
(TRAY. 332.)—The malice of men should not be
indulged.

1314. **Malum non habet efficientem, sed de-
ficientem causam.** (3 INST. PROEM.)—Evil has
not an efficient, but a deficient, cause.

1315. **Malum non præsumitur.** (4 COKE, 72.)
—Evil is not presumed.

1316. **Malum quo communius eo pejus.**
(WHART. 605.)—The more common an evil is,
the worse.

1317. **Malus usus est abolendus.** (COKE,
LITT. 141. a.)—An evil custom is to be abolished.

1318. **Mandata licita recipiunt strictam interpretationem; sed illicita, latam et extensam.**
(BAC. MAX. 16.)—Lawful commands receive a
strict interpretation; but unlawful, a wide and
broad interpretation.

1319. **Mandatarius terminos sibi positos trans-**
(11)

gredi non potest. (JENK. CENT. 53.)—A mandatary cannot exceed the bounds placed upon him.

1320. Mandatum nisi gratuitum nullum est. (DIG. 17. 1. 1. 4.)—Unless a mandate is gratuitous, it is not a mandate.

1321. Manerium dicitur a manendo, secundum excellentiam, sedes magna, fixa et stabilis. (COKE, LITT. 58. a.)—A manor is called from MANENDO, a seat, according to its excellence, great, fixed, and firm.

1322. Manifesta probatione non indigent. (7 COKE, 40.)—Things manifest need no proof.

1323. Manumittere, idem est quod extra manum vel potestatem ponere. (COKE, LITT. 187. a.)—To manumit is to place beyond hand and power.

1324. Manus mortua, quia possessio est immortalis, manus pro possessione et mortua pro immortali. (COKE, LITT. 2. b.)—Mortmain, because it is an immortal possession; MANUS stands for possession, and MORTUA for immortal.

1325. Maris et fœmina conjunctio est de jure naturæ. (7 COKE, 13.)—The connection of male and female is by the law of nature.

1326. Maritagium est aut liberum aut servitio obligatum. (COKE, LITT. 21. b.)—A marriage portion is either free or bound to service.

1327. Matrimonia debent esse libera. (2 KENT, COM. 102.)—Marriage ought to be free.

1328. **Matrimonium subsequens legitimos facit.** (COKE, LITT. 345. a.)—A subsequent marriage makes the children legitimate.

1329. **Matrimonium subsequens tollit peccatum præcedens.** (2 BOU. 138.)—Subsequent marriage cures preceding criminality.

1330. **Matter en ley ne serra mise en bouche del jurors.** (JENK. CENT. 180.)—Matter of law should not be put into the mouth of jurors.

1331. **Maturiora sunt vota mulierum quam virorum.** (6 COKE, 71.)—The wishes of women are more mature than those of men.

1332. **Maxima illecebra est peccandi impunitatis spes.** (TAYLER, 315.)—The greatest incitement to guilt is the hope of sinning with impunity.

1333. **Maxime ita dicta quia maxima est ejus dignitas et certissima auctoritas, atque quod maxime omnibus probetur.** (COKE, LITT. 11. a.) —A maxim is so called because its dignity is chiefest, and its authority the most certain, and because it is universally approved by all.

1334. **Maxime paci sunt contraria vis et injuria.** (COKE, LITT. 161. b.)—Force and injury are chiefly contrary to peace.

1335. **Maximus erroris populus magister.** (15 BAC. 124.)—The people is the greater master of error.

1336. **Melieur serra prize pour le roy.** (JENK. CENT. 192.)—The best shall be taken for the king.

1337. **Melior dabit nomen rei.** (BRANCH, PR.) —The better gives a name to a thing.

1338. **Melior est causa possidentis.** (DIG. 50. 17. 126.)—The cause of the possessor is to be preferred.

1339. **Melior est conditio defendentis.** (HOB. 199.)—The cause of the defendant is the better.

1340. **Melior est conditio possidentis et rei quam actoris.** (4 INST. 180.)—Better is the condition of the possessor and that of the defendant, than that of the plaintiff.

1341. **Melior est conditio possidentis, ubi neuter jus habet.** (JENK. CENT. 118.)—Better is the condition of the possessor, where neither of the two has a right.

1342. **Melior est justitia vere præveniens, quam severe puniens.** (3 INST. EPIL.)—Better is justice truly preventing, than severely punishing.

1343. **Meliorem conditionem ecclesiæ suæ facere potest prælatus, deteriorem nequaquam.** (COKE, LITT. 101. b.)—A bishop can make the condition of his own church better, but by no means worse.

1344. **Meliorem conditionem suam facere potest minor, deteriorem nequaquam.** (COKE, LITT, 337. b.)—A minor can make his own condition better, but by no means worse.

1345. **Melius est in tempore occurrere, quam post causam vulneratam remedium quærere.** (2

INST. 299.)—It is better to restrain in time than to seek a remedy after the injury inflicted.

1346. **Melius est jus deficiens quam jus incertum.** (LOFFT, 395.)—Better is law deficient, than law uncertain.

1347. **Melius est omnia mala pati quam malo consentire.** (3 INST. 23.)—It is better to suffer every wrong than to consent to wrong.

1348. **Melius est recurrere quam male currere.** (4 INST. 176.)—It is better to recede than to proceed wrongly.

1349. **Melius est ut deoem noxii evadant quam ut unus innocens pereat.** (LOFFT, 129.)—It is better that ten guilty persons escape, than that one innocent person perish.

1350. **Melius et tutius si non festines.** (TAYLER, 316.)—It is better and safer not to be in haste.

1351. **Mens testatoris in testamentis spectanda est.** (JENK. CENT. 277.)—The testator's intention should be regarded in wills.

1352. **Mentiri est contra mentem ire.** (3 BULS. 260.)—To lie, is to go against the mind.

1353. **Mercis appellatio ad res mobiles tantum appertinet.** (DIG. 50. 16. 66.)—The term merchandise belongs to movable things only.

1354. **Mercis appellatione homines non contineri.** (DIG. 50. 16. 207.)—Men are not included under the name of merchandise.

1355. **Merito beneficium legis amittit, qui**

legem ipsam subvertere intendit. (2 INST. 53.)
—He justly loses the benefit of the law who purposes to overturn the law itself.

1356. **Merx est quicquid vendi potest.** (3
METC. 365. 367.)—Merchandise is whatever can
be sold.

1357. **Messis sementem sequitur.** (ERSK.
INST. 174. 26.)—Harvest follows seed-time.

1358. **Meum est promittere et non dimittere.**
(2 ROL. 39.)—It is mine to promise not to dis-
charge.

1359. **Minatur innocentibus, qui parcit nocentibus.** (4 COKE, 45.)—He threatens the innocent who spares the guilty.

1360. **Minima poena corporalis est major
qualibet pecuniara.** (3 INST. 220.)—The smallest
bodily punishment is greater than any pecuniary
one.

1361. **Minime mutanda sunt quae certam
habent interpretationem.** (COKE, LITT. 365. a.)—
Things which have a certain interpretation are
to be changed as little as possible.

1362. **Minimum est nihilo proximum.** (15
BAC. 73.)—The least is next to nothing.

1363. **Ministeria recipiunt vicarium, sed non
item pleraque judiciara.** (LOFFT, 457.)—The
office of judge, as a rule, admits of no substitute,
as do purely ministerial offices.

1364. **Minius est actionem habere quam rem.**
(HALK. 89.)—To have an action is less than to
have the property itself.

1365. **Minor ante tempus agere non potest in casu proprietatis, nec etiam convenire.** (2 INST. 291.)—A minor before majority cannot act in a case of property, nor even agree.

1366. **Minor jurare non potest.** (COKE, LITT. 172. b.)—A minor cannot make oath.

1367. **Minor minorem custodire non debet; alios enim præsumitur male regere qui seipsum regere nescit.** (COKE, LITT. 88. b.)—A minor cannot be guardian to a minor, for he is presumed to direct others badly who knows not how to direct himself.

1368. **Minor non tenetur placitare super hæreditate paterna.** (TRAY. 341.)—A minor is not bound to defend his right to the heritage of his ancestor.

1369. **Minor non tenetur respondere durante minori ætate; nisi in causa dotis, propter favorem.** (3 BULS. 143.)—A minor is not bound to answer during his minority, except as a matter of favor in a cause of dower.

1370. **Minor qui infra ætatem 12 annorum fuerit utlagari non potest nec extra legem poni, quia ante talem ætatem non est sub lege aliqua.** (COKE, LITT. 128. a.)—A minor who is under twelve years of age cannot be outlawed, nor placed without the law, because before such age, he is not under any law.

1371. **Minor 17 annis, non admittitur fore executorum.** (6 COKE, 67.)—A minor under seventeen years of age is not admitted to be an executor.

1372. Minor tenetur in quantum locupletior factus. (TRAY. 342.)—A minor is bound to the extent to which he has been enriched.

1373. Minus solvit, qui tardius solvit; nam et tempore minus solvitur. (DIG. 50. 16. 12. 1.) —He pays little who pays late, for from the delay he is judged not to pay.

1374. Misera est servitus ubi jus est vagum aut incertum. (4 INST. 246.)—Obedience is miserable where the law is vague and uncertain.

1375. Mitiores pœnæ nobis semper placuere. (TRAY. 343.)—A light punishment is always pleasing to the law.

1376. Mitius imperanti melius paretur. (3 INST. 24.)—He is better obeyed who commands leniently.

1377. Mobilia non habet situm. (4 JOHNS. CH. N. Y. 472.)—Movables have no place.

1378. Mobilia personam sequuntur; immobilia situm. (BR. 522.)—Movable things follow the person; immovable, the place.

1379. Modica circumstantia facti jus mutat. (2 BOU. 139.)—A small circumstance attending an act may change the law.

1380. Modus de non decimando non valet. (CRO. ELIZ. 511.)—An agreement not to take tithes avails not.

1381. Modus debet esse certus, rationabilis,

et perantiquus. (LOFFT, 426.)—A custom should be certain, reasonable, and very ancient.

1382. **Modus et conventio vincunt legem.** (2 COKE, 73.)—Custom and agreement overrule law.

1383. **Modus legem dat donationi.** (COKE, LITT. 19. a.)—The manner gives law to a gift.

1384. **Moneta est justum medium et mensura rerum commutabilium; nam per medium monetæ fit omnium rerum conveniens et justa æstimatio.** (DAV. 51.)—Money is the just medium and measure of all commutable things, for by the medium of money a convenient and just estimation of all things is made.

1385. **Monetandi jus comprehenditur in regalibus quæ nunquam a regio sceptro abdicantur.** (DAV. 54.)—The right of coining money is comprehended among those royal rights that are never separated from the royal sceptre.

1386. **Monopolia dicitur, cum unus solus aliquod genus mercaturæ universum emit, pretium ad suum libitum statuens.** (11 COKE, 86.) —It is called monopoly, when one person alone buys up the whole of one kind of commodity, and fixes a price at his own pleasure.

1387. **Monumenta quæ nos recorda vocamus sunt veritatis et vetustatis vestigia.** (COKE, LITT. 118. a.)—Monuments, which we call records, are the vestiges of truth and antiquity.

1388. **Mora reprobatur in lege.** (JENK. CENT. 51.)—Delay is reproved by law.

1389. **Mors dicitur ultimum supplicium.** (3 INST. 212.)—Death is considered the extreme penalty.

1390. **Mors omnia solvit.** (JENK. CENT. 160.) —Death dissolves all things.

1391. **Morte donantis donatio confirmatur.** (HALK. 90.)—A donation is confirmed by the death of the donor.

1392. **Morte legatarii, perit legatum.** (TRAY. 849.)—By the death of the legatee, the legacy perishes.

1393. **Morte mandatoris, perit mandatum.** (TRAY. 350.)—At the death of the mandant the mandate fails.

1394. **Mortgagium scuto magis quam gladia opus est.** (TAYLER, 475.)—A mortgage is used as a shield rather than a sword.

1395. **Mortis momentum est ultimum vitæ momentum.** (4 BRADF. SURR. N. Y. 245. 250.) —The last moment of life is the moment of death.

1396. **Mortuus exitus non est exitus.** (COKE, LITT. 29. b.)—To be dead-born is not to be born.

1397. **Mos pro lege.** (TAYLER, 321.)—Custom stands for law.

1398. **Mos retinendus est fidelissimæ vetustatis.** (4 COKE, 78.)—A custom of the truest antiquity is to be retained.

1399. **Mulcta damnum famæ non irrogat.** (CODE, 1. 54.)—A fine does not impose a loss of reputation.

1400. **Mulieres ad probationem status hominis admitti non debent.** (COKE, LITT. 16. b.) —Women ought not to be admitted to proof of the estate of a man.

1401. **Multa conceduntur per obliquum, quæ non conceduntur de directo.** (6 COKE, 47.)— Many things are indirectly conceded that are not conceded directly.

1402. **Multa fidem promissa levant.** (11 CUSH. MASS. 350.)—Many promises lessen faith.

1403. **Multa ignoramus quæ nobis non laterent si veterum lectio fuit nobis familiaris.** (10 COKE, 78.)—We are ignorant of many things that would not be hidden from us if the readings of old authors were familiar to us.

1404. **Multa impediunt matrimonium contrahendum quæ non dirimunt contractum.** (TRAY. 351.)—Many things impede the contracting of a marriage, which do not detract from its validity when contracted.

1405. **Multa in jure communi contra rationem disputandi, pro communi utilitate introducta sunt.** (COKE, LITT. 70. b.)—Many things contrary to the rule of argument are introduced into common law for common utility.

1406. **Multa multo exercitatione facilius quam regulis percipies.** (4 INST. 50.)—You will perceive many things more easily by practice than by rules.

1407. Multa non legibus humanis, sed, foro divino pertinent. (LOFFT, 281.)—Many things pertain not to human laws, but to divine jurisdiction.

1408. Multa non vetat lex quæ tamen tacitæ damnavit. (WHART. 665.)—The law does not forbid many things which yet it has silently condemned.

1409. Multa transeunt cum universitate quæ non per se transeunt. (COKE, LITT. 12. b.)—Many things pass in the whole which would not pass by themselves.

1410. Multi muita, nemo omnia novit. (4 INST. 348.)—Many men know many things; no one knows everything.

1411. Multiplex indistinctum parit confusionem; et quæstiones quo simpliciones, eo lucidores. (HOB. 335.)—Multiplicity and indistinctness produce confusion; and questions, the more simple they are, the more lucid.

1412. Multiplicata transgressione crescat pœnæ inflictio. (3 INST. 479.)—Let infliction of punishment increase with multiplied crime.

1413. Multitudinem decem faciunt. (COKE, LITT. 257. a.)—Ten make a multitude.

1414. Multitudo errantium non parit errori patrocinium. (11 COKE, 75.)—The multitude of those who err gives no excuse for error.

1415. **Multitudo imperitorum perdit curiam.** (2 INST. 219.)—A multitude of ignorant persons destroys a court.

1416. **Multo utilius est pauca idonea effundere quam multis inutilibus homines gravari.** (4 COKE, 20.)—It is more useful to impart a few trustworthy ideas, than to impress men with many useless things.

1417. **Mutata forma interemetur prope substantia rei.** (HALK. 91.)—When the form of a thing is changed, its substance is almost destroyed.

N.

1418. **Nam debes melioris conditionis esse quam actor meus a quo jus in me transit.** (DIG. 50. 14. 175. 1.)—One should not be placed in better condition, than the person to whose rights he succeeds.

1419. **Natura appetit perfectum; ita et lex.** (HOB. 144.)—Nature desires perfection; so does the law.

1420. **Natura non facit saltum; ita nec lex.** (COKE, LITT. 238. b.)—Nature takes no leaps ; nor does the law.

1421. **Natura non facit vacuum, nec lex**

supervacuum. (COKE, LITT. 79. a.)—Nature
makes no vacuum; law no supervacuum.

1422. **Naturæ vis maxima.** (2 INST. 564.)—
The force of nature is greatest.

1423. **Ne ad consilium antequam voceris.**
(RILEY, 7.)—Go not to the council before you are
called.

1424. **Ne curia deficeret in justitia exhibenda.**
(4 INST. 63.)—Nor should the court be deficient
in showing justice.

1425. **Ne fictio plus valeat in casu fictio.
quam veritas in casu vero.** (TRAY. 357.)—A
fiction is of no more value in a fictitious case,
than truth in a real case.

1426. **Ne licitatorem venditor apponat.**
(LOFFT, 620.)—The seller should not appoint a
bidder.

1427. **Ne quære litem cum licet fugere.**
(RILEY, 66.)—Seek not a lawsuit when you can
escape it.

1428. **Ne se ipsum præcipites in discriminem.**
—Be not hasty in judging.

1429. **Nec beneficium pertinet ad eum qui
non debet genere officium.**—No benefit belongs
to him who was not obliged to perform a certain act.

1430. **Neo regibus infinita, aut libera potestas.**
(TAYLER, 385.)—The power of kings is neither
unlimited nor free.

1431. **Neo tempus neo locus occurrit regi.**

(JENK. CENT. 190.)—Neither time nor place bars the king.

1432. Nec veniam, effuso sanguine, casus habet. (3 INST. 57.)—Where blood is spilled the case is unpardonable.

1433. Nec veniam læso Numine, casus habet. (JENK. CENT. 167.)—Where the Divinity is insulted the case is unpardonable.

1434. Necessarium est quod non potest aliter se habere. (BRANCH, PR.)—That is necessary which cannot be otherwise.

1435. Necessitas est lex temporis et loci. (8 COKE, 69.)—Necessity is the law of time and place.

1436. Necessitas excusat aut extenuat delictum in capitalibus, quod non operatur idem in civilibus. (BAC. MAX. 7.)—Necessity excuses or extenuates delinquency in capital cases, which would not operate the same in civil cases.

1437. Necessitas facit licitum quod alias non est licitum. (10 COKE, 61.)—Necessity makes that lawful which otherwise is not lawful.

1438. Necessitas inducit privilegium quoad jura privata. (BAC. MAX. 5.)—Necessity gives a privilege with reference to private rights.

1439. Necessitas non habet legem. (PLOWD. 18.)—Necessity has no law.

1440. Necessitas publica major est quam privata. (BAC. MAX. 5.)—Public necessity is greater than private.

1441. Necessitas, quod cogit, defendit. (1 HALE, PL. CR. 54)—Necessity defends what it compels.

1442. Necessitas sub lege non continetur, quia quod alias non est licitum necessitas facit licitum. (2 INST. 326.)—Necessity is not restrained by law; since what otherwise is not lawful, necessity makes lawful.

1443. Necessitas vincit legem; legum vincula irridet. (HOB. 144.)—Necessity overcomes the law; it breaks the chains of justice.

1444. Necessity creates equity. (2 BOU. 140).

1445. Nefarium est per formulas legis laqueos innectere innocentibus. (LOFFT, 87.)—It is infamous to lay snares for the innocent through forms of law.

1446. Negatio conclusionis est error in lege. (WING. 268.)—The denial of a conclusion is error in law.

1447. Negatio destruit negationem, et ambæ faciunt affirmativum. (COKE, LITT. 146. b.)—A negative destroys a negative, and both make an affirmative.

1448. Negatio duplex est affirmatio. (WHART. 678.)—A double negative is an affirmative.

1449. Negatio non potest probari. (LOFFT, 381.)—Denial cannot be proved.

1450. Negligentia semper habet infortunium comitem. (COKE, LITT. 246. b.)—Negligence always has misfortune for a companion.

1451. **Neminem cum alterius detrimento et injuria fieri locupletiorum.** (TAYLER, 266.)—No one can be made richer to the detriment and injury of another.

1452. **Neminem oportet esse sapientiorem legibus.** (COKE, LITT. 97. b.)—No one need be wiser than the laws.

1453. **Nemini in alium plus licet quam concessum est legibus.** (LOFFT, 155.)—More is allowed to no one against another, than is conceded by the laws.

1454. **Nemo ad littus maris accedere prohibetur.** (HALK. 96.)—No one is prohibited from approaching the sea-shore.

1455. **Nemo admittendus est inhabilitare seipsum.** (JENK. CENT. 40.)—No one is allowed to incapacitate himself.

1456. **Nemo agit in seipsum.** (JENK. CENT. 40.)—No one acts against himself.

1457. **Nemo alienæ rei, sine satisdatione, defensor idoneus intelligitur.** (1 CURT. C. C. 202.)—Without security, no one is deemed a competent defender of the property of another.

1458. **Nemo alieno nomine lege agere potest.** (DIG. 50. 17. 123.)—No one may sue at law in the name of another.

1459. **Nemo aliquam partem recte intelligere potest antequam totum, iterum atque iterum perlegit.** (3 COKE, 59.)—No one can rightly un-

(12)

derstand part of a thing till he has read through the whole again and again.

1460. **Nemo allegans suam turpitudinem est audiendus.** (4 INST. 279.)—No one alleging his own baseness is to be heard.

1461. **Nemo bis in periculum veniet pro eodem delicto.** (LOFFT, 431.)—No one should come twice into danger for the same crime.

1462. **Nemo cogi potest praecise ad factum, sed in id tantum quod interesse.** (WHART. 681.) —No person can be compelled precisely to the act, but to so much only as interests him.

1463. **Nemo cogitur rem suam vendere, etiam justo pretio.** (4 INST. 275.)—No one is obliged to sell his own property, even for the full value.

1464. **Nemo condemnari debet inauditus nec summonitus.** (HALK. 96.)—No one should be condemned unheard, or unsummoned.

1465. **Nemo contra factum suum venire potest.** (2 INST. 66.)—No one can come against his own deed.

1466. **Nemo damnum facit, nisi qui id fecit quod facere jus non habet.** (DIG. 50. 17. 151.) —No one does damage, unless he is doing what he has no right to do.

1467. **Nemo dat qui non habet.** (JENK. CENT. 250.)—No one gives who does not possess.

1468. **Nemo de domo sua extrahi potest.**

(DIG. 50. 17. 103.)—No one may be dragged from his own house.

1469. **Nemo debet bis punire pro uno delicto: et Deus, non agit bis in ipsum.** (4 COKE, 43.) —No one should be punished twice for the same fault, and God punishes not twice against himself.

1470. **Nemo debet bis vexari, si constet curiæ quod sit pro una et eadem causa.** (5 COKE, 61.)—No man should be twice punished, if it appear to the court that it is for one and the same cause.

1471. **Nemo debet ex alieno damno lucrari.** (TRAY. 365.)—No one should be enriched by the loss of another.

1472. **Nemo debet ex aliena jactura lucrari.** (WHART. 681.)—No person ought to gain by another's loss.

1473. **Nemo debet immiscere se rei alienæ —ad se nihil pertinenti.** (JENK. CENT. 18.)— No one should interfere in another's business— in nothing relating to him.

1474. **Nemo debet in communione invitus teneri.** (1 JOHNS. N. Y. 106. 114.)—No one should be retained in partnership against his will.

1475. **Nemo debet rem suam sine facto aut defectu suo amittere.** (COKE, LITT. 263. a.)— No one should lose his property without his own act or negligence.

1476. Nemo duobus utatur officiis. (4 INST. 100.)—No one should fill two offices.

1477. Nemo ejusdem tenementi simul potest esse hæres et dominus. (1 REEVES, 106.)—No one can be at the same time heir and lord of the same fief.

1478. Nemo est cogendus quis ad substituendum. (HALK. 180.)—No one is compelled to substitute another in his own place.

1479. Nemo est hæres viventis. (COKE, LITT. 22. b.)—No one is the heir of a living man.

1480. Nemo est supra leges. (LOFFT, 142.)—No one is beyond the law.

1481. Nemo ex alterius detrimento fieri debet locupletari. (JENK. CENT. 4.)—No one ought to be made rich out of another person's injury.

1482. Nemo ex alterius facto prægravari debet. (2 KENT, COM. 646.)—No one should be burdened by the act of another.

1483. Nemo ex consilio obligatur. (DIG. 17. 1. 2. 6.)—No one is bound by the advice he gives.

1484. Nemo ex dolo suo proprio relevetur, aut auxilium capiat. (JUR. CIV.)—No one is relieved, or gains an advantage from his own proper deceit.

1485. Nemo ex proprio dolo consequitur actionem. (TRAY. 366.)—No one can acquire a right of action through his own fraud.

1486. **Nemo ex suo delicto meliorem suam conditionem facere potest.** (DIG. 50. 17. 134. 1.) —No one can improve his condition by his own wrong.

1487. **Nemo factum a se alienum tenetur scire.** (LOFFT, 53.)—No one is bound to know the private act of another, unless done with himself.

1488. **Nemo habetur agere dolose qui jure se utitur.** (TRAY. 866.)—No one is held to act fraudulently who acts in exercise of his rights.

1489. **Nemo inauditus nec summonitus condemnari debet, si non sit contumax.** (JENK. CENT. 18.)—No one should be condemned unheard and unsummoned, unless for contumacy.

1490. **Nemo invitus compellitur ad communionem.** (TAYLER, 337.)—No one can be compelled into co-partnership against his will.

1491. **Nemo militans Deo implicetur secularibus negotiis.** (COKE, LITT. 70. b.)—No man warring for God should be troubled by secular business.

1492. **Nemo mori potest pro parte testatus pro parte intestatus.** (TRAY. 867.)—No one can die partly testate and partly intestate.

1493. **Nemo moriturus præsumitur mentiri.** (2 How. ST. TR. 18.)—No one at the point of death is presumed to lie.

1494. **Nemo nascitur artifex.** (COKE, LITT. 97. b.)—No one is born an artificer.

1495. Nemo patriam in qua natus est exuere neo ligeantiæ debitum ejurare possit. (COKE, LITT. 129. a.)—No one can renounce the country in which he was born, nor abjure the bond of allegiance.

1496. Nemo plus commodi hæredi suo relinquit quam ipse habuit. (DIG. 50. 17. 120.) —No one should leave a greater benefit to his heir than he had himself.

1497. Nemo plus juris ad alienum transferre potest, quam ipse habet. (COKE, LITT. 309. b.) —No one can transfer to another a greater right than he has himself.

1498. Nemo potest contra recordum verificare per patriam. (2 INST. 880.)—No one can verify by jury against a record.

1499. Nemo potest episcopo mandare præter regem. (LOFFT, 311.)—No one can give a mandate to a bishop except the king.

1500. Nemo potest esse dominus et hæres. (HALE, HIST. C. L. 7.)—No one can be both owner and heir.

1501. Nemo potest esse simul actor et judex. (13 Q. B. 327.)—No one can be at the same time suitor and judge.

1502. Nemo potest esse tenens et dominus. (GILB. TEN. 152.)—No one can be both tenant and lord (of the same tenement).

1503. Nemo potest facere per alium, quod per se non potest. (JENK. CENT. 237.)—No one can do by another what he cannot do by himself.

1504. **Nemo potest facere per obliquum quod non potest facere per directum.** (1 EDEN, 512.) —No one can do that indirectly which cannot be done directly.

1505. **Nemo potest gladii potestam sibi vel cujus alterius coercitionis ad alium transferre.** (HALK. 98.)—No one to whom is delegated a power of coercion, can himself transfer it to another.

1506. **Nemo potest habere duas militias nec duas dignitates.** (4 COKE, 118.)—No man can fill two offices, or two dignities.

1507. **Nemo potest immittere in alienum.** (TRAY. 368.)—No one can send anything into the domains of another.

1508. **Nemo potest mutare consilium suum in alterius injuriam.** (DIG. 50. 17. 75.)—No one should change his mind to the injury of another.

1509. **Nemo potest nisi quod de jure potest.** (LOFFT, 5.)—No man can do anything except what he can do lawfully.

1510. **Nemo potest renunciare juri publico.** (TRAY. 368.)—No one can renounce a public right.

1511. **Nemo potest sibi debere.** (2 BOU. 141.) —No one can be his own debtor.

1512. **Nemo potest sibi mutare causam pos-**

sessionis. (HALK. 98.)—No one can change for himself the cause of his possession.

1513. **Nemo prædo est qui pretium numeravit.** (HALK. 97.)—No one is a pirate who has counted out the price.

1514. **Nemo præsens nisi intelligat.** (2 BOU. 141.)—One is not present unless he understands.

1515. **Nemo præsumitur alienam posteritatem suæ prætulisse.** (COKE, LITT. 373. a.)—No one is presumed to have preferred the posterity of another to his own.

1516. **Nemo præsumitur donare.** (WHART. 682.)—No one is presumed to give.

1517. **Nemo præsumitur esse immemor suæ æternæ salutis, et maxime in articulo mortis.** (6 COKE, 76.)—No one is presumed to be forgetful of his own eternal welfare, and particularly at the point of death.

1518. **Nemo præsumitur ludere in extremis.** (WHART. 682.)—No one is presumed to trifle at the point of death.

1519. **Nemo præsumitur malus.** (WHART. 682.)—No one is presumed to be bad.

1520. **Nemo prohibetur plures negotiationes sive artes exercere.** (11 COKE, 54.)—No one is prohibited from exercising several kinds of business or arts.

1521. **Nemo prohibetur pluribus defensionibus uti.** (COKE, LITT. 304. b.)—No one is prohibited from using several defenses.

1522. **Nemo prudens punit ut præterita revocentur, sed ut futura præveniantur.** (3 Buls. 179.)—No wise man punishes, that things done may be revoked, but that future wrongs may be prevented.

1523. **Nemo punitur pro alieno delicto.** (Wing. 336.)—No one is to be punished for the crime of another.

1524. **Nemo punitur sine injuria, facto, seu defalto.** (2 Inst. 287.)—No one is punished unless for some injury, deed, or default.

1525. **Nemo qui condemnare potest, absolvere non potest.** (Dig. 50. 17. 37.)—No one who is able to condemn, is unable to acquit.

1526. **Nemo redditum invito domino percipere, et possidere potest.** (Coke, Litt. 323. b.) —No one can take, and enjoy the rent without consent of the owner.

1527. **Nemo rem suam amittat, nisi ex facto aut delicto suo, aut neglectu.** (Lofft, 40.)—No one can lose his own property, except by his own deed, transgression, or neglect.

1528. **Nemo repente turpissimus.**—No one becomes bad in an instant.

1529. **Nemo sibi esse judex, vel suis jus dicere debet.** (12 Coke, 113.)—No man ought to be his own judge, or to administer justice in cases in which he is interested.

1530. **Nemo sine actione experitur, et hoc non sine breve sive libello conventionali.**

(BRACT. 112.)—No one goes to law without an action, and no one can bring an action without a writ or bill.

1531. **Nemo tenetur ad impossibile.** (JENK. CENT. 7.)—No one is bound to an impossibility.

· 1532. **Nemo tenetur armare adversarium suum contra se.** (COKE, LITT. 36. a.)—No one is bound to arm his adversary against himself.

1533. **Nemo tenetur divinare.** (4 COKE, 28.) —No one is bound to foretell.

1534. **Nemo tenetur edere instrumenta contra se.** (BELL, DIC.)—No one is bound to produce writings against himself.

1535. **Nemo tenetur informare qui nescit, sed quisquis scire quod informat.** (LANE, 110.) —No one who is ignorant is bound to give information, but everyone ought to know that of which he gives information.

1536. **Nemo tenetur jurare in suam turpitudinem.** (BELL, DIC.)—No one is bound to testify to his own baseness.

1537. **Nemo tenetur prodere seipsum.** (1 GR. EV. 224.)—No one is bound to expose himself.

1538. **Nemo tenetur seipsum accusare.** (3 BULS. 50.)—No one is bound to accuse himself.

1539. **Nemo tenetur seipsum infortuniis et periculis exponere.** (COKE, LITT. 253. b.)—No one is bound to expose himself to misfortunes and dangers.

1540. Nemo videtur fraudare eos qui sciunt et consentiunt. (DIG. 20. 17. 145.)—No one is considered as defrauding those who know and consent.

1541. Neque leges neque senatus consulta ita scribi possunt ut omnis casus qui quando que in sed. riunt comprehendantur. (HALK. 100.)— Neither laws nor acts of parliament can be so written as to include all possible cases.

1542. Nihil aliud potest rex quam quod de jure potest. (11 COKE, 74.)—The king can do nothing but what he can do by law.

1543. Nihil consensui tam contrarium est quam vis atque metus. (DIG. 50. 17. 116.)— Nothing is so contrary to consent as force and fear.

1544. Nihil cuiquam expedit quod per leges non licet. (HALK. 103.)—No one can profit by what is contrary to law.

1545. Nihil dat qui non habet. (2 BOU. 141.) —He who has nothing gives nothing.

1546. Nihil est ad conciliandum gratius verecundia. (WHART. 689.)—There is nothing more agreeable to conciliation than mutual respect.

1547. Nihil est enim liberale quod non idem justum. (2 KENT, COM. 441.)—There is nothing generous which is not at the same time just.

1548. Nihil facit error nominis cum de corpore constat. (11 COKE, 21.)—An error of name is nothing when there is certainty as to the person.

1549. Nihil fit a tempore; quamquam nihil non fit in tempore. (Tray. 374.)—Nothing is done by time, although everything is done in time.

1550. Nihil habet forum ex scena. (2 Bou. 141.)—The court has nothing to do with what is not before it.

1551. Nihil in lege intolerabilius est, eandem rem diverso jure censeri. (4 Coke, 93.)—Nothing in law is more intolerable than to rule a similar case by a diverse law.

1552. Nihil infra regnum subditos magis conservat in tranquillitate et concordia quam debita legum administratio. (2 Inst. 158.)—Nothing more preserves in tranquillity and concord those subjected to the government than a due administration of the laws.

1553. Nihil iniquius quam æquitatem nimis intendere. (Halk. 103.)—Nothing is so unjust as to extend equity too far.

1554. Nihil interest ipso jure quis actionem non habeat an per exceptionem infirmetur. (Halk. 101.)—The law does not concern itself as to who may not have the right to an action, or who may be injured by an exception.

1555. Nihil magis justum est quam quod necessarium est. (Dav. 32.)—Nothing is more just than what is necessary.

1556. **Nihil nequam est præsumendum.** (2 P WILL. 583.)—Nothing wicked is to be presumed.

1557. **Nihil perfectum est dum aliquid restat agendum.** (9 COKE, 9.)—Nothing is perfect while something remains to be done.

1558. **Nihil peti potest ante id tempus, quo per rerum naturam persolvi possit.** (DIG. 50. 17. 186.)—Nothing can be demanded before that time when, in the nature of things, it can be paid.

1559. **Nihil possumus contra veritatem.** (DOCT. & STUD. 2. 6.)—We can do nothing against truth.

1560. **Nihil præscribitur nisi quod possidetur.** (5 BAR. & ALD. 277.)—There is no prescription for that which is not possessed.

1561. **Nihil quod est contra rationem est licitum.** (COKE, LITT. 97. b.)—Nothing which is against reason is lawful.

1562. **Nihil simile est idem.** (TAYLER, 343.)—Nothing similar is identical.

1563. **Nihil simul inventum est et perfectum.** (COKE, LITT. 230. a.)—Nothing is invented and perfected at the same moment.

1564. **Nihil tam conveniens est naturali æquitati, quam unumquodque dissolvi eo ligamine quo ligatum est.** (4 INST. 28.)—Nothing is so consonant to natural equity, as that the same thing be dissolved by the same means by which it was bound.

1565. Nihil tam conveniens est naturali æquitati, quam voluntatem domini rem suam in alium transferre, ratum habere. (1 COKE, 100.) —Nothing is so consonant to natural equity as to regard the wish of the owner in transferring his own property to another.

1566. Nihil tam proprium est imperio quam legibus vivere. (2 INST. 63.)—Nothing is so becoming to authority, as to live according to the law.

1567. Nil agit exemplum litem quod lite resolvit. (15 WEND. 44. 49.)—An example does no good which settles one question by asking another.

1568. Nil sine prudenti fecit ratione vetustas. (COKE, LITT. 65. a.)—Antiquity did nothing without a good reason.

1569. Nil temere novandum. (JENK. CENT. 163.)—Nothing should be rashly changed.

1570. Nil utile aut honestum quod legibus contrarium. (LOFFT, 95.)—Nothing is useful or honorable that is contrary to law.

1571. Nimia certitudo certitudinem ipsam destruit. (LOFFT, 244.)—Too great certainty destroys certainty itself.

1572. Nimia subtilitas in jure reprobatur. (4 COKE, 5.)—Too great subtlety is disapproved in law.

1573. Nimium altercando veritas amittitur. (Hob. ᴠ 334.)—By too much altercation truth is lost.

1574. No man can hold the same land immediately of two several landlords. (Coke, Litt. 152. b).

1575. No man shall set up his infamy as a defense. (2 Bou. 142).

1576. No man shall take by deed, but by parties, unless in remainder. (2 Bou. 142).

1577. No one can grant or convey what he does not own. (25 Barb. N. Y. 284. 301).

1578. No statute is to have a retrospect beyond the time of its commencement. (Whart. Max. 316).

1579. Nobiles magis plectuntur pecunia; plebes vero in corpore. (3 Inst. 220.)—The higher classes are more punished in money; but the lower in person.

1580. Nobiles sunt qui arma gentilitia antecessorum suorum proferre possunt. (2 Inst. 595.)—The gentry are those who are able to produce armorial bearings, derived by descent from their own ancestors.

1581. Nobiliores et benigniores præsumptiones in dubiis sunt præferendæ. (Jur. Civ.) —In cases of doubt the more generous and more benign presumptions are to be preferred.

1582. Nobilitas est duplex, superior et inferior. (2 Inst. 583.)—There are two sorts of nobility, the higher and the lower.

1683 **Nomen dicitur a noscendo,' quia notitiam facit.** (6 COKE, 65.)—A name is called from the word to know, because it makes recognition.

1584. **Nomen est quasi rei notamen.** (11 COKE, 20.)—A name is as it were, the note of a thing.

1585. **Nomen non sufficit si res non sit de jure aut de facto.** (4 COKE, 107.)—A name does not suffice, if the thing does not exist either by law or by fact.

1586. **Nomina si nescis perit cognitio rerum.** (COKE, LITT. 86. b.)—If you know not the names of things, the knowledge of things themselves perishes.

1587. **Nomina sunt mutabilia, res autem immobilis.** (6 COKE, 66.)—Names are mutable, but things immutable.

1588. **Nomina sunt symbola rerum.** (GODB.) —Names are the symbols of things.

1589. **Non accipi debent verba in demonstratio nem falsam quæ competunt in limitationem veram.** (BAC. MAX. 13.)—Words which agree in a true meaning should not be received in a false sense.

1590. **Non alienat qui duntaxat omittit possessionem.** (HALK. 104.)—He does not alienate who merely gives up possession.

1591. **Non alio modo puniatur aliquis, quam secundum quod se habet condemnatio.** (3 INST.

217.)—A person may not be punished differently than according to what the sentence enjoins.

1592. Non aliter a significatione verborum recedi oportet quam cum manifestum est aliud sensisse testatorem. (DIG. 32. 69. PR.)—The usual meaning of words should not be departed from, unless it is manifest that the testator used them in another sense.

1593. Non autem deperditæ dicuntur, si postea recuperantur. (TAYLER, 345.)—Nothing may be said to be lost which is afterwards recovered.

1594. Non concedantur citationes priusquam exprimatur super qua ne fieri debet citatio. (12 COKE, 47.)—Summonses should not be granted before it is expressed upon what grounds the summons should be made.

1595. Non consentit qui errat. (BRACT. 44.) —He who errs does not consent.

1596. Non creditur referenti, nisi constet de relato. (TRAY. 381.)—The reference is not to be credited, unless the thing referred to be proved.

1597. Non crimen per se neque privatum damnum, sed publicum malum, leges spectant. (LOFFT, 467.)—The law regards a crime not only as a private injury in itself, but as a public evil.

1598. Non dat qui contra leges dat. (LOFFT, 258.)—He gives nothing who gives contrary to law.

(13)

1599. Non debet adduci exceptio ejus rei cujus petitur dissolutio. (JENK. CENT. 37.)—An exception of the thing whose abolition is sought, ought not to be adduced.

1600. Non debet alteri per alterum iniqua conditio inferri. (DIG. 50. 17. 74.)—No one should be placed in a bad position by the act of another.

1601. Non debet, cui plus licet, quod minus est, non licere. (DIG. 50. 17. 21.)—He who is allowed to do the greater may with more reason do the less.

1602. Non decet homines dedere causa non cognita. (4 JOHNS. CH. N. Y. 106. 114.)—It is not proper to surrender the persons of men when no cause is shown.

1603. Non decipitur qui scit se decipi. (5 COKE, 60.)—He is not deceived who knows himself to be deceived.

1604. Non defendere videtur qui præsens negat se defendere. (HALK. 106.)—He who does not defend himself when present is considered as submitting.

1605. Non differunt quæ concordant re, tametsi non in verbis iisdem. (JENK. CENT. 70.) —Those things which agree in substance, though not in the same words, do not differ.

1606. Non definitur in jure quid sit conatus. (6 COKE, 42.)—What an attempt is, is not defined in law.

1607. **Non dubitatur, etsi specialiter venditor evictionem non promiserit, re evicta, ex empto competere actionem.** (DOCT. & STUD. 2. 47.)—It is certain that although the vendor has not given a special guarantee, an action EX EMPTO lies against him, if the purchaser be evicted.

1608. **Non effecit affectus nisi sequatur effectus. Sed in atrocioribus delictis punitur affectus, licet non sequatur effectus.** (2 ROL. 89.) —The intention fulfils nothing unless an effect follows. But in deeper delinquencies the intention is punished, though no effect follow.

1609. **Non est arctius vinculum inter homines quam jusjurandum.** (JENK. CENT. 126.)—There is no stronger link among men than an oath.

1610. **Non est deleganda reipublicæ cura personæ non idoneæ.** (LOFFT, 329.)—The affairs of the republic should not be delegated to improper persons.

1611. **Non est disputandum contra principia negantem.** (COKE, LITT. 343. a.)—There is no disputing against a man denying principles.

1612. **Non est lex sed servitus, ad ea teneri quibus non consenseris.** (LOFFT, 11)—It is not law but servitude to be held by what we have not consented to.

1613. **Non est novum ut priores legis ad posteriores trahantur.** (DIG. 1. 3. 26.)—It is no new thing that prior statutes give place to later ones.

1614. **Non est regula quin fallat.** (OFF. EX. 212.)—There is no rule which may not fail.

1615. **Non est singulis concedendum, quod per magistratum publice possit fieri.** (DIG. 50. 17. 176.)—That is not to be conceded to individuals which may be publicly done by a magistrate.

1616. **Non ex opinionibus singulorum, sed ex communi usu, nomini exaudiri debent.** (DIG. 83. 10. 7. 2.)—Names of things should be understood according to common usage, not according to the opinions of individuals.

1617. **Non exemplis, sed legibus, judicandum.** (TRAY. 383.)—Things should be judged by laws, not by examples.

1618. **Non facias malum ut inde veniat bonum.** (11 COKE, 74.)—You are not to do evil that good may come of it.

1619. **Non impedit clausula derogatoria, quo minus ab eadem potestate res dissolvantur a qua constituuntur.** (BAC. MAX. 19.)—A derogatory clause does not prevent acts from being dissolved by the same power which constituted them.

1620. **Non in legendo sed in intelligendo leges consistunt.** (8 COKE, 167.)—The laws consist not in being read but in being understood.

1621. **Non jus ex regula, sed regula ex jure.** (TRAY. 384.)—The law does not arise from the rule, but the rule from the law.

1622. **Non jus, sed seisina, facit stipitem.**

(FLETA, 6. 14.)—Not right; but seisin, makes a stock.

1623. **Non licet quod dispendio licet.** (COKE, LITT. 127. a.)—That which is permitted at a loss is not permitted.

1624. **Non multum distant a brutis qui ratione carent.** (4 COKE, 126.)—Not far removed from brutes are those who are wanting in reason.

1625. **Non obligat lex nisi promulgata.** (2 BOU. 143.)—A law is not obligatory unless it be promulgated.

1626. **Non observata forma infertur adnullatio actus.** (12 COKE, 7.)—When form is not observed it is inferred that the act is annulled.

1627. **Non officit conatus nisi sequatur effectus.** (11 COKE, 98.)—The attempt does no harm unless the consequence follow.

1628. **Non omne damnum inducit injuriam.** (3 BLACK. COM. 219.)—Not every loss produces an injury.

1629. **Non omne quod licet honestum est.** (DIG. 50. 17. 144.)—Not everything which is permitted by law is honorable.

1630. **Non omnium quæ a majoribus nostris constituta sunt ratio reddi potest.** (DIG. 1. 3. 20.) —A reason cannot be given for all the things which were instituted by our ancestors.

1631. **Non pertinet ad judicem secularem cognoscere de iis quæ sunt mere spiritualia annexa.** (2 INST. 488.)—It pertains not to the secular judge to take cognizance of things purely spiritual.

1632. **Non possessori incumbit necessitas probandi possessiones ad se pertinere.** (BR. 714.)—The necessity of proving possession of his own property is not incumbent upon the owner.

1633. **Non potest adduci exceptio ejusdem rei, cujus petitur dissolutio.** (BAC. MAX. 2.)—A plea of the same matter whose dissolution is sought, cannot be made.

1634. **Non potest probari quod probatum non relevat.** (1 EXCH. 91. 92. 102.)—That cannot be proved, which when proved is irrelevant.

1635. **Non potest quis sine brevi agere.** (FLETA, 1. 2. 13.)—No one can sue without a writ.

1636. **Non potest rex gratiam facere cum injuria et damno aliorum.** (3 INST. 236.)—The king cannot confer a favor on one subject which occasions injury and loss to others.

1637. **Non potest videri desisse habere, qui nunquam habuit.** (DIG. 50. 17. 208.)—He may not be regarded as having ceased to have a thing, who never had it.

1638. **Non præstat impedimentum quod de jure non sortitur effectum.** (JENK. CENT. 162.)—An impediment which does not by law produce a consequence, avails nothing.

1639. **Non quod dictum est, sed quod factum est, inspicitur.** (COKE, LITT. 36. a.)—Not what is said, but what is done, is to be regarded.

1640. **Non recusat ad minora dimittere lex.** (RILEY, 7.)—The law does not refuse to descend to the smallest details.

1641. **Non refert an quis assensum suum præbet verbis, an rebus ipsis et factis.** (10 COKE, 52.)—It matters not whether a man gives his assent by words, or by acts and deeds.

1642. **Non refert quid notum sit judici, si notum non sit in forma judicii.** (3 BULS. 115.)—It matters not what is known to the judge, if it be not known to him judicially.

1643. **Non refert quid ex æquipollentibus fiat.** (5 COKE, 122.)—That which is gathered from equivalent expressions is of no consequence.

1644. **Non refert verbis an factis fit revocatio.** (CRO. CAR. 49.)—It matters not if a revocation is made by word or deed.

1645. **Non respondebit minor nisi in causa dotis, et hoc pro favore doti.** (2 BOU. 143.)—A minor shall not answer, unless in a case of dower, and this in favor of dower.

1646. **Non solent quæ abundant vitiare scripturas.** (DIG. 50. 17. 94.)—Superfluity does not usually vitiate writings.

1647. **Non solet deterior conditio fieri eorum qui litem contestati sunt quam si non, sed plerumque melior.** (HALK. 107.)—Those who contest a suit, do not make their condition worse than if they had not, but rather better.

1648. **Non solum quid licet, sed quid est**

conveniens considerandum; quia nihil quod inconveniens est licitum. (COKE, LITT. 66. a.)—Not only what is permitted, but what is proper, is to be considered; because nothing which is improper is illegal.

1649. Non sunt longa ubi nihil est quod demere possis. (VAUGH. 138.)—There is no prolixity where there is nothing which can be spared.

1650. Non temere credere, est nervus sapientiæ. (5 COKE, 114.)—Not to believe rashly is the nerve of wisdom.

1651. Non valet impedimentum quod de jure non sortitur effectum. (4 COKE, 31.)—An impediment is of no consequence, which by law has no effect.

1652. Non verbis sed ipsis rebus, leges imponimus. (CODE, 6. 43. 2.)—We impose law upon things themselves, not upon words.

1653. Non videntur qui errant consentire. (DIG. 50. 17. 116.)—Those who err are not considered as consenting.

1654. Non videtur perfecte cujusque id esse, quod ex casu auferri potest. (DIG. 50. 17. 159. 1.)—That is not considered as truly belonging to any one, which upon occasion, can be taken from him.

1655. Non videtur quisquam id capere quod ei necesse est alii restituere. (DIG. 50. 17. 51.)—One is not regarded as owning a thing which he is obliged to restore.

1656. Non videntur rem amittere quibus propria non fuit. (DIG. 50. 17. 85.)—They cannot be said to lose a thing whose own it was not.

1657. Non videtur consensum retinuisse si quis ex præscripto minantis aliquid immutavit. (BAC. MAX. 22.)—He does not appear to have retained consent who has changed anything through the menaces of a party threatening.

1658. Non videtur vim facere, qui jure suo utitur, et ordinaria actione experitur. (DIG. 50. 17. 155. 1.)—He is not regarded as using force, who exercises his own right, and proceeds by ordinary action.

1659. Noscitur a sociis. (BR. 588.)—The meaning of a word may be ascertained by reference to the meaning of words associated with it.

1660. Noscitur ex socio qui non cognoscitur ex se. (MOORE, 817.)—He who cannot be known from himself, may be known from his associates.

1661. Nothing shall be void, which by possibility may be good. (NOY, 23).

1662. Nothus nullius est filius. (LOFFT, 223.)—A bastard is nobody's son.

1663. Nova constitutio futuris formam imponere debet, non præteritis. (2 INST. 292.)—A new enactment ought to impose form upon what is to come, not upon what is past.

n præsumitur. (HALK. 109.)
to be presumed.

n tam utilitate prodest quam
(JENK. CENT. 167.)—Novelty
by its utility, as it disturbs by

iiicium non dat jus novum,
im. (10 COKE, 42.)—A new
iake a new law, but declares

itur caput. (HEIN. EL. JUR.
s the person.
tio obligationem non parit.
naked promise does not make

actum est ubi nulla subest
entionem; sed ubi subest
it parit actionem. (PLOWD.
act is where there is no con-
t the agreement; but where
on, an obligation exists, and

ctum inefficax ad agendum.
ed agreement is insufficient

ria mala ducunt. (TAYLER,
serious harm.
a advantage de son tort
713.)—No one can take ad-
vrong.

1673. **Nul sans damage avera error ou attaint.** (JENK. CENT. 323.)—No one shall have error or attaint without loss.

1674. **Nulla curia quæ recordum non habet potest imponere finem neque aliquem mandare carceri; quia ista spectant tantummodo ad curias de recordo.** (8 COKE, 60.)—No court which has not a record, can impose a fine, or commit any person to prison; because those powers belong only to courts of record.

1675. **Nulla impossibilia aut inhonesta sunt præsumenda; vera autem, et honesta, et possibilia.** (COKE, LITT. 78. b.)—No impossible, or dishonest things are to be presumed; but things true, honorable and possible.

1676. **Nulla pactione effici potest ut dolos præstetur.** (DIG. 2. 14. 27. 3.)—It cannot be effected by any agreement, that there is no accountability for fraud.

1677. **Nulla pæna capitis nulla quæ hominum remve ejus destruat esse potest nisi legibus præfinita.** (LOFFT, 466.)—There can be no capital punishment destructive either to the individual or his property, which is not established by law before the fact.

1678. **Nulla res vehementius rempublicam continet quam fides.** (LOFFT, 618.)—Nothing binds the Republic more closely than the fidelity of its citizens.

1679. **Nulle regle sans faute.** (2 BOU. 144.)—There is no rule without fault.

1680. Nulle terre sans seigneur. (GUY. INST. FEOD. 28.)—No land without a lord.

1681. Nulli enim res sua servit jure servitutis. (DIG. 8. 2. 26.)—No one can have a servitude over his own property.

1682. Nulli vendemus, nulli negabimus, aut differimus justitiam vel rectum. (LOFFT, 64.)—Neither justice nor right shall be sold, denied, or delayed, to any one.

1683. Nullius charta legibus potest derogare. (LOFFT, 245.)—No written deed can derogate from the laws.

1684. Nullius hominis auctoritas apud nos valere debet, ut meliora non sequeremur si quis attulerit. (COKE, LITT. 383. a.)—The authority of no man ought to prevail with us, so that we should not follow better opinions, should another present them.

1685. Nullum crimen majus est inobedientia. (JENK. CENT. 77.)—No crime is greater than disobedience.

1686. Nullum crimen patitur is qui non prohibet cum prohibere non potest. (HALK. 110.)—He is not guilty of a crime who fails to prevent what he cannot prevent.

1687. Nullum damnum sine remedio. (LOFFT, 36.)—There is no loss without a remedy.

1688. Nullum exemplum est idem omnibus. (COKE, LITT. 212. a.)—No example is the same to all.

1689. **Nullum iniquum est in jure præsumendum.** (4 COKE, 72.)—No iniquity is to be presumed in law.

1690. **Nullum matrimonium, ibi nulla dos.** (4 BARB. N. Y. 192. 194.)—No marriage, no dower.

1691. **Nullum medicamentum est idem omnibus.** (COKE, LITT. 417. b.)—No medicine is the same to all.

1692. **Nullum tempus aut locus occurrit reipublicæ.** (11 GRAT. 572.)—Neither time nor place affects the republic.

1693. **Nullum tempus occurrit regi.** (2 INST. 273.)—Lapse of time does not bar the right of the crown.

1694. **Nullus alius quam rex possit episcopo de mandare inquisitionem faciendam.** (COKE, LITT. 134. b.)—No other than the king can command the bishop to make an inquisition.

1695. **Nullus commodum capere potest de injuria sua propria.** (COKE, LITT. 148. b.)—No one shall obtain an advantage by his own wrong.

1696. **Nullus debet agere de dolo, ubi alia actio subest.** (4 COKE, 92.)—Where another form of action is given, no one ought to sue in the action DE DOLO.

1697. **Nullus dicitur accessorius post feloniam sed ille qui novit principalem feloniam fecisse, et illum receptavit et comfortavit.** (3 INST. 138.)— No one is called an accessory after the fact, but he who knew the principal to have committed a felony, and received and comforted him.

1698. **Nullus dicitur felo principalis nisi actor, aut qui præsens est, abettans aut auxilians ad feloniam faciendam.** (3 INST. 138.) —No one shall be called a principal felon except the party actually committing the felony, or the party present, aiding and abetting in its commission.

1699. **Nullus jus alienum forisfacere potest.** (FLETA, 1. 28. 11.)—No man can forfeit the right of another.

1700. **Nullus recedat e curia cancellaria sine remedio.** (YEAR B. 4. H. VII. 4.)—Let no one depart from the court of chancery without a remedy.

1701. **Nullus videtur dolo facere qui suo jure utitur.** (DIG. 50. 17. 55.)—No one should be esteemed a wrong doer who uses his own legal right.

1702. **Numerus certus pro incerto ponitur.** (TAYLER, 359.)—A certain number is to be substituted for one which is uncertain.

1703. **Nummus est mensura rerum commutandarum.** (WHART. 709.)—Money is the measure of things that are to be changed.

1704. **Nunquam concluditur in falso.** (WHART. 710.)—Nothing is falsely concluded.

1705. **Nunquam crescit ex post facto præteriti delicti æstimatio.** (DIG. 50. 17. 138. 1.)—

The character of a past offence is never aggravated by a subsequent act.

1706. **Nunquam decurritur ad extraordina-rium sed ubi deficit ordinarium.** (4 INST. 84.)—We are never to recur to what is extraordinary, until what is ordinary fails.

1707. **Nunquam nimis dicitur quod nunquam satis dicitur.** (COKE, LITT. 375. b.)—What is never sufficiently said is never said too much.

1708. **Nunquam præscribitur in falso.** (BELL, DIC.)—There is never prescription in case of false-hood.

1709. **Nunquam res humanæ prospere suc-cedunt ubi negliguntur divinæ.** (COKE, LITT. 95. b.)—Human affairs never prosper where things divine are neglected.

1710. **Nuptias non concubitas, sed consensus, facit.** (COKE, LITT. 33. a.)—Not cohabitation, but consent makes the marriage.

O.

1711. **Ob reverentiam personarium et metum perjurii.** (HALK. 113.)—The embarrassment of a witness proceeds from his respect for an oath, and his dread of perjury.

1712. **Obtemperandum est consuetudini ra-**

tionabili tanquam legi. (4 COKE, 38.)—A reasonable custom is to be obeyed as law.

1713. Occultatio thesauri inventi fraudulosa. (3 INST. 133.)—The concealment of discovered treasure is fraudulent.

1714. Occupantis fiunt derelicta. (1 PET. ADM. 58.)—Things abandoned become the property of the occupant.

1715. Odio et amore judex careat. (LOFFT, 59.)—Let a judge be free from hatred and love.

1716. Odiosa et inhonesta non sunt in lege præsumenda. (COKE, LITT. 78. b.)—Odious and dishonest things are not to be presumed in law.

1717. Officers may not examine the judicial acts of the court. (2 BOU. 145).

1718. Officia judicialia non concedantur antequam vacent. (11 COKE, 4.)—Judicial offices are not to be granted before they are vacant.

1719. Officia magistratus non debent esse venalia. (COKE, LITT. 234. a.)—The offices of magistrates ought not to be sold.

1720. Officium nemini debet esse damnosum. (BELL, DIC.)—An office ought to be injurious to no one.

1721. Officit conatus, si effectus sequatur. (JENK. CENT. 55.)—The attempt becomes of consequence if the effect follow.

1722. Omissio eorum quæ tacite insunt nihil operatur. (2 BULS. 131.)—The omission of those things that are silently expressed is of no consequence.

1723. **Omne actum ab intentione agentis est judicandum; a voluntate procedit causa vitii atque virtutis.** (JUR. CIV.)—Every act is to be estimated by the intention of the doer; the cause of vice and virtue proceeds from the will.

1724. **Omne crimen ebrietas et incendit et detegit.** (COKE, LITT. 247. a.)—Drunkenness both lights up and reveals every crime.

1725. **Omne jus aut consensus fecit, aut necessitas constituit, aut firmavit consuetudo.** (DIG. 1. 3. 40.)—Every law has either been created by consent, or established by necessity, or confirmed by custom.

1726. **Omne magnum exemplum habet aliquid ex iniquo, quod publica utilitate compensatur.** (HOB. 279.)—Every great example has something of injustice, which is compensated by its public utility.

1727. **Omne sacramentum debet esse de certa scientia.** (4 INST. 279.)—Every oath ought to be founded on certain knowledge.

1728. **Omne testamentum morte consummatum est.** (3 COKE, 29.)—Every will is completed by death.

1729. **Omne verbum de ore fideli cadit in debitum.** (TRAY. 404.)—Every word sincerely spoken constitutes an obligation.

1730. **Omnes homines aut liberi sunt aut servi.** (FLETA, 1. 1. 2.)—All men are either freemen or slaves.

1731. Omnes in defensionem reipublicæ vita bonisque omnibus cives tenentur. (LOFFT, 172.) —All citizens are bound to defend the republic with all their lives and possessions.

1732. Omnes licentiam habere his quæ pro se indulta sunt, renunciare. (CODE, 2. 3. 29.)— All shall have liberty to renounce those things which have been established in their favor.

1733. Omnes sorores sunt quasi unus hæres de una hæreditate. (COKE, LITT. 67. a.)—All sisters are as it were, one heir to one inheritance.

1734. Omnes subditi sunt regis servi. (JENK. CENT. 126.)—All subjects are the king's servants.

1735. Omnia delicta in aperto leviora sunt. (8 Coke, 127.)—All crimes done openly are lighter.

1736. Omnia honeste et ordine fiant. (LOFFT, 138.)—Let all things be done honestly and in order.

1737. Omnia libere et legaliter facienda. (TAYLER, 369.)—All things should be done freely and legally.

1738. Omnia præsumuntur contra spoliatorem. (WHART. 717.)—All things are to be presumed against a wrong doer.

1739. Omnia præsumuntur legitime facta donec probetur in contrarium. (COKE, LITT. 232. b.)—All things are presumed to be legitimately done, until it be proved to the contrary.

1740. Omnia præsumuntur solemniter esse

acta. (COKE, LITT. 6. b.)—All things are presumed to be done solemnly.

1741. **Omnia quæ jure contrahuntur, contrario jure pereunt.** (DIG. 50. 17. 100.)—All contracts made under a law, perish under a contrary law.

1742. **Omnia quæcunque causæ cognitionem desiderant per libellum expedire non possunt.** (HALK. 115.)—It is not possible to explain in a memorial all things requiring cognizance.

1743. **Omnia quæ movent ad mortem sunt deodanda.** (3 INST. 57.)—All things which move to death are deodands.

1744. **Omnia uxoris durante conjugio mariti sunt.** (LOFFT, 215.)—All things belonging to the wife are also the husband's while the marriage continues.

1745. **Omnibus infra regnum orantibus legis remedium patet.** (LOFFT, 152.)—The remedy of the law lies open to all within the kingdom who ask it.

1746. **Omnis actio est loquela.** (COKE, LITT. 292. a.)—Every action is a complaint.

1747. **Omnis conclusio boni et veri judicii sequitur ex bonis et veris præmissis et dictis juratorum.** (COKE, LITT. 226. b.)—Every conclusion of a good and true judgment arises from good and true premises, and sayings of juries.

1748. **Omnis contractus turpitudinis legibus invisus.** (LOFFT, 190.)—Every dishonorable contract is odious to the laws.

1749. Omnis definitio in jure periculosa est, parum est enim ut non subverti possit. (DIG. 50. 17. 202.)—Every definition in law is dangerous, for there is but little that can not be overthrown.

1750. Omnis indemnatus pro innoxio legibus habetur. (LOFFT, 121.)—Every uncondemned person is held by the law as innocent.

1751. Omnis innovatio plus novitate perturbat quam utilitate prodest. (2 BULS. 338.)—Every innovation disturbs more by its novelty, than benefits by its utility.

1752. Omnis interpretatio, si fieri potest, ita fienda est in instrumentis, ut omnes contrarietates amoveantur. (JENK. CENT. 96.)—Every interpretation, if it can be done, is to be so made in instruments, that all contradictions may be removed.

1753. Omnis lascivia legibus vetita. (LOFFT, 106.)—All lasciviousness is contrary to law.

1754. Omnis nova constitutio futuris temporibus formam imponere debet, non præteritis. (2 INST. 95.)—Every new statute should give a form to future times, not to past.

1755. Omnis privatio præsupponit habitum. (COKE, LITT. 339. a.)—Every privation presupposes former enjoyment.

1756. Omnis prohibitio mandato equiparatur. (TAYLER, 308.)—Every prohibition is equivalent to a command.

1757. Omnis querela et omnis actio injuriarum limita est infra certa tempora. (COKE, LITT. 114. b.)—Every plaint and every action for injuries is limited within certain times.

1758. Omnis ratihabitio retro trahitur et mandato priori aequiparatur. (COKE, LITT. 207. a.)—Every ratification of an act already done has a retrospective effect, and is equal to a prior command.

1759. Omnis regula suas patitur exceptiones et omnis exceptio est regula. (2 BOU. 146.)—Every rule is subject to its own exceptions, and every exception is a rule.

1760. Omnium rerum quarum usus est, potest esse abusus, virtute solo excepta. (DAV. 79.)—There may be an abuse of everything of which there is a use, virtue alone excepted.

1761. Once a fraud, always a fraud. (13 VIN. ABR. 539).

1762. Once a mortgage, always a mortgage. (1 HILL. REAL PROP. 378).

1763. Once a recompense, always a recompense. (19 VIN. ABR. 277).

1764. Once quit and cleared, ever quit and cleared. (2 BOU. 146).

1765. One may not do an act to himself. (2 BOU. 146).

1766. One should be just before he is generous. (2 BOU. 146).

1767. One thing shall inure for another. (NOY, 41).

1768. Opinio quæ favet testamento est tenenda. (1 W. BL. 13. ARG.)—That opinion is to be followed which favors the will.

1769. Oportet quod certa res deducatur in judicium. (JENK. CENT. 84.)—A thing certain must be brought to judgment.

1770. Oportet quod certa sit res quæ venditur. (BRACT. 61.)—A thing which is to be sold, must be certain.

1771. Oportet quod certæ personæ, certæ terræ, et certi status, comprehendantur in declaratione usuum. (9 COKE, 9.)—It is right that certain persons, lands, and certain estates should be comprehended in a declaration of uses.

1772. Oportet legum brevum esses, quo facilius ab imperitis teneatur. (RILEY, 201.)—Laws should be short, that they may be more easily comprehended by the ignorant.

1773. Opposita juxta se posita magis elucescunt. (15 BAC. 139.)—Things opposite when placed together appear in a clearer light.

1774. Optima est legum interpres consuetudo. (DIG. 1. 3. 37.)—Custom is the best interpreter of laws.

1775. Optima est lex quæ minimum relinquit arbitrio judicis. (BAC. APH. 46.)—That law is the best which leaves least to the discretion of the judge.

1776. Optima evidentia rei prævalebit. (TAYLER, 371.)—The best evidence of the matter will prevail.

1777. Optima statuti interpretratrix est (omnibus particulis ejusdem inspectis) ipsum statutum. (8 COKE, 117.)—The best interpreter of a statute is (all the separate parts being considered) the statute itself.

1778. Optimus interpres rerum usus. (2 INST. 282.)—Usage is the best interpreter of things.

1779. Optimus interpretandi modus est sic leges interpretare ut leges legibus concordant. (8 COKE, 169.)—The best mode of interpretation, is so to interpret that the laws may accord with the laws.

1780. Optimus judex, qui minimum sibi. (BAC. APH. 46.)—He is the best judge who relies least upon his own opinion.

1781. Ordine placitandi servato, servatur et jus. (COKE, LITT. 303. a.)—The order of pleading being preserved, the law is preserved.

1782. Origine propria neminem posse voluntate sua eximi manifestum est. (1 BLACK. COM. 10.)—It is manifest that no one can by his own will renounce his natural allegiance.

1783. Origo rei inspici debet. (COKE, LITT. 248. b.)—The origin of a thing ought to be regarded.

P.

1784. Paci sunt maxime contraria, vis et injuria. (COKE, LITT. 161. b.)—Violence and injury are especially contrary to peace.

1785. Pacta conventa, quæ neque contra leges, neque dolo malo inita sunt, omni modo observanda sunt. (CODE, 2. 3. 29.)—Contracts which are not against law, and do not originate in fraud, are in all respects to be observed.

1786. Pacta dant legem contractui. (HALK. 118.)—Agreements give the law to the contract.

1787. Pacta privata juri publico derogare non possunt. (7 COKE, 23.)—Private contracts cannot derogate from public right.

1788. Pacta quæ contra leges constitutionesque vel contra bonos mores fiunt, nullam vim habere, indubitati juris est. (CODE, 2. 3. 6.)—That contracts which are made against law or against good morals, have no force, is a principle of undoubted law.

1789. Pacta quæ turpem causam continent non sunt observanda. (DIG. 2. 14. 27. 4.)—Contracts founded upon an immoral consideration are not to be observed.

1790. Pacta reciproca vel utrosque ligant vel neutrum. (LOFFT, 193.)—Mutual contracts bind either both parties, or neither one.

1791. Pacta traditione firmantur. (HALK. 175.)—Agreements are confirmed by delivery.

1792. Pacto aliquid licitum est, quod sine pacto non admittitur. (COKE, LITT. 166. a.)—By a contract something is permitted, which, without it, could not be admitted.

1793. Pactum de assedatione facienda et ipsa assedatione æquiparantur. (TRAY. 417.)—An agreement to grant a lease is equivalent to the lease itself.

1794. Par in parem imperium non habet. (JENK. CENT. 174.)—An equal has no power over an equal.

1795. Parens est nomen generale ad omne genus cognationis. (COKE, LITT. 80. b.)—Parent is a general name for every kind of relationship.

1796. Parentum est liberos alere etiam nothos. (LOFFT, 222.)—The parents of a bastard are liable for his support.

1797. Paria copulantur cum paribus. (15 BAC. 41.)—Like things unite with like.

1798. Paribus sententiis reus absolvitur. (4 INST. 64.)—When opinions are equal the defendant is acquitted.

1799. Paries oneri ferundo uti nunc est ita sit. (TRAY. 423.)—The party wall is to remain intact for both tenements forever.

1800. Parium eadem est ratio, idem jus. (WHART. 738.)—Of things equal, the reason and the law is the same.

1801. **Parte quacunque integrante sublata, tollitur totum.** (8 COKE, 41.)—An integral part being taken away, the whole is taken away.

1802. **Participes plures sunt quasi unum corpus, in eo quod unum jus habent.** (COKE, LITT. 164. a.)—Many partners are as one body, inasmuch as they have one right.

1803. **Parties are presumed to know the law upon the undisputed facts of their case.** (37 BARB. N. Y. 476. 479).

1804. **Partus ex legitimo thoro non certius noscit matrem quam genitorem suum.** (FORTESC. 42.)—The offspring of a legitimate bed knows not his mother more certainly than his father.

1805. **Partus sequitur ventrem.** (2 BLACK. COM. 390.)—The offspring follows the mother.

1806. **Parum differunt quæ re concordant.** (2 BULS. 86.)—Things differ but little which agree in substance.

1807. **Parum est latam esse sententiam, nisi mandetur executioni.** (COKE, LITT. 289. b.)—It is not enough that sentence be given unless it be carried to execution.

1808. **Parum proficit scire quid fieri debet, si non cognoscas quo modo sit facturum.** (2 INST. 503.)—It profits little to know what ought to be done, if you know not how it is to be done.

1809. **Pater est quem nuptiæ demonstrant.** (1 BLACK. COM. 446. 454.)—He is the father whom marriage indicates.

1810. Pater et mater et puer sunt una caro. (WHART. 754.)—The father, mother and son are of one flesh.

1811. Paterfamilias ab alterius culpam tenetur sive servi sive liberi. (TAYLER, 377.)—The father is responsible for the misconduct of his child or his slave.

1812. Patria laboribus et expensis non debet fatigari. (JENK. CENT. 6.)—A jury ought not to be fatigued by labors and expenses.

1813. Patria potestas in pietate debet, non in atrocitate consistere. (TAYLER, 377.)—Parental power should consist in affection, not in barbarity.

1814. Patronum faciunt dos, ædificatio, fundus. (DOD. ADM. 6.)—Dower, building, and the land make the patron.

1815. Peccata contra naturam sunt gravissima. (3 INST. 20.)—Crimes against nature are the most heinous.

1816. Peccatum peccato addit qui culpæ quam facit patrocinium defensionis adjungit. (5 COKE, 49.)—He adds sin to sin who, when he commits an offense, joins the protection of a defense.

1817. Pendente lite nihil innovetur. (COKE, LITT. 344. b.)—Pending a suit nothing should be changed.

**1818. Per alluvionem id videtur adjici, quod ita paulatim adjicitur, ut intelligere non possumus quantum quoquo momento temporis adjiciatur. (DIG. 41. 1. 7. 1.)—That is considered to be added by alluvion, which is so added little by little that we cannot tell how much is added at any one moment of time.

1819. **Per rationes, pervenitur ad legitimam rationem.** (LITT. § 386.)—By reasoning we come to legal reason.

1820. **Per varios actus, legem experientia facit.** (4 INST. 50.)—By various acts experience frames the law.

1821. **Pereat unus ne pereant omnes.** (WHART. 764.)—Let one perish, rather than all.

1822. **Perfectum est cui nihil deest secundum suæ perfectionis, vel naturæ modum.** (HOB. 51.)—That is perfect to which nothing is wanting, according to the measure of its perfection or nature.

1823. **Periculosum est res novas et inusitatas inducere.** (COKE, LITT. 379. a.)—It is perilous to introduce new and untried things.

1824. **Periculosum existimo quod bonorum virorum non comprobatur exemplo.** (9 COKE, 97.)—I think that dangerous which is not warranted by the example of good men.

1825. **Periculum rei venditæ, nondum traditæ, est emptoris.** (2 KENT, COM. 498. 499.)—The risk of an article sold, and not yet delivered, is the purchaser's.

1826. **Perjuri sunt qui servatis verbis juramenti decipiunt aures eorem qui accipiunt.** (8

INST. 166.)—They are perjured, who, preserving the words of an oath, deceive the ears of those who receive it.

1827. Perjurii poena divina exitium; humana dedecus. (LOFFT, 46.)—The divine punishment of perjury is destruction ; the human punishment is disgrace.

1828. Perpetua lex est, nullam legem humanam ac positivam perpetuam esse. (BAC. MAX. 19.)—It is a perpetual law that no human or positive law can be perpetual.

1829. Perpetuitatibus lex obsistit. (HALK. 123.)—The law is opposed to perpetuities.

1830. Persona conjuncta aequiparatur interesse proprio. (BAC. MAX. 18.)—A union with a person is equivalent to one's own interest.

1831. Persona est homo, cum statu quodam consideratus. (HEIN. EL. JUR. CIV. 1. 3. 75.)—A person is a man considered in relation to a certain status.

1832. Personae vice fungitur municipium et decuria. (23 WEND. N. Y. 103. 144.)—Towns and boroughs act as if persons.

1833. Personal things cannot be done by another. (FINCH, LAW. 1. 3. 14).

1834. Personal things cannot be granted over. (FINCH, LAW. 1. 3. 15).

1835. Personal things die with the person. (FINCH, LAW. 1. 3. 16).

1836. Perspicua vera non sunt probanda.

(COKE, LITT. 16. b.)—Plain truths need not to be proved.

1837. **Pirata est hostis humani generis.** (3 INST. 113.)—A pirate is an enemy of the human race.

1838. **Placita debent apte concludere.** (LOFFT, 416.)—Pleas ought to conclude properly.

1839. **Placita ex directo esse debent, et nil per inductionem supponere.** (LOFFT, 417.)—The wills of superiors should be directly expressed, and nothing supposed by way of inference.

1840. **Placita negativa duo exitum non faciunt.** (LOFFT, 415.)—Two negative pleas form no issue.

1841. **Placitorum alia dilatoria; alia peremptoria.** (LOFFT, 398.)—Pleas are either dilatory or peremptory.

1842. **Placitum aliud personale, aliud reale, aliud mixtum.** (COKE, LITT. 284. b.)—Pleas are personal, real, and mixed.

1843. **Placitum mendax non est placitum.** (LOFFT, 410.)—A lying will is no will.

1844. **Placitum nemo cessabit, nisi melius dando.** (HALK. 125.)—A plea in abatement must give a better plea.

1845. **Plena et celeris justitia fiat partibus.** (4 INST. 67).—Let full and speedy justice be done to the parties.

1846. **Plura corpus quam membra supplicia.** (RILEY, 8.)—The whole body is capable of greater suffering than any one member.

1847. **Pluralis numerus est duobus contentus.** (1 Rol. 476.)—The plural number is contained in two.

1848. **Pluralities are odious in law.** (2 Bou. 148.)

1849. **Plures cohæredes sunt quasi unum corpus, propter unitatem juris quod habent.** (Coke, Litt. 163. b.)—Several co-heirs are as one body, by reason of the unity of right which they possess.

1850. **Plures eandem rem in solidum possidere non possunt.** (Tray. 446.)—Several persons cannot each have, at the same time, an equal right to the same thing.

1851. **Plus enim valet quod agitur quam quod simulate concipitur.** (Tray. 446.)—That which is done is of more avail than that which is pretended to be done.

1852. **Plus exempla quam peccata nocent.** (Whart. 799.)—Examples hurt more than crimes.

1853. **Plus peccat auctor quam actor.** (5 Coke, 99.)—The instigator offends more than the performer.

1854. **Plus valet unus oculatus testis quam auriti decem.** (4 Inst. 279.)—One eye-witness is better than ten ear-witnesses.

1855. **Plus valet vulgaris consuetudo quam regalis concessio.** (Halk. 125.)—Common custom is better than royal grant.

1856. **Plus vident oculi quam oculus.** (4 Inst. 160.)—Two eyes see more than one.

1857. Pœna ad paucos, metus ad omnes perveniat. (LOFFT, 139.)—Let punishment come to few, fear to all.

1858. Pœna ex delicto defuncti, hæres teneri non debet. (2 INST. 198.)—The heir ought not to be bound by a penalty for the crime of the dead.

1859. Pœna gravior, ultra legem posita æstimationem conservat. (4 INST. 66.)—A heavier punishment put beyond the law preserves esteem.

1860. Pœna non debet ante ire crimen. (LOFFT, 120.)—Punishment should not precede a crime.

1861. Pœna non potest, culpa perennis erit. (21 VIN. ABR. 271.)—Punishment cannot be, crime will be, perpetual.

1862. Pœnæ potius molliendæ quam exasperandæ sunt. (3 INST. 220.)—Punishments should rather be softened than aggravated.

1863. Pœnæ sunt restringendæ. (JENK. CENT. 29.)—Punishments should be restrained.

1864. Pœnæ suos tenere debet, actores et non alios. (BRACT. 380.)—Punishment ought to find its own authors and not others.

1865. Politiæ legibus non leges politiis adaptandæ. (HOB. 154.)—Politics are to be adapted to the laws, and not the laws to politics.

1866. Ponderantur testes non numerantur. (1 STARK. EV. 554.)—Witnesses are weighed not counted.

1867. Posito uno oppositorum negatur alterum.

(2 ROL. 422.)—One of two opposite positions being affirmed, the other is denied.

1868. **Positus in conditione non censetur positus in institutione.** (TRAY. 450.)—A person named in a condition is not necessarily named in the destination.

1869. **Possessio contra omnes valet præter eum cui jus sit possessionis.** (LOFFT, 265.)—Possession is valid against all except him who has the right of possession.

1870. **Possessio est quasi pedis positio.** (3 COKE, 42.)—Possession is, as it were, the resting-place of the foot.

1871. **Possessio fratris de feodo simplici facit sororem esse hæredem.** (3 COKE, 42.)—The brother's possession in fee-simple makes the sister to be heir.

1872. **Possessio pacifica pour anns 60 facit jus.** (JENK. CENT. 26.)—Peaceable possession for sixty years gives a right.

1873. **Possession is a good title where no better title appears.** (20 VIN. ABR. 278).

1874. **Possessor has right against all men but him who has the very right.** (2 BOU. 148).

1875. **Possibilitas post dissolutionem executionis nunquam reviviscatur.** (1 ROL. 321.)—Possibility is never revived after the dissolution or the execution.

1876. **Possibility cannot be on a possibility.** (2 BOU. 148).

1877. Post executionem status lex non patitur possibilitatem. (3 BULS. 108.)—After the execution of an estate, the law suffers not a possibility.

1878. Post factum nullum consilium. (RILEY, 338.)—After the deed counsel is in vain.

1879. Posteriora derogant prioribus. (WHART. 811.)—Things subsequent derogate from things prior.

1880. Postliminium fingit eum qui captus est in civitate semper fuisse. (DIG. 49. 51.)—Postliminy feigns that he who has been captured has never left the state.

1881. Potentia debet sequi justitiam, non antecedere. (3 BULS. 199.)—Power ought to follow, not precede, justice.

1882 Potentia inutilis frustra est. (BRANCH, PR.)—Useless power is vain.

1883. Potentio non est nisi ad bonum. (TAYLER, 324.)—Power is not conferred except for the public good.

1884. Potest quis renunciare pro se, et suis, juri quod pro se introductum est. (BRACT. 20.)—One may relinquish for himself and his heirs, a right which was introduced for his own benefit.

1885. Potestas stricte interpretatur. JENK. CENT. 17.)—A power is to be strictly interpreted.

1886. Potestas suprema seipsum dissolvere potest, ligare non potest. (BAC. MAX. 19.)—Supreme power can dissolve, but cannot bind itself.

1887. Præpropera consilia raro sunt prospera. (4 INST. 57.)—Hasty counsels are seldom prosperous.

1888. Præscriptio est titulus ex usu et tempore substantiam capiens ab auctoritate legis. (COKE, LITT. 113. a.)—Prescription is a title by authority of law, deriving its force from use and time.

1889. Præscriptio in feodo non acquirit jus. (WHART. 817.)—Prescription in fee acquires not a right.

1890. Præscriptio et executio non pertinent ad valorem contractus, sed ad tempus et modum actionis instituendæ. (3 MASS. 84.)—The prescription and execution of a contract do not affect the validity of the contract, but the time and manner of bringing an action.

1891. Præscriptio non datur in bona felonum, nisi per recordum. (LOFFT. 288.)—Prescription is not granted against the goods of felons, except by record.

1892. Præsentare nihil aliud est quam præstodare seu offerre. (COKE, LITT. 120. a.)—To present, is no more than to give or offer on the spot.

1893. Præsentia corporis tollit errorem nominis. (BAC. MAX. 24.)—The presence of the body cures error in the name.

1894. Præstat cautela quam medela. (COKE, LITT. 304. b.)—Caution is better than cure.

1895. Præsumatur pro justitia sententiæ. (BEST. EV. INT. 42.)—The justice of a sentence should be presumed.

1896. Præsumitur pro legitimatione. (5 COKE, 98.)—Legitimacy is to be presumed.

1897. Præsumptio, ex eo quod plerumque fit. (22 WEND. N. Y. 425. 475.)—Presumptions arise from what generally happens.

1898. Præsumptio juris est de jure. (TRAY. 462.)—A legal presumption is a legal rule.

1899. Præsumptio violenta, plena probatio. (COKE, LITT. 6. b.)—Strong presumption is full proof.

1900. Præsumptio violenta valet in lege. (JENK. CENT. 56.)—Strong presumption is of weight in law.

1901. Præsumptiones sunt conjecturæ ex signo verisimili ad probandum assumptæ. (2 BOU. 148.)—Presumptions are conjectures from probable proof, assumed for purposes of evidence.

1902. Prætextu liciti non debet admitti illicitum. (WING. 728.)—Under pretext of legality what is illegal ought not to be admitted.

1903. Praxis judicum est interpres legum. (HOB. 96.)—The practice of the judges is the interpreter of the laws.

1904. Precedents have as much law as justice. (2 BOU. 149).

1905. Precedents that pass sub-silentio are of little or no authority. (16 VIN. ABR. 499).

1906. Pretium succedit in locum rei. (2 Buls. 312.)—The price succeeds in place of the thing.

1907. Previous intentions are judged by subsequent acts. (4 Denio, N. Y. 319. 320).

1908. Prima pars æquitatis æqualitas. (2 Bou. 149.)—The radical part of equity is equality.

1909. Primo executienda est verbi vis, ne sermonis vitio obstruetur oratio, sive lex sine argumentis. (Coke, Litt. 68. b.)—The force of a word is to be first examined, lest by the fault of diction the sentence be destroyed, or the law be without arguments.

1910. Princeps et respublica ex justa causa possunt rem meam auferre. (12 Coke, 13.)—The king, and the republic may, in a just cause, take away my property.

1911. Princeps legibus solutus est. (Dig. 1. 3. 31.)—The emperor is free from laws.

1912. Principalis debet semper excuti antequam perveniatur ad fidei jussores. (2 Inst. 19.)—The principal should always be exhausted before coming upon the sureties.

1913. Principia data sequuntur concomitantia. (Whart. 826.)—Given principles are followed by their concomitants.

1914. Principia probant, non probantur. (3 Coke, 40.)—Principles prove, they are not proved.

1915. Principiis obsta. (Branch, Pr.)—Withstand beginnings.

1916. Principiorum non est ratio. (2 Buls. 239.)—There is no reasoning of principles.

1917. Principium est potissima pars cujusque rei. (10 Coke, 49.)—The principal of a thing is the most powerful part.

1918. Prior possessio cum titulo posteriore melior est priore titulo sine possessione. (Tray. 466.)—Prior possession, with subsequent title, is better than prior title without possession.

1919. Privatio præsupponit habitum. (2 Rol. 419.)—A deprivation presupposes a possession.

1920. Privatis pactionibus non dubium est non lædi jus cæterorum. (Dig. 2. 15. 3.)—There is no doubt that the rights of others cannot be prejudiced by private agreement.

1921. Privatorum conventio juri publico non derogat. (Dig. 50. 17. 45. 1.)—An agreement of private individuals cannot derogate from public law.

1922. Privatum commodum publico cedit. (Jenk. Cent. 223.)—Private yields to public good.

1923. Privatum incommodum publico bono pensatur. (Jenk. Cent. 85.)—Private inconvenience is compensated by public good.

1924. Privilegiatus contra privilegiatum non utitur privilegis. (Tray. 468.)—One privileged person cannot plead his privilege against another privileged person.

1925. Privilegium est beneficium personale

et extinguitur cum persona. (3 Buls. 8.)—A privilege is a personal benefit, and dies with the person.

1926. **Privilegium est quasi privata lex.** (2 Buls. 189.)—A privilege is, as it were, a private law.

1927. **Privilegium non valet contra rempublicam.** (Bac. Max. 5.)—A privilege is of no force against the commonwealth.

1928. **Pro possessore habetur qui dolo injuriave desiit possidere.** (Off. of Ex. 166.)—He is counted a possessor who by fraud or injury discontinues to possess.

1929. **Probandi necessitas incumbit illi qui agit.** (Inst. 2. 20. 4.)—The necessity of proving lies upon him who sues.

1930. **Probationes debent esse evidentes, id est, perspicuæ et faciles intelligi.** (Coke, Litt. 283. a.)—Proofs ought to be evident, that is, clear and easily understood.

1931. **Probatis extremis præsumuntur media.** (1 Gr. Ev. 20.)—The extremes being proved, the intermediate proceedings are presumed.

1932. **Procurationem adversus nulla est præscriptio.** (Dav. 17.)—There is no perscription against procuration.

1933. **Prohibetur ne quis faciat in suo quod nocere possit alieno.** (9 Coke, 59.)—It is prohibited for one to do on his own property that which may injure another's.

1934. Prolem ante matrimonium natam, ita ut post, legitimam, lex civilis et succedere facit in hæreditate parentum. (FORTESC. 39.)—The civil law permits both the offspring born before and after marriage to be the heirs of their parents.

1935. Proles sequitur sortem paternam. (1 SANDF. CH. N. Y. 583. 660.)—The offspring follows the condition of the father.

1936. Propinquior excludit propinquum; propinquus remotum; et remotus remotiorem. (COKE, LITT. 10. b.)—He who is nearer excludes him who is near; he who is near, him who is remote; he who is remote, him who is more remote.

1937. Propositio indefinita æquipollet universali. (WHART. 834.)—An indefinite proposition is equal to a general one.

1938. Proprietas totius navis carinæ causam sequitur. (DIG. 6. 1. 61.)—The property of the whole ship follows the condition of the keel.

1939. Proprietas verborum est salus proprietatum. (JENK. CENT. 16.)—The propriety of words is the safety of property.

1940. Proprietates verborum observandæ sunt. (JENK. CENT. 136.)—The proprieties of words are to be observed.

1941. Prosecutio legis est gravis vexatio; executio legis coronat opus. (COKE, LITT. 289. b.)—The prosecution of the law is a grievous vexation; the execution of the law crowns the work.

1942. Protectio trahit subjectionem, et sub-

jectio protectionem. (COKE, LITT. 65. a.)—Protection draws to it subjection; and subjection, protection.

1943. Proviso est providere præsentia et futura, non præterita. (2 COKE, 72.)—A proviso is to provide for the present and future, not the past.

1944. Proximus est cui nemo antecedit; supremus est quem nemo sequitur. (DIG. 50. 16. 92.)—He is next whom no one precedes; he is last whom no one follows.

1945. Prudentur agit qui præcepto legis obtemperat. (5 COKE, 49.)—He acts prudently who obeys the commands of the law.

1946. Pueri sunt de sanguine parentum, sed, pater et mater non sunt de sanguine puerorum. (3 COKE, 40.)—Children are of the blood of their parents, but the father and mother are not of the blood of the children.

1947. Pupillus pati posse non intelligitur. (DIG. 50. 17. 110. 2.)—A pupil is not considered able to do an act to his own prejudice.

Q.

1948. Quæ ab hostibus capiuntur statim capientium fiunt. (INST. 2. 1. 17.)—Things which are taken from enemies, immediately become the property of the captors.

1949.   Quæ ab initio inutilis fuit institutio, ex post facto convalescere non potest. (DIG. 50. 17. 210.)—An institution which was useless in the beginning cannot acquire force from after matter.

1950.   Quæ accessionum locum obtinent extinguuntur cum principales res peremptæ fuerint. (DIG. 33. 8. 2.)—Things which hold the place of accessories are extinguished when the principal things are destroyed.

1951.   Quæ ad unum finem loquuta sunt, non debent ad alium detorqueri. (4 COKE, 14.)—Words spoken to one end, should not be perverted to another.

1952.   Quæ cohærent personæ a persona separari nequeunt. (JENK. CENT. 28.)—Things which belong to the person should not be separated from the person.

1953.   Quæ communi legi derogant stricte interpretantur. (JENK. CENT. 221.)—Things which derogate from the common law are to be strictly interpreted.

1954.   Quæ contra rationem juris introducta sunt, non debent trahi in consequentiam. (12 COKE, 75.)—Things introduced contrary to the reason of the law ought not to be drawn into a precedent.

1955.   Quæ dubitationis causa tollendæ inseruntur communem legem non lædunt. (COKE, LITT. 205. a.)—Whatever is inserted for the purpose of removing doubt does not affect the common law.

1956. Quæ in curia acta sunt rite agi præsumuntur. (3 BULS. 43.)—Whatever, is done in court is presumed to be rightly done.

1957. Quæ in partes dividi nequeunt solida, a singulis præstantur. (6 COKE, 1.)—Things which cannot be divided into parts are rendered entire by each severally.

1958. Quæ in testamento ita sunt scripta ut intelligi non possint, perinde sunt ac si scripta non essent. (DIG. 50. 17. 73. 3.)—Things which are so written in a will that they cannot be understood, are the same as if they had not been written.

1959. Quæ incontinenti vel certo fiunt in esse videntur. (COKE, LITT. 236. b.)—Things which are done directly and certainly appear already in existence.

1960. Quæ inter alios actæ sunt nemini nocere debent sed prodesse possunt. (6 COKE, 1.)—Things which are done between others, ought not to injure a person, but may benefit him.

1961. Quæ legi communi derogant non sunt trahenda in exemplum. (WHART. 843.)—Things derogatory to the common law are not to be drawn into a precedent.

1962. Quæ legi communi derogant stricte interpretantur. (JENK. CENT. 29.)—Those things which derogate from the common law are to be strictly interpreted.

1963. **Quæ mala sunt inchoata in principio vix bono peragantur exitu.** (4 COKE, 2.)—Things bad in the commencement seldom end well.

1964. **Quæ non fieri debent facta valent.** (TRAY. 484.)—Things which ought not to be done, are yet held valid when they are done.

1965. **Quæ non valeant singula, juncta juvant.** (3 BULS. 132.)—Things which do not avail singly, avail when joined.

1966. **Quæ præter consuetudinem et morem majorum fiunt, neque placent, neque recta videntur.** (4 COKE, 78.)—Things which are done contrary to the custom and usage of our ancestors, neither please nor appear right.

1967. **Quæ propter necessitatem recepta sunt, non debent in argumentum trahi.** (DIG. 50. 17. 162.)—Things which are received on the ground of necessity should not be drawn into question.

1968. **Quæ rerum natura prohibentur, nulla lege confirmata sunt.** (FINCH, LAW. 74.)—Things which are forbidden in the nature of things, are confirmed by no law.

1969. **Quæ sunt minoris culpæ sunt majoris infamiæ.** (COKE, LITT. 6. b.)—Things which are of the lesser guilt are of the greater infamy.

1970. **Quæ sunt temporalia ad agendum sunt perpetua ad excipiendum.** (TRAY. 487.)—Things which afford a ground of action, if raised within a

certain time, may be pleaded at any time, by way
of exception.

**1971. Quæcunque intra rationem legis inveni-
untur, intra legem ipsam esse judicantur.** (2 INST.
689.)—Whatever appears within the reason of the
law, is to be considered within the law itself.

**1972. Quæcunque lex vult fieri non vult
frustra fieri.** (HALK. 136.)—Whatever the law
wishes done, it wishes not to be done in vain.

**1973. Quælibet concessio fortissime contra
donatorem interpretanda est.** (COKE, LITT. 183.
a.)—Every grant is to be most strongly interpreted
against the grantor.

**1974. Quælibet jurisdictio cancellos suos
habet.** (JENK. CENT. 139.)—Every jurisdiction has
its own limits.

**1975. Quælibet narratio super brevi locari
debet in comitatu in quo breve emanavit.**
(WHART. 843.)—Every count upon the writ ought
to be laid in the county in which the writ arose.

**1976. Quælibet pardonatio debet capi secun-
dum intentionem regis, et non ad deceptionem
regis.** (3 BULS. 14.)—Every pardon ought to be
taken according to the intention of the king, and
not to the deception of the king.

**1977. Quælibet pœna corporalis, quamvis
minima, major est qualibet pœna pecuniaria.** (3
INST. 220.)—Every corporal punishment, although
the very least, is greater than any pecuniary punishment.

1978. Quæras de dubiis, legem bene discere sivis. (WHART. 844.)—Inquire into doubtful points if you wish to understand the law well.

1979. Quærere dat sapere quæ sunt legitima vere. (LITT. § 443.)—To investigate is the way to know what things are really true.

1980. Qualitas quæ inesse debet, facile præsumitur (JUR. CIV.)—A quality which ought to form a part is easily presumed.

1981. Quam legem exteri nobis posuere eandem illis ponemus. (TAYLER, 414.)—The same law which foreign nations have shown to us we should show to them.

1982. Quam longum debet esse rationabile tempus, non definitur in lege, sed pendet ex discretione justiciariorum. (COKE, LITT. 56. b.)—How long reasonable time ought to be, is not defined by law, but depends upon the discretion of the judges.

1983. Quamvis aliquid per se non sit malum, tamen si sit mali exempli, non est faciendum. (2 INST. 564.)—Although a thing in itself may not be bad, yet if it hold out a bad example, it is not to be done.

1984. Quamvis lex generaliter loquitur, restringenda tamen est, ut cessante ratione et ipsa cessat. (4 INST. 330.)—Although the law speaks generally, it is to be restrained, since when the reason on which it is grounded fails, it fails.

1985. Quamvis quis pro contumacia et fuga

utlagetur non propter hoc convictus est de facto principiali. (TAYLER, 415.)—Though a person may be outlawed for contempt and flight, he is not, on this account, convicted of the principal fact.

1986. **Quando abest provisio partis, adest provisio legis.** (6 VIN. ABR. 49.)—When the provision of the party is lacking, the provision of the law is at hand.

1987. **Quando aliquid conceditur, conceditur id sine quo illud feri non possit.** (9 BARB. N. Y. 516. 518.)—When anything is granted, that also is granted without which it cannot be of effect.

1988. **Quando aliquid mandatur, mandatur et omne per quod pervenitur ad illud.** (5 COKE, 116.)—When anything is commanded, everything by which it can be accomplished is also commanded.

1889. **Quando aliquid prohibetur ex directo, prohibetur et per obliquum.** (COKE, LITT. 223. b.)—When anything is prohibited directly, it is also prohibited indirectly.

1890. **Quando aliquid prohibetur prohibetur omne, per quod devenitur ad illud.** (COKE, LITT. 223. b.)—When anything is prohibited, all that relates to it is prohibited.

1891. **Quando aliquis aliquid concedit, concedere videtur et id sine quo res uti non potest.** (3 KENT, COM. 421.)—When a person grants a thing, he is supposed to grant that also without which the thing cannot be used.

1992. Quando charta continet generalem clausulam, posteaque descendit ad verba specialia, quæ clausulæ generali sunt consentanea, interpretanda est charta secundum verba specialia. (8 COKE, 154.)—When a deed contains a general clause, and afterwards descends to special words, which are consentaneous to the general clause, the deed is to be interpreted according to the special words.

1993. Quando de una et eadem re, duo onerabiles existunt, unus, pro insufficientia alterius, de integro onerabitur. (2 INST. 277.)—When two persons are liable for one and the same thing, one for the other's default will be charged for the whole.

1994. Quando diversi desiderantur actus ad aliquem statum perficiendum, plus respicit lex actum originalem. (10 COKE, 49.)—When different acts are required to the formation of an estate, the law chiefly regards the original act.

1995. Quando duo jura concurrunt in una persona, æquum est ac si essent in diversis. (4 COKE, 118.)—When two rights concur in one person, it is the same as if they were in separate persons.

1996. Quando jus domini regis et subditi concurrunt jus regis præferri debet. (9 COKE, 129.)—When the right of the sovereign and of the subject concur, the right of the sovereign is to be preferred.

1997. Quando lex aliquid alicui concedit, concedere videtur id sine quo res ipsa esse non potest. (5 COKE, 47.)—When the law grants anything to any one it is considered to grant that also without which the thing itself cannot exist.

1998. Quando lex aliquid alicui concedit, omnia incidentia tacite conceduntur. (2 INST. 326.)—When the law grants anything to any one, all incidents are tacitly granted.

1999. Quando lex est specialis ratio autem generalis, generaliter lex est intelligenda. (2 INST. 83.)—When the law is special, but its reason general, the law is to be understood generally.

2000. Quando licet id quod majus, videtur licere id quod minus. (SHEP. TOUCH. 429.)—When the greater is allowed, the less seems to be allowed also.

2001. Quando plus fit quam fieri debet videtur etiam illud fieri quod faciendum est. (8 COKE, 85.)—When more is done than ought to be done, that which is to be done, is still considered to be done.

2002. Quando res non valet ut ago, valeat quantum valere potest. (COWP. 600.)—When a thing is of no force as I do it, it shall have effect as far as it can.

2003. Quando verba et mens congruunt, non est interpretationi locus. (2 BOU. 151.)—When words and mind agree there is no place for interpretation.

2004. Quanto gradu unusquisque eorum distat stirpite, eodem distat inter se. (TAYLER, 417.) —In so far as each person is removed from the stock, in such degree are they related among themselves.

2005. Quem sequuntur commoda eundem et incommodo sequuntur. (TRAY. 495.)—He who reaps the advantage, must also bear the disadvantage.

2006. Quemadmodum ad quæstionem facti non respondent judices, ita ad quæstionem juris non respondent juratores. (COKE, LITT. 295. b.) —In the same manner that judges do not answer to questions of fact, so jurors do not answer to questions of law.

2007. Qui accusat integræ famæ sit et non criminosus. (3 INST. 26.)—Let him who accuses be of clear fame, and not criminal.

2008. Qui acquirit sibi, acquirit hæredibus. (TRAY. 496.)—He who acquires for himself, acquires for his heirs.

2009. Qui adimit medium dirimit finem. (COKE, LITT. 161. a.)—He who takes away the means destroys the end.

2010. Qui aliquid statuerit parte inaudita altera æquum licet dixerit haud æquum facerit. (6 COKE, 52.)—He who decides anything, one party being unheard, though he may have decided right, has not done justice.

2011. **Qui alterius jure utitur, eodem jure uti debet.** (BR. 421.)—He who uses the right of another ought to use the same right.

2012. **Qui alterum incusat ne in eodem saltem genere sit incusandus.** (HALK. 140.)—He who accuses another should be free from that offence of which he makes accusation.

2013. **Qui bene distinguit, bene docet.** (2 INST. 470.)—He who distinguishes well, teaches well.

2014. **Qui bene interrogat, bene docet.** (3 BULS. 227.)—He who questions well, teaches well.

2015. **Qui cadit a syllaba cadit a tota causa.** (BRACT. 211.)—He who fails in a syllable fails in the whole cause.

2016. **Qui causa decedit, causa cadit.** (HALK. 141.)—He who departs from his cause, falls from his cause.

2017. **Qui concedit aliquid, concedit omne id sine quo concessio est irrita.** (JENK. CENT. 32.)—He who grants anything grants everything without which the grant is fruitless.

2018. **Qui confirmat nihil dat.** (2 BOU. 151.)—He who confirms does not give.

2019. **Qui contemnit præceptum, contemnit præcipientem.** (12 COKE, 96.)—He who contemns a precept, contemns the party giving it.

2020. **Qui cum alio contrahit, vel est, vel esse**

debet, non ignarus conditionis ejus. (DIG. 50. 17. 19.)—He who contracts with another, either is, or ought to be, not ignorant of his condition.

2021. Qui cum aliter tueri se non possunt damni culpam dederint, innoxii sunt. (TAYLER, 424.)—They are guiltless of homicide who cannot defend themselves otherwise than by homicide.

2022. Qui dat finem, dat media ad finem necessaria. (3 MASS. 129.)—He who gives an end gives the means necessary to that end.

2023. Qui doit inheriter al pere, doit inheriter al fitz. (WHART. 855.)—He who ought to inherit from the father, should inherit from the son.

2024. Qui dolo desierit possidere, pro possidente damnatur. (23 N. Y. 267.)—He who has fraudulently dispossessed himself of a thing may be treated as if he still had possession.

2025. Qui evertit causam, evertit causatum futurum. (10 COKE, 51.)—He who overthrows the cause, overthrows the future consequence.

2026. Qui ex damnato coitu nascuntur inter liberos non computantur. (COKE, LITT. 8. a.)— Those who are born of an illicit union, should not be counted among children.

2027. Qui ex parte testamenti aliquid donatum accipit, universo testamento stabit. (HALK. 142.)—He who takes anything by a part of a testament, should stand by the whole testament.

2028. Qui facit id quod plus est, facit id quod

minus est, sed non convertitur. (BRACT. 207.)—
He who does that which is more, does that which
is less, but not vice versa.

2029. Qui fraudem fit frustra agit. (2 ROL.
17.)—He who commits fraud, acts in vain.

2030. Qui jure suo utitur, non potest dici
fraudem committere. (TRAY. 502.)—He who
uses his own right cannot be said to commit a
fraud.

2031. Qui habet jurisdictionem absolvendi,
habet jurisdictionem ligandi. (12 COKE, 59.)—He
who has jurisdiction to loosen, has jurisdiction to
bind.

2032. Qui hæret in litera, hæret in cortice.
(5 COKE, 4.)—He who adheres to the letter, adheres
to the bark.

2033. Qui ignorat quantum solvere debeat,
non potest in probus videre. (DIG. 50. 17. 99.)—
He who does not know what he ought to pay,
does not want probity in not paying.

2034. Qui in jus dominiumve alterius succedit
jure ejus uti debet. (DIG. 50. 17. 177.)—He who
succeeds to the right or property of another, ought
to use his right as the assignor himself would have
used it.

2035. Qui in utero est, pro jam nato habetur
quoties de ejus commodo quæritur. (WHART.
855.)—He who is in the womb is held as born,
whenever it is questioned concerning his benefit.

2036. Qui jure suo utitur, nemini facit injuriam. (BRANCH, PR.)—He who uses his own right harms no one.

2037. Qui jussu judicis aliquod fecerit non videtur dolo malo fecisse, quia parere necesse est. (10 COKE, 76.)—He who does anything by command of a judge, is not supposed to have acted from an improper motive, because it was necessary to obey.

2038. Qui male agit, odit lucem. (7 COKE, 66.)—He who acts badly, hates the light.

2039. Qui mandat, ipse fecissi videtur. (STORY, BAILM. 147.)—He who commands, is held to have done the thing himself.

2040. Qui melius probat, melius habet. (9 VIN. ABR. 235.)—He who proves most, recovers most.

2041. Qui nascitur sine legitimo matrimonio, matrem sequitur. (2 BOU. 152.)—He who is born out of lawful matrimony, follows the condition of the mother.

2042. Qui non habet in ære, luat in corpore. (2 INST. 173.)—He who has nothing in his purse must suffer in person.

2043. Qui non habet potestatem alienandi habet necessitatem retinendi. (HOB. 336.)—He who has not the power of alienating is obliged to retain.

2044. Qui non improbat, approbat. (3 INST. 27.)—He who does not blame, approves.

2045. Qui non libere veritatem pronunciat,

proditor est veritatis. (4 INST. EPIL.)—He who does not freely speak truth, is a betrayer of the truth.

2046. Qui non obstat quod obstare potest, facere videtur. (2 INST. 146.)—He who does not prevent what he can prevent, is considered as doing the thing.

2047. Qui non potest donare non potest confiteri. (1 POTHIER, Ev. 804.)—He who is not able to give is not able to confirm.

2048. Qui non prohibet, cum prohibere possit, jubet. (1 BLACK. COM. 430.)—He who does not forbid when he can forbid, commands.

2049. Qui non prohibet quod prohibere potest assentire videtur. (2 INST. 305.)—He who does not forbid what he can forbid, appears to assent.

2050. Qui non propuisat injuriam quando potest, infert. (JENK. CENT. 271.)—He who does not repel a wrong when he can, occasions it.

2051. Qui obstruit aditum, destruit commodum. (COKE, LITT. 161. a.)—He who obstructs a way destroys a convenience.

2052. Qui omne dicit, nihil excludit. (2 INST. 81.)—He who says all, excludes nothing.

2053. Qui parcit nocentibus, innocentibus punit. (JENK. CENT. 126.)—He who spares the guilty punishes the innocent.

2054. Qui peccat ebrius, luat sobrius. (CARY, 133.)—Let him who sins when drunk, be punished when sober.

2055. **Qui per alium facit per seipsum facere videtur.** (COKE, LITT. 258. a.)—He who does anything through another, is regarded as doing it himself.

2056. **Qui potest et debet vetare, jubet.** (2 KENT. COM. 483.)—He who can, and ought to forbid, commands.

2057. **Qui primum peccat ille facit rixam.** (GODB. .)—He who first offends causes the strife.

2058. **Qui prior est tempore, potior est jure.** (COKE, LITT. 14. a.)—He who is first in time is stronger in right.

2059. **Qui pro me aliquid facit, mihi fecisse videtur.** (2 INST. 501.)—He who does anything for me, is considered as doing it to me.

2060. **Qui providet sibi, providet hæredibus.** (2 WHART. 856.)—He who provides for himself provides for his heirs.

2061. **Qui rationem in omnibus quærunt rationem subvertunt.** (2 COKE, 75.)—They who seek a reason for everything, subvert reason.

2062. **Qui semel actionem renunciaverit, amplius repetere non potest.** (8 COKE, 59.)—He who has once relinquished his action cannot bring it again.

2063. **Qui semel malus, semper præsumitur esse malus in eodem genere.** (CRO. CAR. 318.)—He who is once bad is presumed to be always bad in the same degree.

2064. **Qui sentit commodum, sentire debet et**

onus. (2 INST. 489.)—He who experiences the benefit ought to bear the burden.

2065. Qui suum recipit licet, a non debitore, non tenetur restituere. (TRAY. 505.)—He who receives his due, although not from his debtor, is not held liable in restitution.

2066. Qui tacet consentire videtur. (JENK. CENT. 32.)—He who is silent appears to consent.

2067. Qui tacet consentire videtur ubi tractatur de ejus commodo. (9 MOD. 38.)—He who is silent is regarded as assenting, when it is debated concerning his convenience.

2068. Qui tacet non utique fatetur, sed tamen verum est eum non negare. (DIG. 50. 17. 142.)—He who is silent, does not thereby confess, yet it is true that he does not deny.

2069. Qui tardius solvit, minus solvit. (JENK. CENT. 58.)—He who pays tardily, pays too little.

2070. Qui timent, cavent et vitant. (OFF. OF Ex. 162.)—They who fear, take care and avoid.

2071. Qui vult decipi, decipiatur. (SHEP. TOUCH. 56.)—Let him who chooses to be deceived, be deceived.

2072. Quicquid acquiritur servo, acquiritur domino. (15 VIN. ABR. 327.)—Whatever is acquired by the servant, is acquired for the master.

2073. Quicquid demonstratae rei additur satis demonstratae frustra est. (DIG. 33. 4. 1. 8.)—Whatever is added to the description of a thing already sufficiently described, avails nothing.

2074. Quicquid est contra normam recti est injuria. (3 BULS. 313.)—Whatever is against the rule of right is a wrong.

2075. Quicquid in excessu actum est, lege prohibetur. (2 INST. 107.)—Whatever is done in excess, is prohibited by law.

2076. Quicquid judicis auctoritati subjicitur, novitati non subjicitur. (4 INST. 66.)—Whatever is subject to the authority of a judge is not subject to innovation.

2077. Quicquid plantatur solo, solo cedit. (OFF. OF EX. 145.)—Whatever is planted in the soil, belongs to the soil.

2078. Quicquid recipitur, recipitur secundum modum recipientis. (HALK. 149.)—Whatever is received, is received according to the intention of the recipient.

2079. Quicquid solvitur, solvitur secundum modum solventis. (2 VER. 606.)—Whatever is paid, is paid according to the intention of the payer.

2080. Quicunque habet jurisdictionem ordinarium, est illius loci ordinarius. (COKE, LITT. 344. a.)—Whoever has an ordinary jurisdiction, is ordinary of that place.

2081. Quid sit jus, et in quo consistit injuria, legis est definire. (COKE, LITT. 158. b.)—What right is, and in what consists injury, the law is to declare.

2082. Quidquid multis peccatur inultum est.

(TAYLER, 425.)—The crime which is committed by a multitude passes unpunished.

2083. Quieta non movere. (28 BARB. N. Y. 9. 22.)—Do not disturb things which are established.

2084. Quilibet potest renunciare juri pro se introducto. (2 INST. 183.)—Any one may renounce a right introduced for his own benefit.

2085. Quisque utitur jure auctoris. (TRAY. 512.) —He who exercises a derived right, exercises it as the right of his principal.

2086. Quisquis est qui velit juris consultus haberi continuet studium, velit a quocunque doceri. (WHART. 856.)—Whoever wishes to be a jurisconsult, let him continually study, and desire to be taught by everything.

2087. Quivis præsumitur bonus, donec probetur contrarium. (TRAY. 512.)—Every man is presumed innocent, until it is proved to the contrary.

2088. Quod a quoque pœnæ nomine exactum est id eidem restituere nemo cogitur. (DIG. 50. 17. 46.)—That which has been exacted as a penalty, no one is obliged to restore.

2089. Quod ab initio non valet in tractu temporis non convalescet. (COKE, LITT. 35. a.)— That which is not valid at the beginning, improves not by lapse of time.

2090. Quod ad jus naturale attinet, omnes homines æquales sunt. (DIG. 58. 17. 32.)—All men are equal as far as the natural law is concerned.

2091. Quod ædificatur in area legata, cedit legato. (BR. 424.)—Whatever is built upon ground given by will, goes to the legatee.

2092. Quod alias bonum et justum est, si per vim vel fraudem petatur, malum et injustum efficitur. (3 COKE, 78.)—What otherwise is good and just, if it be sought by force and fraud, becomes bad and unjust.

2093. Quod alias non fuit licitum necessitas licitum facit. (FLETA, 5. 23. 14.)—What otherwise was not lawful, necessity makes lawful.

2094. Quod approbo non reprobo. (BR. 712.)—What I approve I do not reject.

2095. Quod civile jus non idem continuo gentium; quod autem gentium idem civile esse debet. (HALK. 151.)—All civil law is not the law of nations, but all law of nations is the same as civil law.

2096. Quod constat clare non debet vereficari. (10 MOD. 150.)—What appears clearly, need not be proved.

2097. Quod constat curiæ opere testium non indiget. (2 INST. 662.)—What appears to the court needs not the help of witnesses.

2098. Quod contra legem fit, pro infecto habetur. (4 COKE, 31.)—What is done contrary to law is regarded as not done.

2099. Quod contra rationem juris receptum

est, non est producendum ad consequentias.
(Dig. 50. 17. 141.)—What has been admitted
against the reason of the law, is not to be drawn
into precedents.

2100. Quodcunque aliquis ab tutelam corporis sui fecerit, jure id fecisse videtur. (2 Inst.
598.)—Whatever any one does in defense of his
person, he is considered to have done legally.

2101. Quod datum est ecclesiæ, datum est
Deo. (2 Inst. 2.)—What is given to the church is
given to God.

2102. Quod demonstrandi causa additur rei
satis demonstratæ, frustra fit. (10 Coke, 113.)—
What is added to a thing sufficiently demonstrated, for the purpose of demonstration, is in
vain.

2103. Quod dubitas, ne feceris. (1 Hale,
Pl. Cr. 800.)—Where you doubt, do nothing.

2104. Quod enim semel aut bis existit, prætereunt legislatores. (Dig. 1. 8. 17.)—That which
never happens but once or twice, legislators pass
by.

2105. Quod est ex necessitate nunquam introducitur, nisi quando necessarium. (2 Rol. 502.)
—That which is of necessity, is never introduced
except when necessary.

2106. Quod est inconveniens, aut contra
rationem non permissum est in lege. (Coke,
Litt. 178. a.)—What is inconvenient or contrary
to reason is not allowed in law.

2107. **Quod est necessarium est licitum.** (JENK. CENT. 76.)—What is necessary is lawful.

2108. **Quod factum est, cum in obscuro sit, ex affectione cujusque capit interpretationem.** (DIG. 50. 17. 168. 1)—When there is doubt about an act, it may be interpreted from the known feelings of the actor.

2109. **Quod fieri debet facile præsumitur.** (HALK. 153.)—What ought to be done is easily presumed.

2110. **Quod fieri non debet factum valet.** (5 COKE, 38.)—What ought not to be done, when done, is valid.

2111. **Quod in majore non valet, nec valet in minore.** (TAYLER, 435.)—That which avails not in the greater, avails not in the less.

2112. **Quod in minori valet valebit in majori; et quod in majori non valet nec valebit in minori.** (COKE, LITT. 260. a.)—What is valid in the less shall be valid in the greater; and what is not valid in the greater, shall neither be valid in the · less.

2113. **Quod in uno similium valet, valebit in altero.** (COKE, LITT. 191. a.)—What avails in one of two similar things, will avail in the other.

2114. **Quod inconsulto fecimus, consultius revocemus.** (JENK. CENT. 116.)—What is done without counsel, we revoke upon consideration.

2115. **Quod initio vitiosum est, non potest tractu temporis convalescere.** (DIG. 50. 17. 29.)

—Time cannot render valid an act void in its origin.

2116. **Quod ipsis qui contraxerunt, obstat; et successoribus eorum obstabit.** (Dig. 50. 17. 143.) —That which bars those who have contracted, will bar their successors also.

2117. **Quod juris in toto idem in parte.** (Tray. 516.)—That which is law in regard to the whole, is also law in regard to the part.

2118. **Quod jussu alterius solvitur pro est quasi ipsi solutum esset.** (Dig. 50. 17. 180.)— That which is paid by the order of another is the same as though it were paid to himself.

2119. **Quod meum est sine me auferri non potest.** (Jenk. Cent. 251.)—What is mine cannot be taken away without my consent.

2120. **Quod naturalis ratio inter omnes homines constituit, vocatur jus gentium.** (Dig. 1. 1. 9.)—That which natural reason has established among all men, is called the law of nations.

2121. **Quod necessarie intelligitur id non deest.** (1 Buls. 71.)—What is necessarily understood is not wanting.

2122. **Quod necessitas cogit, defendit.** (1 Hale, Pl. Cr. 54.)—What necessity compels, it justifies.

2123. **Quod non apparet non est.** (2 Inst. 479.)—That which does not appear, does not exist.

2124. **Quod non habet principium non habet**

finem. (COKE, LITT. 345. a.)—That which has no beginning has no end.

2125. Quod non legitur non creditur. (4 INST. 304.)—What is not read is not believed.

2126. Quod non valet in principalia, in accessoria seu consequentia non valebit. (8 COKE, 78.) —That which is not good in its principal, will not be good as to accessories or consequences.

2127. Quod nostrum est, sine facto sive defectu nostro, amitti seu in alium transferri non potest. (8 COKE, 92.)—That which is ours cannot be lost or transferred to another without our own act, or our own fault.

2128. Quod nullius esse potest, id ut alicujus fieret nulla obligatio valet efficere. (DIG. 50. 17. 182.)—No agreement can avail to make that the property of any one, which cannot be acquired as property.

2129. Quod nullum est nullum producit effectum. (TRAY. 519.)—That which is nothing, produces no effect.

2130. Quod nullius est id ratione naturali occupanti conceditur. (DIG. 41. 1. 3.)—That which belongs to no one is by natural reason, given to the occupant.

2131. Quod omnes tangit, ab omnibus debet supportari. (3 HOW. ST. TR. 878. 1087.)—That which concerns all, should be supported by all.

2132. Quod pendet, non est pro eo, quasi sit.

(DIG. 50. 17. 169. 1.)—What is in suspense is considered as not existing, during the suspense.

2133. **Quod per me non possum, neo per alium.** (4 COKE, 24.)—What I cannot do by myself, I cannot do by another.

2134. **Quod per recordum probatum, non debet esse negatum.** (WHART. 858.)—What is proved by record should not be denied.

2135. **Quod populus postremum jussit, id jus ratum esto.** (1 BLACK. COM. 89.)—What the people have last enacted, let that be the established law.

2136. **Quod prius est verius est; et quod prius est tempore potius est jure.** (COKE, LITT. 347. a.)—What is first is true; and what is first in time is best in law.

2137. **Quod pro minore licitum est, et pro majore licitum est.** (8 COKE, 43.)—That which is lawful in the less, is lawful in the greater.

2138. **Quod quis ex culpa sua damnum sentit, non intelligitur damnum sentire.** (DIG. 50. 17. 203.)—He who suffers a damage by his own fault, is not considered as suffering damage.

2139. **Quod quis sciens indebitum dedit hac mente, ut posteo repeteret, repetere non potest.** (DIG. 12. 6. 50.)—That which one has paid, knowing it not to be due, with the intention of redemanding it, he cannot recover.

2140. **Quod quisquis norat in hoo se exerceat.** (11 COKE, 10.)—Let every one employ himself in what he knows.

2141. **Quod remedio destituitur ipsa re valet, si culpa absit.** (BAC. MAX. 9.)—That which is without a remedy is valid by the thing itself, if there be no fault.

2142. **Quod semel meum est, amplius meum esse non potest.** (COKE, LITT. 49. b.)—What is once mine cannot be mine more completely.

2143. **Quod semel placuit in electione, amplius displicere non potest.** (COKE, LITT. 146. a.)— Where choice is once made it cannot be disapproved any longer.

2144. **Quod statim liquidare potest pro jam liquido habetur.** (TRAY. 521.)—That which can be liquidated at once is held to be already liqui- dated.

2145. **Quod sub certa forma concessum vel reservatum est, non trahitur ad valorem vel compensationem.** (BAC. MAX. 4.)—That which is granted or reserved under a certain form, is not to be drawn into a valuation or compensation.

2146. **Quod subintelligitur non deest.** (2 LD. RAYM. 832.)—What is understood, is not wanting.

2147. **Quod tacite intelligitur deesse non videtur.** (4 COKE, 22.)—What is tacitly understood is not considered to be wanting.

2148. **Quod talem eligi faciat qui melius et sciat et velit, et possit officio illio intendere.** (TAYLER, 441.)—That person should be chosen who best understands, and is willing and able to perform the duty of the office.

2149. Quod vanum et inutile est, lex non requirit. (COKE, LITT. 319. b.)—The law does not require what is vain and useless.

2150. Quomodo quid constituitur eodem modo dissolvitur. (JENK. CENT. 74.)—In whatever manner a thing is constituted, in the same manner it is dissolved.

2151. Quorum prætexta, nec auget nec minuit sententiam, sed tantum confirmat præmissa. (PLOWD. 52.)—QUORUM PRÆTEXTA neither increases nor diminishes the meaning, but only confirms that which went before.

2152. Quotiens dubia interpretatio libertatis est, secundum libertatem respondendum erit. (DIG. 50.17. 20.)—When the interpretation between liberty and slavery is doubtful, the decision must be in favor of liberty.

2153. Quotiens idem sermo duas sententias exprimit, ea potissimum excipiatur, quæ rei gerendæ aptior est. (DIG. 50. 17. 67.)—Whenever the same words express two meanings, that is to be taken which is the better fitted for carrying out the proposed end.

2154. Quoties in stipulationibus ambigua oratio est, commodissimum est id accipi quo res de quo agitur in tuto sit. (DIG. 45. 1. 80.)—Whenever in stipulations the expression is ambiguous, it is most fitting that that sense should be taken by which the subject matter may be protected.

2155. Quoties in verbis nulla est ambiguitas ibi nulla expositio contra verba fienda est. (COKE, LITT. 147. a.)—When there is no ambiguity in the words, then no exposition contrary to the words is to be made.

R.

2156. Ræpublicæ cedunt bello parta.—Things taken in war go to the state.

2157. Ratihabatio mandato æquiparatur. (DIG. 46. 3. 12. 4.)—Ratification is equal to a command.

2158. Ratio est formalis causa consuetudinis. (WHART. 864.)—Reason is the formal cause of custom.

2159. Ratio est radius divini luminis. (COKE, LITT. 232. b.)—Reason is a ray of divine light.

2160. Ratio et auctoritas duo clarissima mundi lumina. (4 INST. 320.)—Reason and authority are the two brightest lights in the world.

2161. Ratio in jure æquitas integra. (2 BOU. 155.)—Reason in law is perfect equity.

2162. Ratio legis est anima legis; mutata legis ratione, mutatur et lex. (7 COKE, 7.)—Reason is the soul of law; the reason of law being changed, the law is also changed.

2163. Ratio legis est lex. (JENK. CENT. 45.)—The reason of law is the soul of law.

2164. Ratio non clauditur loco. (2 Bou. 155.) —Reason is not confined to any place.

2165. Ratio potest allegari deficiente lege, sed vera et legalis et non apparens. (COKE, LITT. 191. a.)—Reason may be alleged when the law is defective, but it must be true and legal reason, and not merely apparent.

216́6. Re verbis, scripto, consensu, traditione junctura vestes, sumere pacta solent. (PLOWD. 161.)—Compacts are accustomed to be clothed by the thing itself, by words, by writing, by consent, by delivery.

2167. Receditur a placitis juris potius quam injuriæ et delicta maneant impunita. (BAC. MAX. 12.)—Positive rules of law will be receded from, rather than crimes and wrongs should remain unpunished.

2168. Recorda sunt vestigia vetustatis et veritatis. (2 ROL. 296.)—Records are the traces of antiquity and of truth.

2169. Recuperatio est alicujus rei in causam alterius adductæ per judicem acquisitio. (WHART. 870.)—Recovery is the acquisition, by sentence of the judge, of anything adduced in the cause of another.

2170. Recurrendum est ad extraordinarium quando non valet ordinarium. (WHART. 870.)— We must have recourse to what is extraordinary when what is ordinary fails.

2171. Reddere, nil aliud est quam acceptum

restituere. (COKE, LITT. 142. a.)—To restore, is to give back nothing but what was taken.

2172. **Regula est, juris quidem ignorantiam cuique nocere facti vero ignorantiam non nocere.** (DIG. 22. 6. 9.)—The rule is, that ignorance of the law does not excuse, but that ignorance of a fact may excuse a party from the legal consequences of his conduct.

2173. **Regula pro lege, si deficit lex.** (2 BOU. 155.)—In default of the law, the maxim rules.

2174. **Regulariter non valet pactum de re mea non alienanda.** (COKE, LITT. 223. a.)—Regularly a contract not to alienate my property is not valid.

2175. **Rei depositæ proprietas apud deponentem manet, sed et possessio.** (TRAY. 532.)—The property in a thing deposited, and the possession thereof, remains in the depositor.

2176. **Rei turpis nullum mandatum est.** (DIG. 17. 1. 6. 3.)—A mandate of an illegal thing is void.

2177. **Reipublicæ interest voluntates defunctorum effectum sortiri.** (WHART. 876.)—It concerns the state that the wills of the dead should have their effect.

2178. **Relatio est fictio juris et intenta ad unum.** (3 COKE, 28.)—Relation is a fiction of the law, and intended for one thing.

2179. **Relatio semper fiat ut valeat disposi-**

tio. (6 COKE, 76.)—Reference should always be made so that the disposition may have effect.

2180. **Relation never defeats collateral acts** (18 VIN. ABR. 292).

2181. **Relation shall never make good a void grant or devise of the party.** (18 VIN. ABR. 292).

2182. **Relative words refer to the next antecedent, unless the sense be thereby impaired.** (JENK. CENT. 180).

2183. **Relativorum cognito uno, cognoscitur et alterum.** (CRO. JAC. 539.)—Of things relating to each other, one being known, the other is known.

2184. **Remainder can depend upon no estate but what beginneth at the same time the remainder doth.** (2 BOU. 155).

2185. **Remainder must vest at the same instant that the particular estate determines.** (2 BOU. 155.)

2186. **Remainder to a person not of a capacity to take at the time of appointing it, is void.** (PLOWD. 27).

2187. **Remedies for rights are ever favorably extended.** (18 VIN. ABR. 521.)

2188. **Remedies ought to be reciprocal.** (2 BOU. 155).

2189. **Remissius imperanti melius paretur.** (3 INST. 233.)—One commanding not too strictly is better obeyed.

2190. **Remoto impedimento, emergit actio.**

(5 COKE, 76.)—The impediment being removed, the action arises.

2191. Rent must be reserved to him from whom the state of the land moveth. (COKE, LITT. 143. b).

2192. Repellitur a sacramento infamis. (COKE, LITT. 158. a.)—An infamous person is prevented from taking an oath.

2193. Repellitur exceptione cedendarum actionum. (1 JOHNS. CH. N. Y. 409. 414.)—He is defeated by the plea that the actions have been assigned.

2194. Reprobata pecunia liberat solventem. (9 COKE, 79.)—Money refused liberates the debtor.

2195. Reputatio est vulgaris opinio ubi non est veritas. (4 COKE, 107.)—Reputation is a common opinion, where there is no certain knowledge.

2196. Rerum ordo confunditur, si unicuique jurisdictio non servatur. (4 INST. PROEM.)—The order of things is confounded, if every one preserves not his jurisdiction.

2197. Rerum progressus ostendunt multa, quæ in initio præcaveri seu prævideri non possunt. (6 COKE, 40.)—In the course of events many things are shown, which in the beginning could not be guarded against or foreseen.

2198. Rerum suarum quilibet est moderator et arbiter. (COKE, LITT. 223. a.)—Every one is the manager and disposer of his own affairs.

2199. Res accessoria sequitur rem princi-

palem. (BR. 491.)—An accessory follows its principal.

2200. Res denominatur a principaliori parte. (5 COKE, 47.)—The thing is named from its principal part.

2201. Res est misera ubi jus est vagum et incertum. (2 SALK. 512.)—It is a miserable state of things where the law is vague and uncertain.

2202. Res generalem habet significationem, quia tam corporea, quam incorporea, cujuscunque sunt generis, naturæ sive speciei, comprehendit. (3 INST. 482.)—A *thing* has a general signification, which comprehends corporeal and incorporeal objects, of whatever nature, sort, or species.

2203. Res inter alios acta alteri nocere non debet. (COKE, LITT. 152. b.)—Things done between strangers ought not to injure those who are not parties to them.

2204. Res inter alios judicatæ nullum aliis præjudicium faciant. (DIG. 44. 2. 1.)—Matters adjudged in a cause do not prejudice those who were not parties to it.

2205. Res judicata facit ex albo nigrum, ex nigro album, ex curvo rectum, ex recto curvum. (1 BOU. INST. 840. n.)—A thing adjudged makes white, black; black, white; the crooked, straight; the straight, crooked.

2206. Res judicata pro veritate accipitur. (COKE, LITT. 103. a.)—A thing adjudged is taken for truth.

2207. Res per pecuniam æstimatur, et non pecunia per res. (9 COKE, 76.)—The value of a thing is estimated by its worth in money, and the value of money is not estimated by reference to the thing.

2208. Res perit domino suo. (2 KENT, COM. 591.)—The destruction of the thing is the loss of its owner.

2209. Res propria est quæ communis non est. (8 PAIGE, CH. N. Y. 261. 270.)—A thing is private which is not common.

2210. Res sacra non recipit æstimationem. (DIG. 1. 8. 9. 5.)—A thing sacred admits of no valuation.

2211. Res transit cum suo onere. (FLETA, 3. 10. 3.)—The thing passes with its burden.

2212. Reservatio non debet esse de proficuis ipsis quia ea conceduntur, sed de redditu novo extra proficua. (COKE, LITT. 142. a.)—A reservation ought not to be of the profits themselves, because they are granted, but from the new rent and out of the profits.

2213. Reservatio ut et protestatio non facit jus, sed tuetur. (TRAY. 542.)—Reservation and protest do not create a right, but protect a right.

2214. Resignatio est juris proprii spontanea reputatio. (GODB. 284.)—Resignation is the spontaneous relinquishment of one's own right.

2215. Resoluto jure concedentis resolvitur jus concessum. (MACK. CIV. LAW. 179.)—The right of the grantor being extinguished, the right granted is extinguished.

2216. **Resoluto jure dantis, resolvitur jus accipientis.** (TRAY. 543.)—When the right of the giver becomes void, the right of the receiver ceases.

2217. **Respiciendum est judicanti, nequid aut durius aut remissius construatur quam causa deposcit.** (3 INST. 220.)—It is a matter of import to one adjudicating that nothing should be either more leniently, or more severely construed than the cause itself demands.

2218. **Respondeat raptor qui ignorare non potuit quod pupillum alienum abduxit.** (HOB. 99.)—Let the ravisher answer, for he could not be ignorant that he has taken away another's ward.

2219. **Respondeat superior.** (4 INST. 114.)— Let the principal answer.

2220. **Responsio unius non omnino auditur.** (1 GR. EV. 260.)—The answer of one witness shall not be heard at all.

2221. **Reus excipiendo fit actor.** (BEST, EV. 252. 294.)—The defendant by a plea becomes plaintiff.

2222. **Reus læsæ majestatis punitur, ut pereat unus ne pereant omnes.** (4 COKE, 124.)—A traitor is punished, that one may die lest all perish.

2223. **Rex debet esse sub lege ; quia lex facit regem.** (1 BLACK. COM. 239.)—The king should be subject to the law ; for the law makes the king.

2224. Rex est caput et salus reipublicæ. (4 COKE, 124.)—The king is the guardian and head of the commonwealth.

2225. Rex est legalis et politicus. (LANE, 27.)—The king is both legal and politic.

2226. Rex est lex vivens. (JENK. CENT. 17.) —The king is the living law.

2227. Rex est major singulis, minor universis. (BRACT. 1. 8.)—The king is greater than any single person; less than all.

2228. Rex est persona mixta, medicus regni; pater patriæ; et sponsus regni. (11 COKE, 70.)— The king is a mixed person; the physician of the state, the father of the country, and the husband of the kingdom.

2229. Rex est persona sacra et mixta cum sacerdote. (5 COKE [ECCL. L.], 28.)—The king is a sacred person, and mixed with the priesthood.

2230. Rex hoc solum non potest facere quod non potest injuste agere. (11 COKE, 72.)—The king can do everything but an injury.

2231. Rex in regno suo non habet parem. (WHART. 899.)—The king has no equal in his own kingdom.

2232. Rex non debet esse sub homine sed sub Deo et lege. (BRACT. 5.)—The king should not be under the authority of man, but of God and the law.

2233. Rex non debet judicare sed secundum

legem. (JENK. CENT. 9.)—The king ought to govern only according to law.

2234. **Rex non potest fallere nec falli.** (JENK. CENT. 48.)—The king cannot deceive, nor be deceived.

2235. **Rex non potest peccare.** (2 ROL. 804.)—The king can do no wrong.

2236. **Rex nunquam moritur.** (1 BLACK. COM. 249.)—The king never dies.

2237. **Rex præsumitur habere omnia jura in scrinio pectoris sui.** (COKE, LITT. 99. a.)—The king is presumed to have all the laws in the recess of his own breast.

2238. **Rex prosequi in judicis potest in qua curia sibi visum fuerit.** (WHART. 900.)—The king can proceed to judgment in whatever court he pleases.

2239. **Rex quod injustum est facere non potest.** (JENK. CENT. 9.)—The king cannot do what is unjust.

2240. **Rex summus dominus supra omnes.** (2 INST. 501.)—The king is the great lord over all.

2241. **Rex tuetur legem, et lex tuetur jus.** (COKE, LITT. 130. a.)—The king protects the law, and the law protects the right.

2242. **Rights never die.** (2 BOU. 156).

2243. **Riparum usus publicus est jure gentium, sicut ipsius fluminis.** (DIG. 1. 8. 5.)—The use of river-banks is by the law of nations public, like that of the stream itself.

2244. Roy n'est lie per asoun statute, si il ne soit expressement nosme. (JENK. CENT. 307.)— The king is not bound by any statute, if he is not expressly named.

S.

2245. Sacramentum habet in se tres comites, veritatem, justitiam et judicium; veritas habenda est in jurato; justitia et justicium in judice. (3 INST. 160.)—An oath has in it three component parts, truth, justice, and judgment; truth in the party swearing; justice and judgment in the judge administering the oath.

2246. Sacramentum si fatuum fuerit, licet falsum, tamen non committit perjurium. (2 INST. 167.)—A foolish oath, though false, makes not perjury.

2247. Sacrilegus omnium praedonum cupiditatem et scelerem superat. (4 COKE, 106.)—A sacrilegious person transcends the cupidity and wickedness of all other robbers.

2248. Saepe constitutum est, res inter alios judicatas aliis non praejudicare. (DIG. 42. 1. 63.) —It has often been settled that matters adjudged between others ought not to prejudice those who were not parties.

2249. Saepe viatorem nova, non vetus orbita fallit. (4 INST. 34.)—Often it is the new track, not the old one, which deceives the traveler.

2250. Sæpenumero ubi proprietas verborum attenditur, sensus veritatis amittitur. (7 COKE,. 27.)—Frequently, where the propriety of words is attended to, the meaning of truth is lost.

. **2251. Salus populi est suprema lex.** (13 COKE, 139.)—The health of the people is the first law.

2252. Salus ubi multi consiliarii. (4 INST. 1.) —In many counselors there is safety.

2253. Salutem civum civitatumque incolumnitatem conditæ leges sunt. (CICERO.)—Laws were made for the safety of citizens and for the security of states.

2254. Sanguinis conjunctio benevolentia devincit homines et caritate. (5 JOHNS. CH. N. Y, 1. 18.)—A tie of blood overcomes men through benevolence and family affection.

2255. Sapiens incipit a fine, et quod primum est in intentione, ultimum est in executione. (10 COKE, 25.)—A wise man begins with the last, and what is first in intention, is last in execution.

2256. Sapiens omnia agit cum consilio. (4 INST. 4.)—A wise man does everything advisedly.

2257. Sapientia legis nummario pretio non est æstimanda. (JENK. CENT. 168.)—The wisdom of the law cannot be valued by money.

2258. Sapientis judicis est cogitare tantum sibi esse permissum, quantum commissum et creditum. (4 INST. 163.)—It is the part of a wise judge to think so much only permitted to him, as is committed and intrusted to him.

2259. Satisfaction should be made to that fund which has sustained the loss. (2 Bou. 156).

2260. Scientia utriumque par pares contra-hentes facit. (3 Burr. 1905. 1910.)—Equal knowledge on both sides makes the contracting parties equal.

2261. Scientii' et volunti non fit injuria. Bract. 20.)—A wrong is not done to one who knows and wills it.

2262. Scire debes cum quo contrahis. (2 Bou. 156.)—You ought to know with whom you contract.

2263. Scire et scire debere æquiparantur in jure. (Tray. 551.)—What one knows, and what one ought to know are regarded in law as equivalent.

2264. Scire leges, non hoc est verba earum tenere, sed vim et potestatem. (Dig. 1. 3. 17.)—To know the laws, is not to observe their mere words, but their force and power.

2265. Scire proprie est, rem ratione et per causam cognoscere. (Coke, Litt. 183. b.)—To know properly, is to know a thing in its reason, and by its cause.

2266. Scribere est agere. (2 Rol. 89.)—To write is to act.

2267. Scriptæ obligationes scriptis tolluntur, et nudi consensus obligatio, contrario consensu

dissolvitur. (2 Bou. 157.)—Written obligations are superseded by writings, and obligations of naked assent is dissolved by naked assent to the contrary.

2268. **Secta quæ scripto nititur a scripto variari non debet.** (JENK. CENT. 65.)—A suit which relies upon a writing ought not to vary from the writing.

2269. **Secundum naturam est, commoda cujusque rei eum sequi, quam sequentur incommoda.** (DIG. 50. 17. 10.)—It is natural that he who bears the charge of a thing should receive the profits.

2270. **Securius expediuntur negotia commissa pluribus.** (4 COKE, 46.)—Business intrusted to many, is more securely dispatched.

2271. **Seisina facit stipitem.** (2 BLACK. COM. 209.)—Seisin makes the stock.

2272. **Semel civis, semper civis.** (TRAY. 555.)—Once a citizen, always a citizen.

2273. **Semper in dubiis id agendum est, ut quam tutissimo loco res sit bona fide contracta, nisi quum aperte contra leges scriptum est.** (DIG. 34. 5. 21.)—Always in doubtful cases that is to be done by which a *bona fide* contract may be in the greatest safety, unless when it has been openly made against law.

2274. **Semper in obscuris quod minimum est sequimur.** (DIG. 50. 17. 9.)—In cases of obscurity we always follow that which is least.

2275. **Semper in stipulationibus et in cæteris**

contractibus id sequimur quod actum est. (Dig. 50. 17. 34.)—In stipulations and other contracts we always follow that which was done.

2276. Semper ita fiat relatio ut valeat dispositio. (6 Coke, 76.)—Reference should always be so made that the disposition may avail.

2277. Semper necessitas probandi incumbit ei qui agit. (2 Bou. 157.)—The necessity of proving is always incumbent upon him who acts.

2278. Semper praesumitur pro legitimatione puerorum; et filiatio non potest probari. (5 Coke, 98.)—The presumption is always in favor of the legitimacy of children, for filiation cannot be proved.

2279. Semper praesumitur pro negante. (2 Bou. 157.)—The presumption is always in favor of the one who denies.

2280. Semper praesumitur pro sententia. (3 Buls. 42.)—The presumption is always in favor of the sentence.

2281. Semper qui non prohibet pro se intervenire, mandare creditur. (Dig. 14. 6. 16.)—He who does not prohibit the intervention of another in his behalf, is supposed to authorize it.

2282. Semper sexus masculinus etiam foemininum continet. (Dig. 32. 62.)—The male sex always includes the female.

2283. Semper specialia generalibus insunt. (Dig. 50. 17. 147.)—Special clauses are always included in general ones.

2284. Senatores sunt partes corporis regis. (4 INST. 53.)—Senators are part of the body of the king.

2285. Sensus verborum est anima legis. (5 COKE, 2.)—The meaning of words is the spirit of the law.

2286. Sensus verborum est duplex, mitis et asper, et verba semper accipienda sunt in mitiore sensu. (4 COKE, 13.)—The meaning of words is two-fold, mild and rough, and words are always to be received in their milder sense.

2287. Sensus verborum ex causa dicendi accipiendus est. (4 COKE, 13.)—The sense of words is to be taken from the occasion of speaking them.

2288. Sententia a non judice lata nemini debet nocere. (FLETA, 6. 6. 7.)—A sentence passed by one who is not a judge should not harm any one.

2289. Sententia contra matrimonium nunquam transit in rem judicatam. (7 COKE, 43.)—A sentence against marriage never passes in a matter judged.

2290. Sententia facit jus, et legis interpretatio 'legis vim obtinet. (ELLES. POST. 55.)—The sentence makes the law, and the interpretation of law obtains the force of law.

2291. Sententia facit jus et res judicata pro veritate accipitur. (ELLES. POST. 55.)—Judgment creates the right, and what is adjudicated is taken for truth.

2292. Sententia interlocutoria revocari potest, definitiva non potest. (BAC. MAX. 20.)—An interlocutory sentence may be revoked, but not a final.

2293. Sententia non fertur de rebus non liquidis. (JENK. CENT. 7.)—Sentence is not given upon matters that are not clear.

2294. Sequamur vestigia patrum nostrorum. (WHART. 929,)—Let us follow in the footsteps of our fathers.

2295. Sequi debet potentia justitiam, non præcedere. (2 INST. 454.)—Power should follow justice, not precede it.

2296. Serjeantia idem est quod servitium. (COKE, LITT. 105. b.)—Serjeantry is the same as service.

2297. Sermo relatus ad personam, intelligi debet de conditione personæ. (4 COKE, 16.)—A speech referring to a person, ought to be understood of the condition of the person.

2298. Sermones semper accipiendi sunt secundum subjectam materiam, et conditionem personarum. (4 COKE, 14.)—Discourses are to be understood according to their subject, and the condition of the persons.

2299. Servanda est consuetudo loci ubi causa agitur. (3 JOHNS. CH. N. Y. 190. 219.)—The custom of the place where the action is brought is to be observed.

2300. **Servitia personalia sequuntur personam.** (2 INST. 374.)—Personal services follow the person.

2301. **Satius est petere fontes quam sectari rivulos.** (10 COKE, 118.)—It is better to seek the fountain than to follow the streamlet.

2302. **Servitus est constitutio de jure gentium, qua quis domino alieno contra naturam subjicitur.** (COKE, LITT. 116. b.)—Slavery is an institution by the law of nations, by which a man is subjected to a foreign master, contrary to nature.

2303. **Si a jure discedas vagus eris, et erunt omnia omnibus incerta.** (COKE, LITT. 227. b.)—If you depart from the law you will wander, and all things will be uncertain to every one.

2304. **Si alicujus rei societas sit, et finis negotio impositus est, finitur societas.** (16 JOHNS. N. Y. 438. 489.)—If there is a partnership in any matter, and the business is ended, the partnership ceases.

2305. **Si aliquid ex solemnibus deficiat, cum æquitas poscit subveniendum est.** (1 KENT, COM. 157.)—If any one of certain required forms be wanting, when equity requires, it will be aided.

2306. **Si assuetis mederi possis nova non sunt tentanda.** (10 COKE, 142.)—If you can be relieved by accustomed remedies new ones should not be tried.

2307. Si duo in testamento pugnantia reperientur, ultimum est ratum. (LOFFT, 251.)—If two conflicting provisions appear in a testament, the last prevails.

2308. Si judicas, cognosce. (2 Bou. 157.)—If you judge, understand.

2309. Si meliores sunt quos ducit amor, plures sunt quos corrigit timor. (COKE, LITT. 392. b.)—If those are better who are led by love, those are the greater number corrected by fear.

2310. Si non appareat quid actum est erit consequens, ut id sequamur quod in regione in qua actum est, frequentatur. (DIG. 50. 17. 34.)—If it does not appear what was agreed upon, the consequence will be that we must follow that which is the usage of the place where the agreement was made.

2311. Si nulla sit conjectura quæ ducat alio, verba intelligenda sunt ex proprietate, non grammatica sed populari ex usu. (2 KENT, COM. 555.)—If there be no inference which leads to a different result, words are to be understood according to their proper meaning, not in a grammatical, but in a popular and ordinary sense.

2312. Si plures conditiones ascriptæ fuerunt donationi conjunctim omnibus est parendum. (COKE, LITT. 225. a.)—If several conditions are conjunctively written in a gift, the whole of them must be complied with.

2313. **Si plures sunt fidejussores, quodquit erunt numero, singuli in solidum tenentur.** (INST. 8. 21. 4.)—If there are more sureties than one, however many they may be, they shall each be held for the whole.

2314. **Si quid universitati debetur singulis non debetur, nec quod debet, universitas singuli debent.** (DIG. 8. 4. 7.)—If anything is due to a corporation, it is not due to the individual members of it, nor do the members individually owe what the corporation owes.

2315. **Si quidem in nomine, cognomine, præ-nomine, agnomine legatarii enaverit; cum de persona constat, nihilominus valet legatum.** (INST. 2. 20. 29.)—If the testator has erred in the name, cognomen, prænomen, or title of the legatee, whenever the person is rendered certain, the legacy is nevertheless, valid.

2316. **Si quis custos fraudem pupillo fecerit, a tutela removendus est.** (JENK. CENT. 39.)—If a guardian behave fraudulently to his ward, he shall be removed from the guardianship.

2317. **Si quis prægnantem uxorem reliquit, non videtur sine liberis decessisse.** (2 BOU. 158.) —If a man leave his wife pregnant, he shall not be considered to have died without children.

2318. **Si quis unum percusserit, cum alium percutere vellet, in felonia tenetur.** (3 INST. 51.)

—If a man kill one, meaning to kill another, he is held guilty of felony.

2319. **Si suggestio non sit vera, literæ patentes vacuæ sunt.** (10 COKE, 113.)—If the suggestion of a patent is false, the patent itself is void.

2320. **Sic enim debere quem meliorem agrum suum facere, ne vicini deteriorem faciat.** (3 KENT, COM. 441.)—Every one ought so to improve his land as not to injure his neighbor's.

2321. **Sic interpretandum est ut verba accipiantur cum effectu.** (3 INST. 80.)—Such an interpretation is to be made that the words may be received with effect.

2322. **Sic utere tuo ut alienum non lædas.** (9 COKE, 59.)—So use your own as not to injure another's property.

2323. **Sicut ad quæstionem facti, non respondent judices, ita ad quæstionem juris, non respondent juratores.** (COKE, LITT. 295. b.)—Inasmuch as the judges do not decide on questions of fact, so the jury do not decide on questions of law.

2324. **Sicut natura nil facit per saltum, ita nec lex.** (COKE, LITT. 238. b.)—As nature does nothing by a leap, so neither does the law.

2325. **Sicut subditus regi tenetur ad obedientiam, ita rex subdito tenetur ad protectionem.** (7 COKE, 5.)—Inasmuch as a subject is bound to obey the king, so the king is bound to protect the subject.

2326. Sigillum est cera impressa, quia cera sine impressione non est sigillum. (3 INST. 169.) —A seal is a piece of wax impressed, because wax without an impression is not a seal.

2327. Silence shows consent. (6 BARB. N. Y. 28. 35.)

2328. Silentium in senatu est vitium. (12 COKE, 94.)—Silence in the senate is a fault.

2329. Silent leges inter arma. (4 INST. 70.)— Laws are silent amidst arms.

2330. Similitudo legalis est casuum diversorum inter se collatorum similis ratio; quod in uno similium valet, valebit in altero. (COKE, LITT. 191. a.)—Legal similarity is the like reason of different cases when compared with each other; for what avails in one similar case avails in the other.

2331. Simonia est voluntas sive desiderium emendi vel vendendi spiritualia vel spiritualibus adhærentia. (HOB. 167.)—Simony is the will or desire or buying or selling spiritualities, or things pertaining thereto.

2332. Simplex commendatio non obligat. (DIG. 4. 3. 37.)—A simple recommendation does not bind.

2333. Simplex et pura donatio dici poterit, ubi nulla est adjecta conditio neo modus. (BRACT. 17.)—A gift is said to be pure and simple when no condition or qualification is annexed.

2334. Simplicitas est legibus amica, et nimia

subtilitas in jure reprobatur. (4 COKE, 5.)—Simplicity is favorable to the laws, and too much
subtlety in law is to be reprobated.

**2335. Sine possessione usucapio procedere
non potest.** (2 Bou. 158.)—There can be no prescription without possession.

2336. Singuli in solidum tenentur. (6 JOHNS.
CH. N. Y. 242. 252.)—Each is bound for the
whole.

**2337. Sive tota res evincatur, sive pars habet
regressum emptor in venditorem.** (DIG. 21. 2. 1.)
—The purchaser who has been evicted in whole, or
in part, has an action against the vendor.

2338. Socagium idem est quod servitium socæ.
(COKE, LITT. 86. a.)—Socage is the same as service
of the plough.

2339. Socii mei socius, meus socius non est.
(DIG. 50. 17. 47. 1.)—The partner of my partner is
not my partner.

**2340. Sodomie est crime de majestie vers le
Roy Celestre.** (3 INST. 58.)—Sodomy is high
treason against the King of Heaven.

2341. Sol sine homine generat herbam. (OFF.
OF EX. 57.)—The sun makes the grass grow without man's assistance.

**2342. Sola ac per se senectus donationem
testamentum aut transactionem non vitiat.** (5
JOHNS. CH. N. Y. 148. 158.)—Old age does not of
itself and alone, vitiate a will or a gift.

2343. Solemnitas intervenire debet in muta-

tione liberi tenementi, ne contingat donationem deficere pro defectu probationis. (COKE, LITT. 48. a.)—Solemnity ought to be observed in an exchange of free tenement, lest it happen that the gift fail through want of proof.

2344. **Solemnitates juris sunt observandæ.** (JENK. CENT. 13.)—The solemnities of law are to be observed.

2345. **Solus cum sola in loco suspecto suspectus.** (TRAY. 567.)—A man alone with a woman in a suspicious place is to be suspected.

2346. **Solus Deus facit hæredem, non homo.** (COKE, LITT. 5. a.)—God alone makes the heir, not man.

2347. **Solutio pretii, emptionis loco habetur.** (JENK. CENT. 56.)—The payment of the price is held in the place of a sale.

2348. **Solvendo esse nemo intelligitur nisi qui solidum potest solvere.** (DIG. 50. 16. 114.)— No one is considered to be solvent unless he can pay the whole.

2349. **Solvitur adhuc societas etiam morte socii.** (DIG. 17. 2.)—A partnership is moreover dissolved by the death of a partner.

2350. Some things are to be construed according to the end thereof. (NOY, 7).

2351. Some things are to be construed according to the original cause thereof. (NOY, 5).

2352. **Spes est vigilantis somnium.** (4 INST. 203.)—Hope is the dream of the vigilant.

2353. **Spes impunitatis continuum affectum tribuit delinquendi.** (3 INST. 236.)—The hope of impunity holds out a continual temptation to crime.

2354. **Spoliatus debet ante omnia restitui.** (3 INST. 714.)—Spoil ought to be restored before anything else.

2355. **Spondet peritiam artis.** (2 KENT, COM. 588.)—He promises the skill of his art.

2356. **Sponsalia dicuntur futurarum nuptiarum conventio et repromissio.** (COKE, LITT. 34. a.)—A betrothal is the agreement and promise of a future marriage.

2357. **Sponsalia, inter minores contracta, ante septem annos, nulla sunt.** (JENK. CENT. 95.)—Betrothals contracted between parties under seven years of age are void.

2358. **Sponte virum mulier fugiens et adultera facta, dote sua careat, nisi sponte retracta.** (COKE, LITT. 32. b.)—A woman leaving her husband of her own accord, and committing adultery, loses her dower, unless her husband takes her back of his own accord.

2359. **Stabit præsumptio donec probetur in contrarium.** (COKE, LITT. 373. b.)—A presumption shall stand until the contrary is proved.

2360. **Stare decisis, et non quieta movere.** (22 BARB. N. Y. 97. 106.)—To stand by precedents, and not to disturb settled points.

2361. **Stat pro ratione voluntas.** (1 BARB.

N. Y. 408. 411.)—The will stands in place of a reason.

2362. **Stat pro ratione voluntas populi.** (25 BARB. N. Y. 344. 376.)—The will of the people stands in place of a reason.

2363. **Statuta ita interpretanda ut innoxiis ne obsint.** (LOFFT, 596.)—Statutes should be so interpreted that they may not hurt the innocent.

2364. **Statuta pro publico commodo late interpretantur.** (JENK. CENT. 21.)—Statutes made for the public good ought to be liberally construed.

2365. **Statutum affirmativum non derogat communi legi.** (JENK. CENT. 24.)—An affirmative statute does not take from the common law.

2366. **Statutum generaliter est intelligendum quando verba statuti sunt specialia, ratio autem generalis.** (10 COKE, 101.)—When the words of a statute are special, but the reason of it general, it is to be understood generally.

2367. **Statutum speciale statuto speciali non derogat.** (JENK. CENT. 199.)—One special statute does not take from another special statute.

2368. **Sublata causa tollitur effectus.** (2 BLACK. COM. 203.)—Remove the cause, and the effect will cease.

2369. **Sublata veneratione magistratuum, respublica ruit.** (JENK. CENT. 43.)—When respect for magistrates is taken away, the commonwealth falls.

2370. Sublato fundamento cadit opus. (JENK. CENT. 106.)—Remove the foundation, the work falls.

2371. Sublato principali tollitur adjunctum. (COKE, LITT. 389. a.)—If the principal be taken away, the adjunct is also taken away.

2372. Subornare est quasi subtus in aure ipsum male ornare, unde subornatio dicitur de falsi expressione, aut de veri suppressione. (3 INST. 167.)—To suborn is, as it were, to adorn subtilely to the ear what is bad; whence to express what is false, or suppress what is true, is called subornation.

2373. Subrogatio est transfusio unius creditoris in alium, eadem vel mitiori conditione. (MERLIN, QU. DE DR.)—Subrogation is the substituting one creditor in the place of another, in the same, or a better condition.

2374. Succurritur minori; facilis est lapsus juventutis. (JENK. CENT. 47.)—A minor is to be aided; a mistake of youth is easy.

2375. Summa caritas est facere justitiam singulis et omni tempore quando necesse fuerit. (11 COKE, 70.)—The greatest charity is to do justice to individuals, and at any time whenever it may be necessary.

2376. Summa est lex quæ pro religione facit. (10 MOD. 117. 119.)—That is the highest law which favors religion.

2377. Summa ratio est quæ pro religione

facit. (5 COKE, 14.)—That reason is strongest which operates in favor of religion.

2378. Summum jus, summa injuria. Summa lex, summa crux. (HOB. 125.)—The higher the law, the greater the injury. The higher the law, the higher the punishment.

2379. Super fidem chartarum, mortuis testibus, erit ad patriam de necessitate recurrendum. (COKE, LITT. 6. b.)—The truth of charters is necessary to be referred to a jury, when the witnesses are dead.

2380. Superflua non nocent. (JENK. CENT. 184.)—Superfluities do no harm.

2381. Suppressio facti tollit æquitatem. (LOFFT, 381.)—The suppression of a fact takes away equity.

2382. Suppressio veri, expressio falsi. (11 WEND. N. Y. 374. 417.)—Suppression of the truth is equal to the expression of the false.

2383. Suppressio veri, suggestio falsi. (23 BARB. N. Y. 521. 525.)—Suppression of the truth equals the suggestion of the false.

2384. Suprema potestas seipsam dissolvere potest. (WHART. 966.)—Supreme power can dissolve itself.

2385. Supremus est, quem nemo sequitur. (DIG. 50. 16. 92.)—He is last whom no one follows.

2386. Surplusagium non nocet. (3 BOU. INST. 2949.)—Surplusage does no harm.

2387. **Surrogatum capit naturam surrogati.** (TRAY. 577.)—A thing substituted takes the nature of that for which it is substituted.

T.

2388. **Tacita quædam habentur pro expressis.** (FLETA, 3. 12. 1.)—Silent things are sometimes regarded as expressed.

2389. **Talis interpretatio semper fienda est, ut evitetur absurdum, et inconveniens, et ne judicium sit illusorium.** (1 COKE, 52.)—Interpretation is always to be made in such a manner that what is absurd and inconvenient is to be avoided, lest the judgment be illusory.

2390. **Talis non est eadem, nam nullum simile est idem.** (4 COKE, 18.)—What is like, is not the same, for nothing similar is the same.

2391. **Tantum bona valent, quantum vendi possunt.** (3 INST. 805.)—Things are worth what they will sell for.

2392. **Tempus enim modus tollendi obligationes et actiones.** (FLETA, 4. 5. 12.)—Time is a means of destroying obligations and actions.

2393. **Tenor est qui legem dat feudo.** (2 BLACK. COM. 310.)—It is the tenor which gives law to the fee.

2394. **Tenor est pactio contra communem feudi naturam ac rationem, in contractu interposita.** (WRIGHT, TEN. 21.)—Tenure is a compact contrary to the common nature and reason of the fee, put into a contract.

2395. **Tenor investituræ est inspiciendus.** (WRIGHT, TEN. 21.)—The tenor of an investiture is to be searched into.

2396. **Terminus annorum certus debet esse et determinatus.** (COKE, LITT. 45. b.)—A term of years ought to be certain and determinate.

2397. **Terminus et feodum non possunt constare simul in una eademque persona.** (PLOWD. 29.)—A term, and the fee cannot both be in one and the same person at the same time.

2398. **Terra manens vacua occupanti conceditur.** (1 SID. 347.)—Land lying unoccupied is given to the occupant.

2399. **Terra sterilis, ex vi termini, est terra infœcunda, nullum ferens fructum.** (2 INST. 665.) —Sterile land is by force of the term barren, bearing no fruit.

2400. **Terra transit cum onere.** (COKE, LITT. 231. a.)—Land passes with its incumbrances.

2401. **Testamenta latissimam interpretationem habere debent.** (JENK. CENT. 81.)—Wills ought to have the broadest interpretation.

2402. **Testamentum est voluntates nostra justa sententia, de eo quod quis post mortem suam fieri velit.** (DIG. 28. 1. 1.)—A testament is the just expression of one's will concerning that which one wishes done after his death.

2403. **Testamentum omne morte consummatum.**

(COKE, LITT. 322. b.)—Every will is completed by death.

2404. **Testatoris ultima voluntas est perimplenda secundum veram intentionem suam.** (COKE, LITT. 322. b.)—The last will of a testator is to be fulfilled according to his real intention.

2405. **Testes qui postulat debet dare eis sumptus competentes.** (JUR. CIV.)—Whoever demands witnesses, must find them in competent provision.

2406. **Testibus deponentibus in pari numero dignioribus est credendum.** (4 INST. 279.)—Where the number of witnesses is equal on both sides, the more worthy are to be believed.

2407. **Testibus, non testimonis, credendem est.** (TRAY. 585.)—Credence is to be given to the witnesses, not to the testimony.

2408. **Testimonia ponderanda, non numeranda sunt.** (BELL. DIC.)—Evidences are to be weighed, not numbered.

2409. **Testis de visu præponderat aliis.** (4 INST. 279.)—An eye-witness outweighs others.

2410. **Testis lupanaris sufficit ad factum in lupanari.** (MOORE, 817.)—A strumpet is a sufficient witness to a deed committed in a brothel.

2411. **Testis nemo in sua causa esse potest.** (3 BOU. 159.)—No one can be a witness in his own cause.

2412. **Testis** should be able to say from his heart, "Non sum doctus neo instructus, neo curo de victoria, modo ministretur justitia." (4 INST. 279.)—A witness should be able to say from his heart, "I am not taught nor instructed, neither do I care concerning the success of either party, save that justice be administered."

2413. **Testmoignes ne poent testifie le negative, mes l'affirmative.** (4 INST. 279.)—Witnesses cannot witness to a negative, they must witness to an affirmative.

2414. **That which I may defeat by my entry, I make good by my confirmation.** (COKE, LITT. 300. a).

2415. **The fund which has received the benefit should make the satisfaction.** (4 BOU. INST. 8730).

2416. **The husband and wife are but one person in the law.** (32 BARB. N. Y. 250. 260).

2417. **The law favors a man's person before his possession.** (NOY, 20).

2418. **The law favors a thing which is of necessity.** (NOY, 25).

2419. **The law favors a thing which is for the good of the commonwealth.** (NOY, 26).

2420. **The law favors things that are in the custody of the law.** (NOY, 28).

2421. **The law favors works of charity, right, and truth; and abhors fraud, covin, and uncertainties which obscure the truth, contrarieties, delays, unnecessary circumstances, and such like.** (NOY, 32).

2422. The owner of property is not divested of his title by a larceny of it. (5 LANS. N. Y. 416).

2423. The owner of the bed of the stream does not own the water, but only has a mere right to use it. (85 N. Y. 520. 525).

2424. Theftbote est emenda furti capta, sine consideratione curiæ domine regis. (3 INST. 134.)—Theftbote is the paying money to have stolen goods returned, without respect for public justice.

2425. There are no accessories in treason, trespass, or petit larceny. (4 BLACK. COM. 35).

2426. Thesaurus non competit regi, nisi quando nemo scit qui abscondit thesaurum. (3 INST. 132.)—Treasure does not belong to the king, unless no one knows who hid it.

2427. Things accessary are of the nature of the principal. (FINCH, LAW. 1. 8. 25).

2428. Things are construed according to that which was the cause thereof. (FINCH, LAW. 1. 8. 4).

2429. Things are dissolved as they be contracted. (FINCH, LAW. 1. 8. 7).

2430. Things grounded upon an ill and void beginning cannot have a good perfection. (FINCH, LAW. 1. 8. 8).

2431. Things in action, entry, or re-entry cannot be granted over. (2 BOU. 160).

2432. Things incident cannot be severed. (FINCH, LAW. 8. 1. 12).

2433. Things incident shall pass by the grant of the principal, but not the principal by the grant of the incident. (COKE, LITT. 152. a).

2434. Things of a higher nature determine things of a lower nature. (NOY, 15).

2435. Things shall not be void which may possibly be good. (2 BOU. 160).

2436. Three things needful and pertaining to every deed are, writing, sealing, and delivery. (NOY, 54).

2437. Timores vani sunt æstimandi qui non cadunt in constantem virum. (7 COKE, 17.)—Fears which do not affect a brave man are accounted vain.

2438. Titulus est justa causa possidendi id quod nostrum est. (8 COKE, 153.)—A title is the just right of possessing that which is our own.

2439. Tolle voluntatem et erit omnis actus indifferens. (BRACT. 2.)—Take away the will and every action will be indifferent.

2440. Tort a le ley est contrarie. (COKE, LITT. 158. b.)—Tort is contrary to the law.

2441. Totius navis proprietas carinæ causam sequitur. (DIG. 6. 1. 61.)—The proprietorship of the whole ship follows the ownership of the keel.

2442. Totum præfertur unicuique parti. (3 COKE, 41.)—The whole is preferable to any single part.

2443. Tout ce que la loi ne defend pas est permis. (2 Bou. 160.)—All that the law does not forbid is permitted.

2444. Toute exception non surveillee tend a prendre la place du principe. (2 Bou. 160.)—Every exception not watched, tends to take the place of the rule.

2445. Tractent fabrilia fabri. (3 Coke, Epist.) —Let smiths do the work of smiths.

2446. Traditio loqui facit chartam. (5 Coke, 1.)—Delivery makes the deed speak.

2447. Traditio nihil amplius transferre debet vel potest, ad eum qui accipit, quam est apud eum qui tradit. (Dig. 41. 1. 20.)—Delivery neither can nor ought to transfer to him who receives, more than was in possession of him who made the delivery.

2448. Transgressione multiplicata, crescat pœna inflictio. (2 Inst. 479.)—Where transgression is multiplied, let the infliction of punishment be increased.

2449. Transit in rem judicatam. (18 Johns. N. Y. 463.)—It passes into a matter adjudged.

2450. Tres faciunt collegium. (Dig. 50. 16. 85.)—Three form a corporation.

2451. Triatio ibi semper debet fieri, ubi juratores meliorem possunt habere notitiam. (7 Coke, 1.)—Trial ought always to be had where the jury can have the best knowledge.

2452. Trusts survive. (2 Bou. 160).

2453. Turpis est pars quæ non convenit cum suo toto. (PLOWD. 161.)—That part is bad which does not agree with the whole.

2454. Tuta est custodia quæ sibime, creditur. (HOB. 340.)—That guardianship is secure which trusts to itself alone.

2455. Tutius errare ex parte mitiore. (3 INST. 220.)—It is safer to err on the side of mercy.

2456. Tutius est rei incumbere quam personæ. (TRAY. 587.)—Real security is safer than personal security.

2457. Tutius semper est errare acquietando quam in puniendo; ex parte misericordiæ quam ex parte justitiæ. (2 HALE, PL. CR. 290.)—It is always safer to err in acquitting, than in punishing; on the side of mercy, than on the side of justice.

2458. Tutor incertus non dari potest. (TRAY. 588.)—A doubtful person should not be appointed a guardian.

2459. Tutor præsumitur intus habere ante redditas rationes. (TRAY. 588.)—A guardian is presumed to have funds belonging to his trust, until he has rendered his accounts.

2460. Tutor rem pupilli emere non potest. (TRAY. 588.)—A guardian may not purchase the property of his ward.

U.

2461. Ubi aliquid impeditur propter unum, eo remoto, tollitur impedimentum. (5 COKE, 77.)—When anything is impeded by one single cause, that cause being removed, the impediment is removed.

2462. Ubi cessat remedium ordinarium ibi decurritur ad extraordinarium. (4 COKE, 92.)—When an ordinary remedy ceases to be of service, recourse must be had to an extraordinary one.

2463. Ubi culpa est, ibi pœna subesse debet. (JENK. CENT. 325.)—Where there is culpability, there ought the punishment to be undergone.

2464. Ubi damna dantur, victus victori in expensis condemnari debet. (2 INST. 289.)—Where damages are given, the losing party should be condemned in costs to the victor.

2465. Ubi eadem ratio, ibi idem jus. (COKE, LITT. 10. a.)—Like reason doth make like law.

2466. Ubi et dantis et accipientis turpitudo versatur, non posse repeti dicimus; quotiens autem accipientis turpitudo versatur, repeti posse. (17 MASS. 562.)—Where there is a turpitude on the part of both giver and receiver, we say it cannot be recovered back, but as often as the turpitude is on the side of the receiver alone, it can be recovered.

2467. Ubi factum nullum, ibi fortia nulla. (4 COKE, 42.)—Where there is no act, there can be no force.

2468. Ubi jus, ibi remedium. (1 EAST. 220.)—Where there is a right, there is a remedy.

2469. Ubi jus incertum, ibi jus nullum. (2 BOU. 160.)—Where the law is uncertain, there is no law.

2470. Ubi lex aliquem cogit ostendere causam, necesse est quod causa sit justa et legitima. (2 INST. 269.)—Where the law compels a man to show cause, it is necessary that the cause be just and legal.

2471. Ubi lex deest, prætor supplet. (TRAY. 593.)—Where the law is deficient, the judge supplies the deficiency.

2472. Ubi lex est specialis, et ratio ejus generalis, generaliter accipienda est. (2 INST. 43.)—Where the law is special, and the reason of it general, it ought to be taken as being general.

2473. Ubi lex non distinguit, nec nos distinguere debemus. (7 COKE, 5.)—Where the law does not distinguish, we ought not to distinguish.

2474. Ubi major pars est, ibi totum. (MOORE, 578.)—Where the greater part is, there is the whole.

2475. Ubi matrimonium, ibi dos. (BRACT. 92.)—Where there is marriage, there is dower.

2476. Ubi non adest norma legis, omnia quasi pro suspectis habenda sunt. (BAC. APH. 25.)—

When the law fails to serve as a rule, almost everything should be suspected.

2477. Ubi non est annua renovatio, ibi decimæ non debent solvi. (WHART. 1026.)— Where there is no annual renovation, there tithes should not be paid.

2478. Ubi non est condendi auctoritas, ibi non est parendi necessitas. (DAV. 190.)—Where there is no authority to enforce, there is no necessity to obey.

2479. Ubi non est directa lex, standum est arbitrio judicis, vel procedendum ad similia. (ELLES. POST. 41.)—Where there is no direct law, the opinion of the judge is to be taken, or reference made to similar cases.

2480. Ubi non est lex, ibi non est transgressio quoad mundum. (4 COKE, 16.)—Where there is no law there is no transgression, as it regards the world.

2481. Ubi non est manifesta injustitia, judices habentur pro bonis viris, et judicatum pro veritate. (1 JOHNS. CH. N. Y. 341. 345.)—Where there is no manifest injustice, the judges are to be considered as honest men, and their judgment as truth.

2482. Ubi non est principalis, non potest esse accessorius. (4 COKE, 43.)—Where there is no principal, there can be no accessory.

2483. Ubi nullum matrimonium, ibi nulla dos.

(COKE, LITT. 32. a.)—Where there is no marriage, there is no dower.

2484. Ubi periculum, ibi et lucrum collocatur. (2 Bou. 161.)—Where there is risk, there should the profits be received.

2485. Ubi pugnantia inter se in testamento juberentur, neutrum ratum est. (DIG. 50. 17. 188.)—Where conflicting directions are contained in a will, neither is held valid.

2486. Ubi quid generaliter conceditur, in est hæc exceptio, si non aliquid sit contra jus fasque. (10 COKE, 78.)—Where a thing is conceded generally, this exception arises, that there shall be nothing contrary to law and right.

2487. Ubi quis delinquit, ibi punietur. (6 COKE, 47.)—Where a man offends, there shall he be punished.

2488. Ubi verba conjuncta non sunt, sufficit alteratum esse factum. (DIG. 50. 17. 110.)—Where words are not conjoined, it is sufficient that either one of the things expressed be performed.

2489. Ubicunque est injuria, ibi damnum sequitur. (BRANCH, PR.)—Where there is an injury, there a loss follows.

2490. Ultima ratio spoliata ante omnia restituenda. (TAYLER, 554.)—It is of the greatest importance, that before all else, stolen property should be restored.

2491. Ultima voluntas caset libera. (TAYLER,

554.)—The last will should be made without restraint.

2492. Ultimum supplicium esse mortem solam interpretamur. (DIG. 48. 19. 21.)—The extremest punishment we consider to be death alone.

2493. Ultra posse non potest esse, et vice versa. (WING. 100.)—What is beyond possibility cannot exist, and *vice versa.*

2494. Un ne doit prise advantage de son tort demesne. (2 AND. 38. 40.)—One ought not to take advantage of his own wrong.

2495. Una persona vix potest supplere vices duarum. (4 COKE, 118.)—One person can scarcely supply the places of two.

2496. Unius omnino testis responsio non audiatur. (3 BLACK. COM. 370.)—The answer of one witness shall not be heard at all.

2497. Uniuscujusque contractus initium spectandum est, et causa. (DIG. 17. 1. 8.)—The beginning and cause of every contract must be considered.

2498. Universalia sunt notioca singularibus. (2 ROL. 294.)—Things universal are better known than things particular.

2499. Universitas vel corporatio non dicitur aliquid facere nisi id sit collegialiter deliberatum, etiamsi major pars id faciat. (DAV. 131.)—An university or corporation is not said to do anything, unless it be deliberated upon collegiately, although the majority should do it.

2500. Universus terminus in lege dies unus. (LOFFT, 486.)—One day is a complete term in law.

2501. Uno absurdo dato, infinita sequuntur. (1 COKE, 102.)—One absurdity being allowed, an infinite number follow.

2502. Unumquodque est id quod est principalius in ipso. (HOB. 123.)—That which is the principal part of a thing, is the thing itself.

2503. Unumquodque ligamen dissolvitur eodem ligamine quod ligatur. (12 BARB. N. Y. 366. 375.)—Every obligation is dissolved in the same manner in which it is contracted.

2504. Unumquodque principiorum est sibimetipsi fides; et perspicua vera non sunt probanda. (COKE, LITT. 11. b.)—Every principle is its own evidence, and plain truths are not to be proved.

2505. Usucapio constituta est ut aliquis litium finis esset. (DIG. 41. 10. 5.)—Prescription was instituted that there might be an end to litigation.

2506. Usura dicitur quia datur pro usu æris. (2 INST. 89.)—Usury is so called because it is given for the use of money.

2507. Usury is odious in law. (2 BOU. 161).

2508. Usus est dominium fiduciarium. (2 BOU. 161.)—A use is a fiduciary ownership.

2509. Usus et status sive possessio potius differunt secundum rationem fori, quam secundum rationem rei. (WHART. 1038.)—Use, estate, and possession, differ more in the rule of the forum than in the rule of the matter.

2510. Usus fit ex iteratis actibus. (TRAY. 600.)—Repeated acts constitute usage.

2511. Ut pœna ad paucos, metus ad omnes perveniat. (4 INST. 63.)—Though punishment may happen to a few, the fear of it affects all.

2512. Ut res magis valeat quam pereat. (10 EAST, 427.)—That the thing may rather have effect than be destroyed.

2513. Utile per inutile non vitiatur. (3 COKE, 10.)—The useful is not vitiated by the useless.

2514. Utlagatus est quasi extra legem positus. (7 COKE, 14.)—An outlaw is, as it were, out of the protection of the law.

2515. Uxor et filius sunt nomina naturæ. (4 BAC. 350.)—Wife, and son, are names of nature.

2516. Uxor furi desponsata non tenebitur ex facto viri. (3 INST. 108.)—The wife of a thief shall not be bound by the act of her husband.

2517. Uxor non est sui juris, sed sub potestate viri. (3 INST. 108.)—A wife has no power of her own, but is under the government of her husband.

2518. Uxor sequitur domicilium viri. (TRAY. 606.)—A wife follows the domicil of her husband.

V.

2519. **Vagabundum nuncupamus eum qui nullibi domicilium contraxit habitationis.** (PHILL. DOM. 23.)—We call him a vagabond who has nowhere contracted a domicile of residence.

2520. **Valeat quantum valere potest.** (COWP. 600.)—It shall have effect, as far as it can have effect.

2521. **Vana est illa potentia quæ nunquam venit in actum.** (2 COKE, 51.)—Vain is that power which never comes into action.

2522. **Vani timoris justa excusatio non est.** (DIG. 50. 17. 184.)—A vain fear is not a legal excuse.

2523. **Vectigal, origine ipsa, jus Cæsarum et regum patrimoniale est.** (DAV. 33.)—Tribute in its origin is the patrimonial right of kings and emperors.

2524. **Vehiculam vel jumentum agendi non etiam est jus iter eundi ambulandi.** (COKE, LITT. 56. a.)—The right of driving anywhere in a carriage is not included in a right to walk to that place on 'oot.

2525. **Vel declarat, vel extendat, vel restringit omnis interpretatio.** (JENK. CENT. 96.)—An interpretation either declares, extends, or restricts the clause or thing interpreted.

2526. **Velle non creditur qui obsequitur im-**

perio patris vel domini. (DIG. 50. 17. 4.)—He is not considered to consent, who obeys the orders of his father or master.

2527. **Vendens eandem rem duobus falsarius est.** (JENK. CENT. 107.)—It is fraudulent to sell the same thing to two persons.

2528. **Veniæ facilitas incentivum est delinquendi.** (3 INST. 236.)—Facility of pardon is an incentive to crime.

2529. **Vera perspicua non sunt probando.** (COKE, LITT. 16. b.)—Plain truths need not be proved.

2530. **Verba accipienda sunt secundum subjectum materiam.** (COKE, LITT. 36. a.)—⸚ords are to be interpreted according to the ⸚ect-matter.

2531. **Verba accipienda ut sortientur effectum.** (15 BAC. 120.)—Words are to be taken so that they may have some effect.

2532. **Verba æquivoca ac in dubio sensu posita, intelliguntur digniori et potentiori sensu.** (6 COKE, 20.)—Words equivocal and those in a doubtful sense are to be taken in the more worthy and effective sense.

2533. **Verba aliquid operari debent—debent intelligi ut aliquid operentur.** (8 COKE, 94.)—Words ought to have some effect—they should be so interpreted as to give them some effect.

2534. **Verba artis ex arte.** (2 KENT, COM.

556.)—Terms of art should be explained from the art.

2535. Verba attendenda, non os loquitur. (TAYLER, 566.)—Words should be regarded, not the speaker.

2536. Verba chartarum fortius accipiuntur contra proferentem. (COKE, LITT. 36. a.)—The words of deeds are to be taken most strongly against the person offering them.

2537. Verba cum effectu sunt accipienda. (BAC. MAX. 3.)—Words are to be taken with effect.

2538. Verba currentis monetæ, tempus solutionis designant. (DAV. 73.)—The words *current money* refer to the time of payment.

2539. Verba dicta de persona, intelligi debent de conditione personæ. (2 ROL. 72.)—Words spoken of the person, are to be understood of the condition of the person.

2540. Verba generalia generaliter sunt intelligenda. (3 INST. 76.)—General words are to be understood generally.

2541 Verba generalia restringuntur ad habilitatem rei vel aptitudinem personæ. (BAC. MAX. 10.)—General words should be restricted to the capacity of the thing or the aptitude of the person.

2542. Verba homicidium non excusant. (LOFFT, 349.)—Words cannot excuse a homicide

2543. Verba illata inesse videntur. (WHART.

1045.)—Words referred to are considered to be incorporated.

2544. Verba in differenta materia per prius, non per posterius, intelligenda sunt. (CAL. LEX.) —Words on a different subject are to be understood by what precedes, not by what follows.

2545. Verba intelligenda sunt in casu possibili. (CAL. LEX.)—Words are to be understood in a possible case.

2546. Verba intentioni, et non e contra, debent inservire. (8 COKE, 94.)—Words should wait upon the intention, and not the reverse.

2547. Verba ita sunt intelligenda, ut res magis valeat, quam pereat. (BAC. MAX. 3.)— Words are to be so understood that the subject-matter may rather be preserved than destroyed.

2548. Verba mere aequivoca, si per communem usum loquendi in intellectu certo sumuntur, talis intellectus praeferendus est. (CAL. LEX.)—When words are merely equivocal, if by common usage of speech they acquire a certain meaning, such meaning is to be preferred.

2549. Verba nihil operari melius est quam absurde. (CAL. LEX.)—It is better that words should have no operation than to operate absurdly.

2550. Verba non tam intuenda, quam causa et natura rei, ut mens contrahentium ex eis potius quam ex verbis appareat. (CAL. LEX.)— Words are not to be looked at so much as the cause and nature of the thing, since the intention of the contracting parties may appear from these rather than from the words.

2551. **Verba offendi possunt, imo ab eis recedere licet, ut verba ad sanum intellectum reducantur.** (CAL. LEX.)—Words may be opposed, nay, they may be receded from altogether, in order that words may be restored to a sound meaning.

2552. **Verba ordinationis quando verificari possunt in sua vera significatione, trahi ad extraneum intellectum non debent.** (CAL. LEX.)—When the words of an ordinance can be made true in their true signification, they ought not to be drawn to a foreign intendment.

2553. **Verba posteriora propter certitudinem addita, ad priora quæ certitudine indigent, sunt referenda.** (WING. 53.)—Subsequent words added for the purpose of certainty, are to be referred to preceding words which require certainty.

2554. **Verba pro re et subjecta materia accipi debent.** (CAL. LEX.)—Words ought to be received most favorably to the thing and the subject-matter.

2555. **Verba quæ aliquid operari possunt non debent esse superflua.** (CAL. LEX.)—Words which can have any effect, should not be treated as surplusage.

2556. **Verba quantumvis generalia, ad aptitudinem restringuntur, etiamsi nullam aliam paterentur restrictionem.** (CAL. LEX.)—Words, however general, are restrained to fitness, though they may admit of no other restriction.

2557. **Verba relata hoc maxime operantur per referentiam ut in eis inesse videntur.** (COKE, LITT. 159. a.)—Words to which reference is made in an instrument have the same effect and operation as if they were inserted in the clause referring to them.

2558. **Verba secundum materiam subjectam intellige nemo est qui nescit.** (CAL. LEX.)—There is no one who does not know that words are to be understood according to the subject-matter.

2559. **Verba semper accipienda sunt in mitiori sensu.** (4 COKE, 13.)—Words are always to be taken in their milder sense.

2560. **Verba stricta significationis ad latam extendi possunt, si subsit ratio.** (CAL. LEX.)—Words of a narrow signification, may be extended to a wide meaning, if reason require.

2561. **Verbis standum ubi nulli ambiguitas.** (TRAY. 612.)—Where there is no ambiguity, words stand as written.

2562. **Verbum imperfecti temporis rem adhuc imperfectam significat.** (6 WEND. N. Y. 103. 120.)—The imperfect tense of the verb indicates an incomplete matter.

2563. **Veredictum, quasi dictum veritatis; ut judicium quasi juris dictum.** (COKE, LITT. 226.

a.)—A verdict is, as it were, the saying of the truth, as the judgment is the saying of the law.

2564. **Veritas demonstrationis tollit errorem nominis.** (1 LD. RAYM. 303.)—The truth of the description removes the error of the name.

2565. **Veritas habenda est in juratore; justitia et judicium in judice.** (BRACT. 186.)—Truth is the desideratum in a juror; justice and judgment, in a judge.

2566. **Veritas nihil veretur nisi abscondi.** (9 COKE, 20.)—Truth fears nothing but concealment.

2567. **Veritas nimium altercando amittitur.** (HOB. 344.)—By too much altercation truth is lost.

2568. **Veritas nominis tollit errorem demonstrationis.** (BAC. MAX. 25.)—The truth of the name removes the error of description.

2569. **Veritas quæ minime defensatur, opprimitur.** (3 INST. 27.)—Truth which is not sufficiently defended, is oppressed.

2570. **Veritatem qui non libere pronunciat, proditor est veritatis.** (4 INST. EPIL.)—He who does not speak the truth freely, is a traitor to the truth.

2571. **Via antiqua via est tuta.** (1 JOHNS. CH. N. Y. 527. 530.)—The old way is the safe way.

2572. **Via trita est tutissima.** (10 COKE, 142.)—The beaten way is the safest.

2573. Vicarius non habet vicarium. (2 Bou. Inst. 1300.)—A deputy cannot have a deputy.

2574. Vicini viciniora facta præsumuntur scire. (4 Inst. 172.)—Neighbors are presumed to know the acts done in the neighborhood.

2575. Videbis ea sæpe committi, quæ sæpe vindicantur. (3 Inst. Epil.)—You will see those things frequently committed that are frequently vindicated.

2576. Videtur qui surdus et mutus ne poet faire alienation. (4 Johns. Ch. N. Y. 441. 444.)—It is seen that a deaf and dumb man cannot alienate.

2577. Vigilantibus et non dormientibus jura subveniunt. (Bract. 175.)—The laws serve the vigilant, and not those who sleep.

2578. Vim vi repellere licet, modo fiat moderamine inculpatæ tutelæ, non ad sumendam vindictam, sed ad propulsandam injuriam. (Coke, Litt. 162. a.)—It is lawful to repel force by force; but let it be done with the moderation of blameless defense; not to take revenge, but to repel injury.

2579. Violenta præsumptio aliquando est plena probatio. (Coke, Litt. 6. b.)—Violent presumption is sometimes full proof.

2580. Viperina est expositio quæ corrodit viscera textus. (11 Coke, 34.)—That is a viperous exposition which corrodes the bowels of the text.

2581. Vir et uxor consentur in lege una per-

sona. (JENK. CENT. 27.)—Husband and wife are regarded in law as one person.

2582. **Vires acquirit eundo.** (1 JOHNS. CH. N. Y. 231. 237.)—It gains strength by continuance.

2583. **Vis legibus est inimica.** (3 INST. 176.)—Force is inimical to the laws.

2584. **Vitium clerici nocere non debet.** (JENK. CENT. 23.)—Clerical errors ought not to prejudice.

2585. **Vitium est quod fugi debet, ne, si rationem non invenias, mox legem sine ratione esse clames.** (ELLES. POST. 86.)—It is a fault that ought to be avoided, that if you cannot discover the reason, you should presently exclaim that the law is without reason.

2586. **Vix ulla lex fieri potest quæ omnibus commoda sit, sed si majori parti prospiciat, utilis est.** (PLOWD. 369.)—Scarcely any law can be made which is beneficial to all; but if it benefit the majority it is useful.

2587. **Vocabula artium explicanda sunt secundum definitiones prudentium.** (GROTIUS, DE JUR. BEL. 2. 16. 3.)—Terms of art should be explained according to the definitions of the learned in that art.

2588. **Void things are as no things.** (2 BOU. 163).

2589. **Volenti non fit injuria.** (PLOWD. 501.)—An injury is not done to the willing.

2590. Voluit, sed non dixit. (4 KENT, COM. 538.)—He willed, but did not say.

2591. Voluntas donatoris, in charta doni sui manifeste expressa observetur. (COKE, LITT. 21. a.)—The will of the donor manifestly expressed in his deed of gift is to be observed.

2592. Voluntas et propositum distinguunt maleficia. (BRACT. 2.)—The will and the purpose distinguish crimes.

2593. Voluntas facit quod in testamento scriptum valeat. (DIG. 30. 1. 12. 3.)—The will of the testator gives validity to what is written in the will.

2594. Voluntas in delictis non exitus spectatur. (2 INST. 57.)—In offenses the will, not the consequence, is to be regarded.

2595. Voluntas reputatur pro facto. (3 INST. 69.)—The will is to be taken for the deed.

2596. Voluntas testatoris ambulatoria est usque ad mortem. (4 COKE, 61.)—The will of a testator is ambulatory until death.

2597. Voluntas testatoris habet interpretationem latam et benignam. (JENK. CENT. 260.)—The will of a testator has a broad and benignant interpretation.

2598. Vox emissa volat; litera scripta manet. (1 JOHNS. N. Y. 529. 571.)—Words spoken vanish; words written remain.

2599. Vox populi vox Dei.—The voice of the people is the voice of God.

W.

2600. Warrantus potest excipere quod querens non tenet terram de qua petit warrantiam, et quod donum fuit insufficiens. (HOB. 21.) —A warrantor may except, that the complainant does not hold the land of which he seeks the warranty, and that the gift was insufficient.

2601. What a man cannot transfer, he cannot bind by articles. (2 BOU. 163).

2602. When an agreement is reduced to writing, all previous treaties are resolved into that. (1 JOHNS. N. Y. 453. 461).

2603. When many join in one act, the law says it is the act of him who could best do it; and things should be done by him who has the best skill. (NOY, 88).

2604. When no time is limited, the law appoints the most convenient. (2 BOU. 163).

2605. When the common law and statute law concur, the common law is to be preferred. (4 COKE, 71).

2606. When the foundation fails, all fails. (2 BOU. 163).

2607. When the law gives anything, it gives a remedy for the same. (2 BOU. 163).

2608. When the law presumes the affirmative, the negative is to be proved. (1 ROL. 88).

2609. When two titles concur, the best is preferred. (FINCH, LAW. 1. 4. 82).

2610. Where there is equal equity, the law must prevail. (4 BOU. INST. 3727).

2611. Where two rights concur, the more ancient shall be preferred. (2 BOU. 163).

2612. Wife cannot be produced a witness for or against her husband, for they are two souls in one flesh. (COKE, LITT. 6. b).

2613. Wife cannot devise to her husband. (COKE, LITT. 112. b).

INDEX.

A.

ABBREVIATIONS, sense of, 14.
ABDUCTION, 2218.
ABRIDGMENTS, 260.
ABSENTEE, 15, 16, 619, 788, 864.
ABUSE, 580, 1760.
ACCESSORY, 841, 1950, 2126, 2425, 2427, 2482; follows principal, 21, 22, 23, 199, 2199; under jurdisdiction, 369; conviction of, 1078; after the fact, 1697.
ACCUSER, 615, 667, 2007, 2012; of himself, 25; see EVIDENCE.
ACTION, 10, 35, 330, 584, 592, 593, 594, 600, 601, 608, 906, 1283, 1530, 1607, 1746, 1890, 2038; shows intention, 27, 43, 1128; against deceased, 29; right to sue, 30, 616, 617; not to one uninjured, 31; intention of, 32, 53, 991; penal, 33, 888; personal, 34, 37; form of, 36, 38, 39; criminal, 379; when of force, 650, 1364; *in rem*, 934; to recover, 1021; punishment of, 1188; *de dolo*, 1696; for injuries, 1757; in suspense, 2132.
ACTS, 724, 1228, 1663, 1994, 2266, 2467; of court, 45, 1717; of God, 46; when recalled, 47; when binding, 48; legal, 49, 50, 51, 1134, 1269: without consent, 52; repugnant, 54; of servant, 55, 934; one's own, 133, 651: criminal, 865, 866; not performed, 895; of religion, 1073; when annulled, 1626; ratification of, 1757; void in origin, 2115. See INTENTION.
ADJOURNMENT, 58.
ADJUDICATION, 224, 1058, 2204, 2205, 2206, 2217, 2248, 2291, 2449.
ADMIRALTY COURT, 59.
ADULTERY, 2358.
ADVANTAGE, 363, 534, 558, 598, 1484, 1672, 1695, 2005, 2494.
ADVICE. See COUNSEL.

[315]

H.

I.

gives honors, 454; has no equal, 487, 2231; injury to, 981; rights of, 1070, 1693, 1694; ruled by law, 1162, 2223, 2232; power of, 1430, 1542, 2233, 2238, 2240.

L.

LAND, 368, 771, 2398, 2400; held in fee, 676; sterile, 2399. See WATERCOURSE; REAL PROPERTY.
LANGUAGE, 1236; misuse of, 169, 1288.
LARCENY. See THEFT.
LAW, 290, 305, 307, 308, 817, 318, 328, 331, 341, 411, 444, 445, 448, 496, 502, 509, 518, 569, 571, 572, 574, 585, 589, 613, 615, 621, 623, 629, 631, 637, 652, 668, 709, 721, 734, 735, 795, 802, 809, 820, 823, 833, 885, 892, 893, 894, 914, 956, 964, 965, 973, 1024, 1028, 1035, 1052, 1059, 1061, 1081, 1088, 1090, 1091, 1092, 1100, 1104, 1105, 1107, 1111, 1126, 1128, 1129, 1130, 1154, 1155, 1155, 1157, 1158, 1160, 1162, 1186, 1199, 1200, 1201, 1204, 1205, 1206, 1209, 1219, 1226, 1231, 1249, 1250, 1273, 1452, 1569, 1621, 1745, 1753, 1775, 1823, 1986, 2093, 2223, 2324; no receding from, 11, 1480; applies to intention, 144; of cases omitted, 206; of chattels, 209; favors dower, &c., 211, 501, 664, 1213; when the reason ceases, 227; construction of, 302, 325, 843, 871, 900, 1011, 1184, 1185, 1136, 1137, 1156, 1167, 1170, 1171, 1172, 1180, 1234, 1245, 1346, 1358, 1419, 1501, 1505, 1541, 1581, 1570, 1639, 1722, 1725, 1772, 1961, 1971, 2000, 2032, 2107, 2110, 2112, 2117, 2136, 2137, 2141, 2149, 2162, 2163, 2253, 2334; common, 309, 316, 322, 391, 407, 409, 1042, 1161, 1169, 2605; of nations, 820, 687, 1131, 1104, 2095, 2120; interpretation of, 333, 513, 532, 959, 960, 966, 1006, 1408, 1410, 1411, 1514, 1525, 1572, 1573, 1606, 1620, 1627, 1652, 1689, 1782, 1739, 1740, 1749, 1750, 1779, 1794, 1903, 1953, 1954, 1955, 1959, 1962, 1999, 2001, 2104, 2151, 2257, 2285, 2290, 2344, 2350, 2351, 2339, 2420, 2421, 2470, 2472, 2479, 2522, 2585, 2586, 2588, 2603; of nature, 285, 409, 796, 1067, 1077, 1097, 1159, 1173, 1179, 1247, 1325, 1419, 1420, 1421, 1422, 1815, 2341; public, 568, 1102, 1103; private, 568, 1102; civil, 568, 712, 1071, 1087, 1283, 2035; strength of, 677, 698, 706, 707, 1047, 1080, 1175, 1182, 1207, 1208, 1209, 1237, 1238, 1625; fiction of, 682, 683; ignorance of, 817, 818, 1248; in deeds. 880; how revealed, 1058; unwritten, 1101; supreme, 1163, 2251, 2376, 2599; retrospective, 1176; execution of, 415, 622, 1181, 1222, 1223, 1224, 1225, 1227, 1228, 1229, 1268, 1318, 1348, 1350, 1357, 1379, 1420, 1453, 1456, 1462, 1463, 1464, 1465, 1468, 1489, 1503, 1504, 1524, 1543, 1551, 1554, 1602, 1615, 1618, 1629, 1648, 1706, 1721, 1736, 1737, 1765, 1821, 1851, 1941, 1956, 1964, 1972, 1984, 2002, 2039, 2048, 2055, 2056, 2098, 2103, 2308, 2443, 2455 2457, 2478, 2488, 2578, 2583, 2607; beneficial, 1197, 1240; should be certain, 1198; safety of, 1211, 2303; unjust, 1217; mercantile, 1220; of the present, 1221; in defining, 1230,

Lightning Source UK Ltd.
Milton Keynes UK
UKHW021228180122
397316UK00003B/200